Reckoning the Racial Reckoning

The demise of the "racial reckoning" that followed George Floyd's death in 2020 occurred without definition, scrutiny or attempts to revive it. In this compelling new book, David Dante Troutt explores the "what," "so what" and "now what" of this period when much of the US sidelined the pandemic to confront racial inequality. It details how a rare focus on embedded racism shifted toward awareness, leaving deep disparities in wealth, health and policing unaddressed, and how this was overpowered by an enduring conservative backlash. Troutt unpacks how legal doctrine favored colorblindness over inequality, and examines government policies that created segregated zones of racial bargaining in health and wealth. The book also exposes deterrence-proof policing rules and explains the problems and promises of DEI. *Reckoning the Racial Reckoning* argues that democratic struggles over local resources are essential for creating justice and well-being for Black American communities, and ultimately for all Americans.

DAVID DANTE TROUTT has been thinking and writing about the possibility of justice for decades. A son of Harlem, he's the author of nonfiction (*The Price of Paradise, After the Storm*), fiction (*The Monkey Suit, The Importance of Being Dangerous*), and numerous law review articles, policy reports and commentaries. He teaches law and public policy at Rutgers Law School in Newark, New Jersey.

"David Troutt has written a searing and essential account of what the 2020 racial reckoning revealed – and what America chose not to confront. With extraordinary clarity, *Reckoning the Racial Reckoning* exposes how systemic racism continues to shape wealth, health, and policing, and why awareness without accountability leaves inequality intact. The book challenges us to move beyond symbolism toward the hard work of structural change. A powerful, urgent book for anyone committed to building a truly multi-racial democracy."

Deborah N. Archer, President, ACLU and Margaret B. Hoppin Professor of Law, NYU Law School

"Clear-eyed and unsparing, this book dismantles a comforting myth – that the nation stood on the brink of a genuine racial reckoning after George Floyd's murder. By tracing why that moment collapsed, it shows where racial justice actually has to be fought, how it must be pursued, and why the reckoning so many expected never stood a chance."

Devon W. Carbado, author of *Unreasonable: Black Lives, Police Power, and the Fourth Amendment*

"Do you remember back in 2020, when it looked like the American people had finally had their fill of racism? Yet here we are, an eyeblink later, with the Border Patrol roaming Chicago to round up anyone with a skin tone darker than porcelain and companies and schools frantically scrubbing the mere word 'diversity' from their websites lest the Trump regime subject them to extrajudicial punishment. David Troutt's book is an essential effort to wrestle with the whiplash and think carefully about why the moment of reckoning precipitated by the murder of George Floyd fell apart in such a nightmarish way."

Paul Gowder, author of *The Rule of Law in the United States: An Unfinished Project of Black Liberation*

"From the insightful and poetic voice of a respected race law expert, comes a much-needed post-mortem of what the brief racial reckoning of 2020 wrought – reflecting the fragility of the stated commitment to racial justice. With this post-mortem, David Troutt powerfully illustrates what has become a restorative justice tenet articulated by Kerrick Arrington: 'Accountability is not absolution. It is the hard labor of repairing what racism has broken brick by brick until justice stands firm.'"

Tanya Kateri Hernandez, author of *Racial Innocence: Unmasking Latino Anti-Black Bias and the Struggle for Equality*

DAVID DANTE TROUTT

RECKONING THE RACIAL RECKONING

From Backlash to Accountability after George Floyd

CAMBRIDGE
UNIVERSITY PRESS

CAMBRIDGE
UNIVERSITY PRESS

Shaftesbury Road, Cambridge CB2 8EA, United Kingdom

One Liberty Plaza, 20th Floor, New York, NY 10006, USA

477 Williamstown Road, Port Melbourne, VIC 3207, Australia

314–321, 3rd Floor, Plot 3, Splendor Forum, Jasola District Centre,
New Delhi – 110025, India

Cambridge University Press is part of Cambridge University Press & Assessment,
a department of the University of Cambridge.

We share the University's mission to contribute to society through the pursuit of
education, learning and research at the highest international levels of excellence.

www.cambridge.org
Information on this title: www.cambridge.org/9781009707350

DOI: 10.1017/9781009707374

When citing this work, please include a reference to the DOI 10.1017/9781009707374

First published 2026

A catalogue record for this publication is available from the British Library

A Cataloging-in-Publication data record for this book is available from the Library of Congress

ISBN 978-1-009-70735-0 Hardback

Inspired by my mother.
For my daughters.
With thanks to my wife.

Contents

Introduction

By the summer of 2020, the nation's centuries-old commitment to racial injustice changed. Something had interrupted the national instinct for racial avoidance inside our institutions. It came with little warning. Some of it was the predictability with which the global Covid pandemic was finding and killing disproportionate numbers of Black people. Some of it was a societal reaction to four vituperative years of Donald Trump, a presidential spectacle of reactionary racism empowered by festering resentment at Barack Obama, the country's first Black president. And clearly, some of it was in defiance of another public lynching of a Black man in police custody, whose plaintive pleas for humanity were callously ignored as the planet looked on. We called the ensuing swell of mass demonstrations, DEI (diversity, equity and inclusion) pledges, retraining conferences, apologetic op-eds and promises to be antiracist a "racial reckoning." It wasn't always clear whether reckoning referred only to awareness or if it extended to an accounting for racial inequality. This confusion proved costly. As did the question of *what* was being reckoned. Police brutality? Covid deaths? Systemic racism? The perennial Black struggle for freedom? At the time, what was briefly certain, if not universally acknowledged, was that Black lives mattered so much you could stake it on a lawn sign or hang it in a window.

Within two years the reckoning was in rapid retreat. Then it was over.

The uniquely American déjà vu of racial backlash was swift, unrelenting and surprisingly effective. Racial reckoning had been reckoned with. It came with threats, mandates and the force of law. Despite Trump's reelection defeat, the Republican campaign against "wokeism" converted more than Republicans to protests against "critical race theory" in schools, against state anti-DEI laws in the workplace and against most efforts at curbing police brutality. Just three summers after the start of racial reckoning, the US Supreme Court all but eviscerated diversity as the last refuge of affirmative action in admissions. Then, in 2024 when issues of race had slipped back into silence nationally, Trump won again, and a counter-racial reckoning was refueled with new energy and an irrepressible vengeance.

There have been no mass protests against the backlash, no antiracism statements and no lost elections.

This book, though, imagines something else. It acknowledges that a racial redress of American institutions was overdue in 2020 and asks what a real racial reckoning would look like. What would we address, for what reasons and how would we approach it? If the goal was not just awareness of the forces that sustain racial inequality but to take just account for them, what would accountability do? For the sake of a single book, I take the racial reckoning of 2020 to be about three issues – systemic racism, lives weakened and shortened by chronic health disparities, and police abuse. While not the entirety of racial inequality, these three elusive features of injustice explain a lot about the motivation for mass protests at the time and the need for actual reckoning now. In the past, moments of reckoning have been subject to pendular swings between exasperation and backlash, which historically have cycled with American partisan politics to produce legal compromises. A principle of this book is that racial justice must be pragmatic, but it cannot be compromised. Another is that we must better define what needs reckoning and how to do it.

What becomes clear on this journey is that the very idea of racial justice is contested, squishy and often diluted by intersecting, if not competing, interests. This ambiguity feeds compromise, especially on the most challenging aspects of white supremacy and its effects. To talk seriously about a racial reckoning, we should agree on two things at the outset. First, we must be able to name Blackness. We have to be able to say "Black," period, and sustain the focus as if addressing racial inequality against African Americans benefits the whole of American democracy in important ways. For that reason, I acknowledge but do not attempt to integrate the many threads of struggle faced by other racial minorities in this book.

Second, we must agree that cumulative harms of racial inequality produce a debt. The debt issue is a quagmire because it provokes accusations of blame, avoidance of guilt, intricate arguments about group exculpation, assertions of eligibility and ultimately the very real transfer of wealth – from some of them to some of us, an "us–them" that must somehow become a "we" again. The debt issue is at the heart of recent efforts to secure racial reparations. This book covers some of the same ground. Like reparations, it asks how we might think about responsibility for generations of specifically defined racial injustices; why we never got around to securing accountability before; and how we can apply it to the three areas of focus in this book. Unlike reparations, this book does not contemplate the whole debt since slavery, nor see it as dischargeable in discrete acts or payments. Instead, it asks how we should understand remedial accountability for the continuing, traceable harms of more contemporary wrongs. Remedies for racial harms should be an ordinary reparative instinct for a society of civil rights. Reparations are extraordinary measures in a society designed for white supremacy. It's a difference of scope (which harms are accounted for) and degree (how much debt is retired), where reparations envision a more comprehensive accounting with, to me, more challenging questions of proof. Reparations work can continue beyond racial reckoning. My focus on accountability, then, requires cumulative loss remediation to undo the demonstrable effects of racial inequality. Where we can show the harmful consequences of responsible conduct – intentional or not – compensation is due in order to bring people back to where they would have been without it. For two precious years, the racial reckoning bypassed remedy in favor of a reconciliation that might never come. It focused too much on racial awareness and not enough on racial accountability. That was a lost opportunity.

The three related areas of remedial focus examined here – systemic racism in wealth creation, racial health disparities and police abuse – illustrate why racial reckoning is long overdue and still necessary.

For systemic racism, I focus on the mostly housing-based institutions that have sustained the racial wealth gap for generations. The 6:1 gap we see today (by 2022 measures) started with the dream of migration to a better life. The Great Migration was a process that by 1970 would transform Southern Blacks into mostly urban Blacks. In the cities to which they went in search of jobs, freedom and democratic rights, Black presence heralded a national interest in segregation policies, less overt but more durable than Jim Crow. The national program of "urban renewal" has escaped responsibility (and scholarly scrutiny) for its profound effects on

Black household wealth and Black urban neighborhoods through government racism, even though it lasted a quarter century from 1949 to 1974. The federal–local program displaced millions of Black migrants from their squalid neighborhoods and separated them from the very wealth opportunities a generous federal government was bestowing upon the wealthiest generation the world has ever known, white baby boomers and their parents. This mass dispossession of Black people's homes and communities was not just a question of housing, but the instantiation of an urban condition that would become known in the decades to follow as "the urban crisis." It is from there that Black Americans become identified not with sharecropping or convict leasing but with ghettoes and public housing. Blacks became the subject of antipoverty policies that come and go, change and diminish. Yet it's the economic effects on land values in Black-identified areas that expand the wealth gap, the high costs and limited availability of credit, and their effects on every kind of investment, from homeownership to the price of eggs. The resulting patterns of systemic devaluation I call "racial bargaining" have set the transactional terms of business in Black neighborhoods long enough to condition predatory and subprime lending, pervasive environmental hazards, gentrification, the loss of public housing, the foreclosure and eviction crises, and profound affordability-instability challenges that remain with us today.

Racial health disparities weaken people unfairly and unnecessarily, producing disability and chronic pain until Black people die – usually earlier than others. Racial health disparities are easier to see than systemic racism because there is so much data about both physical and mental health. For instance, we know that the national difference between Black and white life expectancy in the US, about five years, can differ dramatically from state to state and due to other characteristics. Yet specific health outcomes are often embedded in confidentiality, big numbers and prejudice. Perhaps unwittingly, Black people become the sum of health stereotypes. During Covid, for instance, we sympathized with dying Black folk who faced greater exposure to the risk of death because of either their status as "essential workers" or their high incidence of "underlying conditions" such as kidney disease, heart disease, obesity, diabetes and to some extent hypertension. But we rarely asked why their jobs and housing put them at considerably increased risk. And we certainly never questioned why so many had underlying conditions that, once the virus appeared, turned fatal. My analysis assumes there are two primary explanations for which reckoning is due. One is the prevalence of implicit bias altering the terms and outcomes of the patient–caregiver relationship and the other is the "social determinants of health." Both terms are ungainly. Both require some patience for subtlety. Not surprisingly, both bases for understanding disparate harms have been attacked by a legal and social backlash that began long before the current one.

Finally, there's the issue where all the reckoning began – the mistreatment of Black bodies by armed officers of the state: police abuse and the acquittals that follow. Police brutality is much more than George Floyd's horrific death (or the many others who died that year, the year before or the year after). It is a particular state-inflicted harm reserved specially, though not exclusively, for Black people and has been since the birth of the nation. Every generation of Black person knows the names of multiple people who died or were badly beaten under the most suspicious and incredible circumstances. It is the subject of jokes, parental talks and untold numbers of urban riots, yet it continues almost without accountability. The racial reckoning over police abuse recognized that it was more than the sordid public spectacle of Black death by state action. It was also a symbolic representation of disparate treatment of Black (mostly male) people in the criminal justice system as a whole. The justifications for surveillance, confrontation, arrest, detention and charging would be steps in a pipeline of radically reduced life chances. Disenfranchisement; loss of parenting; loss of education, income and wealth accumulation; lesser health; loss of freedom – Black people saw so much more than the execution of a human being the day George Floyd was mercilessly killed in the street by five police officers. But the larger story is how little stamina the country had for genuine reform and police accountability, reflected in a system of law enforcement oversight that's not designed to deter misconduct.

My goal in this book is to restart a crucial conversation in the United States about African-American well-being and the fair expectations of American democracy, as seen through a brief period of racial reckoning that taught us much about how racial inequality is reproduced and rejected in the twenty-first century. It's a story told in public policy, social science, law and vernacular.

Although some of the research is original – on urban renewal, some legal analyses and the mobility project in the final chapter – my contribution is mostly in the sequence and ordering of ideas and themes. Many recommendations on how to think about the wealth debt, the health debt or criminal justice reform have been made, at least in part, by others. Another aspect of my approach is to overcome the chief legal impediment to racial reckoning: colorblind notions of racial equality. These ideas have long been the lemonade masking the arsenic. Structurally, colorblind doctrine has subverted the meaning of antidiscrimination so that it is at odds with remedying racial inequality. This has undermined the ability of Black people to claim the nature of the racial injuries they've experienced. You don't often hear a Black person describe a basic fact of racial disadvantage – such as being denied housing because of a prior misdemeanor conviction or joining the statistics of people with limbs lost to diabetes – in terms of racist intent. It happens, but that's the language of antidiscrimination lawsuits, not individual harms that flow out of racially inequitable systems. Instead, what diminishes economic, social and physical well-being in a country that has not come to terms with its racism is shown by disparate treatment and disparate impact. Without the ability to show harm this way, it's as if it never happened. Such was the goal of Federalist Society jurisprudence over the last forty years. There are all kinds of creative ways to inflict race-conscious harm on a people without saying so. Not saying so has worked to silence claims in a white noise of false neutrality. But not here. Here, I present proof of harm for the sake of remedy.

ORGANIZATION OF THE BOOK

The book starts with revisiting the racial reckoning of 2020. I invite readers to go back to that remarkable moment in order to understand what it signaled, what it achieved and what, if anything, remains just a few years later. It began as a resistance story and became a battle in a longer American war story, as predictable reactions from the right raged back with unpredictable force. That force often took structural form, which I argue was missing from the articulation of racial reckoning goals. The prospects for correcting course were interrupted by the fierce continuation of white backlash embodied by Trump's second presidency, which resurrected anti-Black themes of "illegal DEI" and reversed discrimination with the full force of the federal government, turning what I call Rules of Avoidance and Denial into political gospel – at least for the time being.

Resistance to racial justice follows a cynical pendulation in US history, so I then turn my attention to understanding why a reckoning is due and how it might remediate inequality, with a pause to consider what we actually mean by racial inequality. After all, there can be no claims to a racial reckoning for or against Blacks without some agreed-upon ways of measuring racial injury and how it occurs in a world of mostly de facto discrimination. A big part of what derailed racial reckoning was the inability to define racial inequality as it's experienced – in locational context, as a continuation of persistent themes, producing cumulative harms through race-neutral means – and to focus on its material consequences. Colorblind constitutionalism obscures these means and ends, righting mostly theoretical wrongs and denying manifest injuries. I argue that inequality is reproduced in plain sight. We see it in place after place, maximizing and minimizing resources by the rules of residential formation in spite of recent Supreme Court decision-making to the contrary. Understanding racial inequality in concrete terms is essential to racial reckoning for Black Americans, who, unlike all other groups except Native Americans, experience a contested idea of progress in key areas of opportunity, such as admissions, employment, income and life expectancy.

After a foundation in racial inequality, I offer the legal and empirical arguments to support reckoning over the denial of wealth accumulation, chronic health disparities and unjust policing. These are stories of migration, underlying conditions and immunities built into law. How did migration condition the terms for wealth creation, and what sustains the racial bargains that resulted? Why *did* so many Black (and Indigenous) people catch Covid and die from it initially – and why do so many suffer daily from "underlying conditions"? Is it possible to hold police officers accountable to the law, and why don't law-and-order basics prevent police brutality the way they're supposed to enforce civilian obedience to law? Because the reckoning was interrupted at the point of DEI, and because conservatives have targeted DEI lest it become a basis for reckoning, we reexamine its origins. How did affirmative action become "diversity," and how did diversity become DEI? Is that the only framework for racial remediation we have? I reevaluate DEI's possibilities and, after a lengthy critique, find some promise in its remedial potential after all.

This brings us closer to the present, explored in the final chapter. There we search for the mythical thing – like "vibranium" in the *Black Panther* movie – that makes Black people move around the US more than any other group in the twenty-first century. Internal migrations have occurred quietly, often reversing the course of the more famous one set in the previous century, but seemingly for the same types of reasons: well-being. Sometimes the movement for racial justice comes down to just that: movement. Most moves are local and reflect a mix of displacement and aspiration. Others are long distance, especially to Southern states under firm Republican control that have legislated a hostility to racial equity initiatives at the local level. Nevertheless, I suspect that what we called "racial reckoning" turns out to be some version of Black well-being. Well-being is pursued in different places, primarily at a local level, to achieve some quality or qualities that are worth moving for. What combination of elements make up that sense of twenty-first century well-being in a country rededicated to white supremacy, and how is it any different from what every other American wants? Maybe migration patterns show that the national battles over democracy have obscured the importance of the many closer to home. Maybe for most of us racial reckoning entails enacting local practices and policies that create opportunity out of our material needs and enhance the bedrock of our collective dignity. Which comes down to our voices – keeping them strong and making them heard, against a concerted attack on First Amendment freedoms. Finally, the epilogue offers a summary of solutions and a framework for action, mostly at the local level.

Overall, what follows offers a mixed picture on the prospects for racial reckoning a quarter way into the twenty-first century. Black interests struggle for attention and can't hold it for long without engendering a punitive response. Even a reckoning of mass awareness during a national crisis could not be defended from attack just months after it was launched. Conservative opposition to remedying racial inequality effectively mobilized legal, political and cultural strategies simultaneously under a banner of colorblindness that has undone principles of racial equity and remediation, elevated white victimhood and now seeks to silence Blackness as it might be studied, celebrated and expressed openly. Accountability reckoning may or may not arise from this in the near future. So the struggle continues.

CHAPTER 1

The 2020 Racial Reckoning Postmortem

There is no word in English to describe what happened in the spring of 2020. Another language might capture the feeling of visceral rage boiling over during each viewing of the nine-minute death of George Floyd at the knee of a police officer, followed by the sublime surprise of mass protests and the unprecedented hope for an overdue racial justice many of us know better than to keep dreaming about. By May 25, 2020, we'd grown used to outrage at the sight or news of an unarmed Black man killed by law enforcement. That's a feeling as old as the Republic. And for as long as anyone alive can recall, the expectation of acquittal after the rare arrest of a police officer is another feeling we've learned to weather like the seasons. As so many Black men before him, Floyd died in the center of three familiar circles – he was alone in the first, a captive in helpless agony; in the next circle were the cops surrounding his body and each other; and finally an outer ring of the public – us – watching, angrily pleading from a careful distance. That outer ring never mattered enough to save the life inside the circle. That outer ring never looked like all of us. Somehow this time it did. People followed each other out of the circle and onto a train whose momentum gathered more people to protest, from place to place, by the millions. The death of George Floyd, just three months into a pandemic that shut down the known world for many months, gave rise to what was called "the racial reckoning." The phrase recalled the kind of historic moment reserved for capitalized but incomplete periods of resistance and promise like Reconstruction and the Civil Rights Movement. It wouldn't last half as long as either.

Both Reconstruction and the Civil Rights Movement persisted well over a decade while the racial reckoning lasted just a few years. Those previous moments had coherent, though contested goals – the first to incorporate a formerly enslaved people into citizens of a constitutional democracy and the second to secure in law the full citizenship rights that had been stripped away over many decades. What exactly was our racial reckoning reckoning?

This book is a long answer to that question, but it begins with questions about the question. What did we actually mean by "reckoning"? Reckoning is a strange word, with slight differences as a verb or a noun, and varied understandings across English-speaking places. The 2020 racial reckoning boiled down to two different ways to reckon – reckoning as awareness and reckoning as accountability. As awareness, reckoning means an acknowledgment of something you should reconsider, a wake-up call. As accountability, reckoning means to settle up and make right. Put another way, if awareness reckoning involves an appraisal of harms, then accountability reckoning requires material relief for material harms.

People from all walks embraced the awareness idea of racial reckoning during its first year and a half or so. Many Black people felt the freedom to talk explicitly about their experience of racism – they were often invited to – and how they struggled to be valued as equals in many areas of their lives. It was a period of truth-telling and listening about racism after years of dismissal, pushback, counterattack and dilution. The reckoning was recognition. The invitation to listen soon engendered statements of awareness and solidarity. The mistreatment of George Floyd's body was a manifestation of deeper harms that dehumanized all Black people, and his death became a metaphor for so many micro and macro injustices. An awareness of anti-Black racism led to learning about the privileges of not being Black, of the myriad unearned entitlements that follow and the actions and attitudes that casually sustain it. People of all races expressed a sense of liberation from this kind of reckoning. Reckoning allowed a freedom from racism in general that would make what happened to Floyd unacceptable to a society committed to fairness and the idea that racism was, as Black folks have long understood, not only evil, but ridiculous.

Awareness reckoning promised that, for the first time in a long time, *racial equity* might be an American value. Racial equity would mean not only that Black lives are equal to all others, but that their constant devaluation may demand processes to make equality demonstrably real. When racial equity is not a core value, the whole idea is negotiable, its existence dependent on who the president is, the balance of the legislature, the victorious candidate in a district attorney race or the make-up of the Supreme Court. A *value* of racial equity makes the *goal* of racial equality possible. In an unjust world, equality without equity is word devoid of purpose.

As a moment of racial awareness, the reckoning was no small achievement for two other reasons. It contravened a cultural norm of American racism: the Rule of Avoidance and Denial. Americans don't talk about race unless they have to, mainly in platitudes, for as briefly as possible. Mention Martin Luther King, then "content of their character," maybe Rosa Parks, and move on. To talk too long about the past or present existence of racial oppression is not only awkward, but dangerous. Race talk is unwelcome and can get the speaker in trouble. Raising race activates the Rule of Denial. Most white Americans are taught to deny and ignore their own race in exchange for racial power.[1] Racial equity challenged all that. The combination of Floyd's brutal death, Black people on ventilators dying alone and stories of implicit bias stifling Black mobility demonstrated to many that equality isn't possible if Black lives aren't treated fairly. After avoidance and denial, white victimization is typically the next stop. But it seemed like nothing could slow this train.

THE STRUGGLE

For many Black people, the rare moment of racial reckoning marched briefly alongside a daily journey called "the Struggle." Some have called it "the Black struggle for freedom," "Black Struggle" or other names, but millions of Black folk since the Middle Passage have engaged in the hard collective work of surviving racism and its many burdens. We hear the Struggle in every form of African-American music and literature. It sits among the chairs in church basements housing court pews and the hard benches of ER waiting rooms. It can be the godfather of cool and the stuff of prayer. Always, the Struggle demands service. You can glimpse it formally in historic labor trends where Black workers, especially women, were vastly overrepresented in the helping occupations, such as teachers and domestics. In the United States at the time of the reckoning, at least a quarter of all the work done by social and human services assistants

(25%), social workers (27%), personal care aids (26%), parking attendants (26%), home health aides (32.5%), sanitation workers (25.8%) and nurse assistants (36%) was performed by African Americans, according to PEW,[2] more than double their share of the population. All of these largely working-class occupations pay modest wages and offer few benefits. The need *to* help reflects the need *for* help, because many of us are also struggling to make ends meet. Not only have Blacks served a disparate share of the nation's personal needs, but an incalculable number serve in the helping traditions of their own families and communities. The extent of the unpaid giving among church members, the life-long service of fraternities and sororities, voluntary participation in community development, drug counseling and gang intervention is hard to count, but it is – and always has been – huge. More than other groups, Blacks bear the sandwich-generation costs of raising children while caring for elderly parents, grandparents and sometimes other family members.[3] We don't all struggle in equal amounts. The Struggle may arise without warning or linger like a heartbeat. In classrooms, boardrooms, courtrooms, social services offices, the streets. Not all the Struggle is easily traceable to racial capitalism or identifiable acts of white supremacy. Some of it is self-imposed. What is and what may not be merge together by the necessity to overcome long odds. Struggle led to the Great Migration discussed in Chapter 3, and to the twenty-first century African-American migrations I reveal in Chapter 7. To a policymaker, the Struggle is the informal safety net. To a social scientist, the Struggle is short for racial inequality. By 2020, many Black folks saw the inequality of a Black life lynched by police hands, Black bodies in the deadly throes of the coronavirus and Black financial resources failing once again to withstand another national shock. What usually goes on in the background of African-American lives, occasionally captured by statistics, was revealed to all like helicopter lights on a crime scene. We'd had enough Struggle and not enough net.

Awareness reckoning looked into every part of that Struggle for about two years. People not only saw Black people's struggles with inequality but their own. Unsurprisingly, awareness reckoning in 2020 attracted Americans who saw the same oppressive dynamics of anti-Black racism reflected in the mistreatment of Latinos, Native Americans, women, immigrants, the LGBTQ community, the disabled – any of a number of groups who are othered by their status. The MeToo movement a few years before brought awareness of profound unaddressed sexism, its many victims demanding accountability in lawsuits. Transgender people demanded awareness through acceptance and equal inclusion. Reckoning protests prominently featured the voices of women and the feminist activists leading the movement for Black lives. Awareness reckoning became inextricably related to issues of identity that had ignited a culture war years before. Beneath it all was a sense of compassion, that sharing about the systemic wrongs would make sharing in the work of recovery easier during a time of unprecedented need where everyone, *everyone* was struggling in some way.

The 2020 racial reckoning reinforced ideas about how to unyoke from marginalization amid national tumult just as the movements for racial justice and Black Power once offered a blueprint for women's justice, immigration, disabled and LGBTQ rights. Historically, these ideas mostly come out of the Civil Rights Movement of the 1950s and 1960s; they then resonated with philosophical notions of multiculturalism in the 1970s and 1980s.[4] The debates about multiethnic curricula in schools, diverse representation in the workplace and undoing stereotypical characterizations in media and Hollywood were united by a demand for recognition and inclusive treatment. People wanted to be reflected in the American frame, which meant white people – especially white men – would have to stop hogging the gaze and all the lines. Most importantly, the group-based hardships during the Trump years fell especially hard on others – undocumented immigrants often identified as Latinos, Muslims, trans and nonbinary people and women, especially in the realm of reproductive autonomy. These groups galvanized their interests under a common enemy of oppressive intolerance. If this was partly a collective effort to take back democratic values, they too demanded to be recognized.

Focusing on awareness had other implications for the direction of racial reckoning. An expansive notion of reckoning invited diversity, equity and inclusion (DEI) programming into the center of national discussion. By 2020, the country was familiar with racial diversity, and, at the time, it raised no legal problems. Inclusion helped widen the diversity lens to nonracial minorities. Equity is based on fair processes and has functioned as the principle that binds diversity and inclusion together. It seemed natural that DEI framing would complement, if not organize, the rising tide of sentiment. Conceptually, awareness reckoning challenges embedded ideas of who matters and forces a recentering of attention. Constitutionally, awareness reckoning is associated with First Amendment rights of free expression and association, while accountability reckoning raises the thorniness of equal protection law. Awareness embodies a multicultural pluralism inspired by (but not always reflective of) Black Struggle. The right to be seen and heard for who one is carries with it the right to be treated with respect and to freely inhabit spaces where your difference may be acknowledged. Belonging is an associational idea. A reckoning adjacent to DEI ideas therefore might have broader appeal than one based on anti-Black racism. On the other hand, racial accountability must take race explicitly into account, which implicates race law, or equal protection, a strategic Pandora's box for a movement, and a windowless trap for civil rights lawyers. This distinction – DEI vs. antiracism, awareness / First Amendment vs. accountability / equal protection – would become a fault line in the years to come.

Nevertheless, in the summer of 2020 Americans in large numbers rose up and became expressively "woke." Within three weeks of his death, the video of Floyd's murder was viewed at least 1.4 *billion* times and was quickly associated with the phrase and the organization Black Lives Matter (or BLM). Awareness and support for BLM grew rapidly. Despite the lack of a Covid vaccine and the virus death toll climbing every day, protests drew the largest crowds since the Civil Rights Movement in over 140 US cities and many more abroad. Though a small number of protesters turned to looting and violence (six people died), Floyd's death mostly produced large, long life-affirming marches, not riots. It came in the aftermath of many high-profile deaths of Black people at the hands of police – Eric Garner, Breonna Taylor, Sandra Bland, Philando Castile, as well as the racist stalking and murder of Ahmaud Arbery. Raw anger around the spectacle of this senseless, racially motivated police brutality resonated in unusual places. There were hundreds of BLM mentions in the social media of Congress members, as the Pew Research Center reported, and a poll showing 67 percent support for BLM among the general public.[5] Black Lives Matter lawn signs were everywhere across suburbia and hanging from windows in city apartments. Former President Obama gave an online speech in June 2020 in which he noted the extraordinary moment of racial consensus, a "broad coalition" of protesters and "a far more representative cross-section of Americans out in the streets" than in the 1960s.[6] This intense flurry of awareness-type reckoning during the most frightening months of the pandemic felt like that elusive non-English word for racial rage-surprise recognition-hope for change-dream of a just society.

The reckoning needed that word. Racial awareness lacks the clarity of racial equity. The range of mostly well-intentioned actors and actions enacted various performative rituals, such as the proliferation of diversity statements, check-your-privilege trainings, corporate pledges and woke logos ("End Racism"). Others were more substantive, instituting some DEI human resources practices, which sought performance metrics and other tangible results of inclusivity. Overall, however, what awareness reckoning demanded we be aware of was so all-inclusive as to be unfocused. This lack of clarity around what to want and how to get it would prove costly later when the reckoning got reckoned with. Once the train becomes symbolic, it's not clear where it's headed and people start getting off.

ACCOUNTABILITY RECKONING

Awareness alone doesn't necessarily fix things. It has no action plan and requires no affirmative rearrangement or sacrifice. It might benefit only the person achieving awareness. Racial reckoning needed to take the further step of accountability. True reckoning should determine responsibility for what was taken, produce the restoration of something owed, in order to repair the harm that was never adequately acknowledged, if not deliberately denied. It ought to take up the demands of justice as if they are serious things to be met.

Accountability reckoning differs from awareness in some crucial respects. To overcome inequality, accountability reckoning focuses on the structural requirements of material opportunity. We look at the institutional structures – like policing rules – that produce measurable, material inequalities – like police shootings of unarmed Black people without prosecution – and expect to be made whole with meaningful policy reforms as a matter of fairness – racial fairness. The rules must work; the harm must be addressed; the unjustified killings must stop. Thoughts and prayers aren't enough. Saying their names isn't enough. Racial harms should merit the same democratic impulse for accountability as we see in our legal system. Every day, we make people whole for proven harms against them in civil and criminal courts and call it justice. In contrast to awareness reckoning, however, this approach is less focused on identity-based indignities and more on remedying material losses.

The racial reckoning of 2020 hardly touched accountability. Indeed, accountability reckoning is so taboo that it's never existed for anti-Black racism in the US. In 2020, death and the fear of death was everywhere. We were sheltering in place and speaking through screens and unable to be our normal selves. The racial vitriol of the Trump presidency had whip-sawed the country in a daily circus of hardening right-wing calumny. Under these extraordinary strains, it was hardly clear why the particular spectacle of Floyd's death suddenly opened the circle of outraged witnesses to millions of people, who for generations had grown numb to occasional police killings, even the videotaped ones. Perhaps recognition of the victims of anti-Black police brutality was step one in a reckoning that would be fulfilled later by the step two of police accountability. Maybe the broader reckoning about racism would take time to crystalize. Or maybe all of it would suffer the Rule of Avoidance and Denial – or worse.

Again, the question, what was the racial reckoning reckoning?

THREE THINGS STILL TO RECKON

That there is no clear answer continues to be the problem for a national reckoning. Yet what most Black people wanted in 2020 is not hard to divine. We wanted to stop all the police killing, the Covid dying and the falling further behind financially. These are the basic demands of justice. They resist the devaluation of one's person, one's body and one's resources.

Beyond that, Black people – individuals, families, households and communities – want to be free of the burden of racism wherever we go, done with the projection of its stain on our lives. We expect to be protected and to get the full value of our labor and what it buys. We want to live as long and as well as other people. We want to be presumed innocent, capable and reasonable. We want the comfort of being stable participants in resource-rich communities. We want our excellence to be known and expected. We want our children to have at least the opportunities we had. All of which means there are also things we don't want. Black people can't keep being caught up in institutions that are chronically impoverished by insufficient resources. We can't be habitually mistaken for threats, thugs, fools and impostors. Reckoning would mean no more occupying secondary status – among minorities, among school children, among professionals, among histories, among pregnancies, among voters, among defendants. Gone go the predators, skimmers, scammers, low appraisers, loan deniers, foreclosers, drug dealers, deniers and false hopers. Black people don't want to bear the Black taxes, because racism is a cost business that devalues, takes and accuses. This is not a complete list, but it gets at what by 2020 had exhausted African Americans to breaking point. Note that these things sit on a continuum from dignitary demands to material expectations, and nearly all of it is systemic. No reckoning could reach them all.

Of course, this list is not only a Black list. These items of Black humanity and struggle are shared by many Americans who believe their democracy is more capable of equity despite so much contrary evidence. Racism represents some of US democracy's most fundamental flaws. Millions marched in 2020 not only against racial capitalism but against the ravages of late-stage capitalism affecting a majority of Americans – increasingly nonwhite but many whites too – who cannot secure a foothold in the middle class. Covid brought a societal collapse that showcased inequalities that had been growing at least since the Great Recession of 2008. These inequalities are mostly material – in educational access, income immobility, citizenship status, health-care burdens, housing instability – yet they were mobilized primarily around issues of identity, as if the bottom-line harms were mostly dignitary. This was a lost opportunity. As we'll see, a democratic reckoning that came wrapped in racial inequality was overcome on that basis. To the detriment of us all.

So, what was the racial reckoning reckoning?

This book argues that 2020 revealed three things that should be reckoned with: police brutality, systemic racism affecting the racial wealth gap and racial health disparities. These matter most because they rose up spontaneously from a background of longstanding inequalities ignored for too long. Police brutality is first because it's the center of the circle and the vicarious experience of all of us standing on the outer ring, feeling our humanity violated and demanding basic justice. The second is systemic racism, maybe not all of it, but more of it than could be reached by DEI trainings, antiracism statements and corporate pledges. Specifically, the systemic racism that must be addressed are those institutional practices that perpetuate a racial wealth gap generations old. The third, racial health disparities, may seem less obvious, but it helps explain why the outer ring grew so large and so angry about casual injustice: dying unnecessary deaths. The number of lives cut short by illness or violence was catastrophic. This is what Covid was showing the country throughout the twenty-odd months of the racial reckoning: that the health of Black lives was too fragile. Even George Floyd, we learned later, had Covid in his lungs when he died.

Though all three of these aspects of embedded racism were addressed during the countless hours of news coverage, organizational meetings, corporate statements and personal discussions, the racial reckoning produced very little evidence of lasting, transformative change. Awareness reckoning might have made clear how racist policing is immune from accountability, why Black lives remain unnecessarily fragile in the most expensive health-care system in the world and why radical Black wealth inequality persists despite all the focus on diversity. But without accountability reckoning, material change was minimal.

And the progress was unstable. We know now that many hiring pledges and DEI statements were performative. Many companies that issued them during the fever of allegiance retracted or dialed them back, sometimes quietly, sometimes not, as the climate cooled.[7] We know that most of the legal attempts to restructure racial outcomes toward equity and basic fairness failed to become law, such as the George Floyd Justice in Policing Act or the John Lewis Voting Rights Act. We know that even the awareness reckoning that proved so poignant in endless discussions – voluntary and mandatory – in workplace trainings and organizational retreats gave way to weariness, criticism and lawsuits *even before the backlash.* For all the organizing involved in the brief period of racial reckoning, there was an acute inability to organize a strategic consensus around what needed to be reckoned and how to engage it in a sustained way. Meanwhile, the attack on democracy was gaining steam.

BETWEEN THE PERSONAL AND THE STRUCTURAL

The three areas I believe should have been the focus of the reckoning are critical aspects of racial inequality, which require a structural analysis of racial injury that goes beyond the typical identity politics discourse. Identity became extremely personal, and a racial reckoning consumed by awareness of personal identity issues became vulnerable to the law and policy of white backlash. The emphasis on personal experience often rendered evidence of racial harm anecdotal and subjective despite the existence of very strong evidence of racial inequality. It wasn't clear what racial harm looked like in 2020. Overemphasizing personal harm also tended to limit solutions to acts of awareness rather than to material changes. There's lots of evidence of material racial harm, as we'll see in coming chapters, but it required reckoning with the problem of an age-old antidiscrimination way of thinking about racist consequences.

Assume we're in a courtroom. Claiming discrimination requires a demonstration of racial injury based on triable fact. It can't just be alleged; it's got to be proven by evidence. So racial injury must be real. But what counts as discrimination? The cop told me he shot me because I'm Black. That would be real, but unlikely. The loan officer denied my application because she said she preferred the white couple in the waiting room behind me. That too would be real, but unlikely. The doctor said he wouldn't bother to waste this clinical trial on me because Black patients don't regularly take their medicine. Also real, just as unlikely. Yet each represents the kind of discrimination our laws unrealistically expect in order to prove racial harm: direct, intentional, atomistic discrimination as if it were 1943 all over again. When, instead, discrimination is based on structure, like an institution's unfair but racially neutral rules or discretionary practices, it can be more challenging to address.

Discrimination against dignitary racial harms is even harder, mainly because it's a fight where the *meaning* of facts is often in dispute. You suffer harm to your sense of dignity when you feel wronged. A microagression, a racial slur, a questionable word by your boss, a deadnaming or misused pronoun – all of these represent dignitary harms. They're insulting, offensive, subjectively wrong acts that usually occur in small numbers and target identity. They become the stuff of painful anecdotes. (As the Trump administration has shown, devaluing identity can be the first step toward devaluing the material lives of those with that identity.) Sometimes identity harms are structural. For instance, a ban on trans student participation in school sports affects all student athletes (and it's discriminatory because it denies trans people the same privileges as others). But identity harms are usually very personal. During the racial reckoning, people often defaulted to the personal character of harmful acts. This is not to say they're not real, but their authenticity can't be challenged because they come from a sense of personal violation. To dispute them can only be to deny them, and to deny them is to dehumanize. The result is a dug-in tendency toward cancellation via petitions and social media campaigns or, increasingly on both sides, litigation. The amount of time, productivity and emotional investment spent in such warfare has roiled a great many organizations to the point of impasse.[8] They struggle to fulfill their missions, even those committed to social justice. Unfortunately, a lot of these struggles were condensed into antagonism for the institutional name we give these conflicts: DEI and its excesses. Lost in this dynamic is the structural inequality that started it all.

The distinction between personal and structural harms is crucial to the kind of accountability I think racial reckoning requires. A structural wrong is significant because the harm is material and reaches far. It can be measured more objectively, and usually has economic impact. We can all see the numbers and count the loss. These material harms affect our economic and social well-being in established, often quantifiable, predictable ways because they're the result of identifiable *policies* in, say, health care, and *practices* by, say, police officers engaged in racial profiling. The policies and practices affect large numbers of people in similar material ways. For instance, a suburban zoning ordinance that regulates almost all housing in a town to single-family homes on large lots appears rational and nonracist in its application. It discriminates against apartment buildings, not Black people. Yet this government action makes economic and racial segregation possible, thereby inflating the value of household wealth for those fortunate non-Blacks to live and vote within its borders and limiting the presence and participation of outsiders. The practice becomes truly exclusionary when it's copied by most of the other towns around it, creating concentrated islands of homogeneous wealth, a no-go zone for others and unaffordable housing markets. As the zoning example shows, a structural wrong has been designed often to do a combination of things, beneficial and costly, but among them provable, broadly applicable material harms to some identifiable group and not as much to others. As we'll see in Chapter 3, this kind of institutional discrimination caused the racial wealth gap. Those harms are measurable and they add up quickly.

By relying on notions of discrimination to distinguish between awareness and accountability reckoning, I am not suggesting that Black people are going to sue this nation into becoming a more perfect union. In fact, the greatest power of the racial reckoning was its potential to produce structural change without resorting to litigation where it would have surely lost. Instead, I'm saying that a more productive racial reckoning would have focused on the structure of racial inequality and committed to remedying that. Taking our eyes off the accountability prize was either a lost opportunity or a stolen one.

THE RECKONING GETS RECKONED WITH

Once again English has no word for the sense of dormant white grievance provoked into organized action to oppose, deny and usurp any protracted racial reckoning. Some of it was the continuation, freshly fueled, of a long conservative movement, especially in law and politics. Other aspects seemed more like spontaneous reactions to a culture war. It began with the police. After a brief pause, Black Lives Matter protests were met by Blue Lives Matter counterprotests and shows of force. The tensions ignited confrontations, especially with ultra-leftist and anarchist groups, like antifa, that turned into rioting in a few places. Once these lines were drawn, battles between a protective right-wing white population that stood for the familiar "law and order" and protesting "thugs" bled into local and national politics. President Donald Trump threatened to use the National Guard to stop protesters. As more cities became centers of extended dissent, cities themselves became associated with the lawlessness. These familiar binaries played out in conspicuous Blue Lives Matter flags, slurs against the urban, even Republican support for Derek Chauvin, the cop who killed George Floyd.[9] Pandemic or not, this national conflict convulsed across the anonymous passages and half thoughts of social media where a competition between Black and Blue

Lives Matter tweets was overwhelming. If social media carried the original reckoning, it carried its backlash, too, a widening conflict between two separate epistemic worlds. Soon, the right was ignited, called into action by increasingly radicalized race rhetoric and violence. Kyle Rittenhouse, a teenager who traveled with an automatic rifle to a protest and killed two people, became a hero, acquitted for "standing his ground" against other protesters. In May 2022, another young white man hunted for Black people in Buffalo, entering the lone supermarket in the East Side neighborhood and slaughtering ten people. Both assailants carried AR-15 rifles, the style preferred by the mass shooters of our time. By the time of both shootings, studies began to reveal the limits of white sympathy for racial injustice against nonwhite people. As represented by the many millions of Make America Great Again (MAGA) Trump supporters in the 2020 election, and the thousands who violently stormed the Capitol Building on January 6, they were not just not woke. They are anti-woke.

We struggle for the word to describe this feeling, its breadth and intensity. "Backlash" denies its inherent predictability. The virulent and sometimes violent anti-woke reaction of a growing number of Americans to the racial reckoning seemed existentially necessary. Breaking the Rule of Avoidance to make demands for racial justice were fighting words. Half the nation seemed provoked to self-defense; "Make America Great Again" meant "stand your ground." The backlash rushed to DEI, a wholesale attack first on the silliness of certain training techniques, then to the suggestion of white guilt some programming seemed to elicit, eventually to the whole idea of white guilt, not as a critique of DEI excesses, but as an antiwhite evil in and of itself. The word I struggle to find in English entails a flipping of the concept of racial harm, so that victim can morph into victimizer even by demanding acts of awareness about their own victimization. This elusive word describes a sense of profound withholding matched by an exasperated unwillingness to await the calculation of another group's losses, an angry *anticipation* of a demand for accounting and a retributive impulse to silence it as a matter of right. Forever. We need a word for this.

Whatever word it is comprehends the hell out of structure. Unlike the racial reckoning, the right-wing racial backlash followed a different theory of change. The white backlash went very rapidly from awareness – the other side are woke thugs trying to guilt and replace us – to accountability – reframe the narrative and change the rules in order to impose lasting structural change. They suffered from no lack of words in English that united their resistance, often by appropriating the reckoning's own language. "Wokeism" became both a dirty word and an ideology to be subdued. Wokeism and wokeness were targeted by organized parent groups demanding and getting curricular changes at school board meetings. In short order, a majority of state legislatures across the country passed anti-Woke Acts and anti-DEI laws.[10] Books were/are being banned for their effect on white minds. While the relentless attack on critical race theory (CRT) seemed misnamed and inane at first, it eventually took on its own reality as a negative label for a broad range of awareness-reckoning work. Once labeled, the sources were easily banned in one place after another. Actual proponents of CRT could not ban racism, systemic or otherwise. Yet the backlash could discredit CRT, and CRT is all about structural inequality. The backlash showed it could take over university boards of trustees and undermine tenure standards, even before the defunding rage of Trump II.[11] As the wins and losses in this conflict ebbed and flowed, the backlash virtually ended the national conversation on racial reckoning. Terms thought liberating just months before had been delegitimated in popular discourse. One obvious result: It weakened the case for racial accountability, which may have been the point all along. By the time Donald Trump was elected a second time in 2024, it already appeared that most people supporting the racial reckoning had gotten off the train.

Before we assess the impact of Trump's reelection on racial reckoning, it's worth noting how divisions during Joe Biden's presidency added to a fatigue with what some liberals were now also pejoratively referring to as wokeness. Generational differences and circumstances colluded to weaken broad public interest. Younger people's demands for an undeclared orthodoxy of language and pronouns, especially around gender, led to intense organizational conflicts. The appeal of certain reforms, such as prison abolition, seemed increasingly to divide over age lines.[12] Circumstances also played a role. Immigration asylum claims skyrocketed, and Southern Republican governors exploited the untested resolve of Democratic mayors in the North, by busing thousands of undocumented migrants to overcrowded shelters in sanctuary cities already impacted by a housing affordability crisis.[13] Indeed, that crisis got much worse during Covid, especially when eviction moratoria expired. Sheltering in place so long and keeping kids out of school was not only unpopular but deadly. Violent crime rose dramatically during the period. The policy responses by the Biden administration prevented a recession and probably saved countless lives. Except for an executive order or two, the administration was mostly silent on the racial reckoning issue that helped usher Biden into office. Nor did it advance accountability in visible ways. Most importantly, it left the structure intact. Predictably, the Rule of Avoidance reasserted itself with cynical pendulation, as if you could set your historical watch to it.

TRUMP II: DEFAME AND DEFUND

Whole books have been written about the authoritarian fury with which Trump's second term began, but reckoning racial reckoning demands we focus on its approach to structure and race. MAGA Republicans combined culture, politics and law in unprecedented, if not often illegal, ways to produce a vituperative festival of racial othering. The fervid sense of racial injury was not matched by the facts or the national mood. DEI had long receded as a campaign issue. Nevertheless, Trump's white nationalist approach completed the reinterpretation of discrimination as something that happens routinely to whites and Asians, not Blacks and others. Laced among the flooded zone of executive orders, mass terminations and funding clawbacks was a recentering of whiteness that "wokeness" had subverted and for which it – and the "lunatic left" – would have to pay dearly. Trump II began not as more backlash but a counter-racial reckoning.

The structural assault had been engineered in the Heritage Foundation's "Project 2025" tome. Within Trump's first 100 days, he moved to cement a theory of centralized federal power (the "unitary executive theory") which asserted that the elected president could remake every facet of the executive branch, including once-independent agencies, in his policy image. He could also destroy them at will. And he could use their funding authority to issue threats. For example, the administration immediately cut foreign aid via the United States Agency for International Development (affecting mostly poor nonwhite people in the world), turned Immigration and Customs Enforcement (ICE) into a weapon against immigration and due process (primarily against nonwhite immigrants), and eviscerated the Department of Education (threatening Title I funds and programming as well as financial aid that would have immediate consequences for poorer districts and college students). The Trump administration sought to collapse the economic model upon which American universities, especially research institutions, had thrived since World War II by canceling federal grants either as vessels of DEI "wokeism" or for their universities' alleged tolerance for antisemitism. And the administration sought retributive justice by threatening the country's biggest, most powerful law firms for a number of pretextual offenses, such as employing lawyers who represented clients adverse to Trump. The list went on and on, a chaotic manifesto of accountability reckoning in service to revenge.

To conservative architects of the MAGA second round, these policy moves don't reflect retribution as much as a structural course correction in which structure is understood to have a causal relationship between culture, politics and law – not siloed spheres. Conservatives have argued that federal law itself, particularly civil rights statutes, set in motion a political and cultural takeover by the left that has threatened free speech since the 1960s, and it has to be repealed.[14] To conservative architects like Chris Rufo, the practices of elite higher education have had undue influence over society in general. "We have insane hatred written into the operating manual of universities."[15]

But deep in the authoritarian ideology was a white racial reckoning, too. It began immediately, as Trump signed post-inauguration executive orders (EO) on January 20 and January 21, 2025, that revived from its late Biden-era slumber the "anti-woke" war over race. This time, the Trump administration had a strategy of defame and defund, in which assertions of illegal discrimination leapfrogged proof, going from an accusatory name – "illegal DEI" – to the punishment of immediate defunding and mass terminations. The DEI-specific controls were based on three EOs: 14151, "Ending Radical and Wasteful Government DEI Programs and Preferencing" ("J20");[16] 14173, "Ending Illegal Discrimination and Restoring Merit-Based Opportunity" ("J21");[17] and 14188, issued on January 29, entitled "Additional Measures to Combat Anti-Semitism" ("J29").[18] All of these executive orders use the language of antidiscrimination to prohibit through termination, certification and enforcement processes "illegal and immoral discrimination programs, going by the name of 'diversity, equity, and inclusion'" (J20). The J21 EO asserted that universities as well as the federal government, corporations, law enforcement and the medical industry "have adopted and actively use dangerous, demeaning, and immoral race- and sex-based preferences under the guise of so-called ... DEI ... and DEIA that *can* violate the civil-rights laws of the Nation" (emphasis added). The Department of Education issued subsequent guidance in a "Dear Colleague Letter" ("DCL")[19] that reemphasized the antidiscrimination theme of these executive policies, specifically decrying discrimination against "white and Asian students, many of whom come from disadvantaged and low-income families." The proof of discrimination was in the allegation. Yet the allegations were strong on adjectives – "repugnant," "divisive," "left-wing radical" – and weak on substantive description, investigation or proof.

Both the vagueness of the terminology and the equivalence between Blackness and discrimination were deliberate. Whatever "DEI" was, it was associated with Blackness. Whatever was Black was associated with the victimization of whites and Asians through the discriminatory suppression of "merit." The onslaught launched a panicked period in which thousands of public and private institutions that did any amount of business with the federal government feverishly scrubbed mentions of "DEI" from their websites, fired DEI departments and professionals, all but repudiating their one-time ridership on the racial reckoning train. The surrender was broad and quick, especially in Southern states. According to one terminated DEI college officer, "The acronym and the word – there's no win in it. There's no win in claiming DEI. Let's just be clear about what we're doing."[20] Even programs that made simple inclusive sense were scrapped. If you were a Puerto Rican lesbian from a working-class family entering college at a predominantly white and wealthy institution in the fall of 2025, there'd be no affinity groups to welcome you, no nod to your distinct and highly unrepresented culture, no institutional hug embracing you a long way from home. You'd just be on your own.

Perhaps more important was Trump's less-noticed attack on equity. I've said that racial equity was almost a value at the original moment of racial reckoning, but that proved fleeting, wrapped more often in rituals of awareness than commitments to accountability. Equity, racial or otherwise, asks what a fair allocation of burdens and benefits is; in law, equitable relief demands that the inequity stop, unfair gains are disgorged and profits returned. Trump ordered everything with the word "equity" in it banned. Conservatives replaced it with references to "meritocracy," a slippery slope, as we'll see in the next chapter. Juxtaposing the two reinforces the idea of inherent Black inferiority, that equity is refuted by merit and that what Blacks achieve comes at the cost of deserved excellence. Many Trump administration policies overreached public approval. Yet the "we're better than you" campaign of Trump II has broad appeal.

REINVENTING DISCRIMINATION IN THE ZERO-SUM PRESIDENCY

Today's Republican MAGA rhetoric has its roots in a powerful legal movement that began when George Floyd was a little boy and long before Donald Trump was a political force. The modern conservative movement in law may have formally begun with the creation of the Federalist Society in 1983, which expanded upon the doctrinal underpinnings of a civil rights backlash that began with the Berger Court in the 1970s. The Federalists' long-term project was to rewrite constitutional interpretation through the persuasive mask of colorblind equality. Almost all civil rights legislation favoring racial justice is couched in neutral terms of equality. Most of it stems from the Fourteenth Amendment, the Reconstruction-era affirmation of the equality principle enshrined in the Declaration of Independence. Its Equal Protection Clause represents the constitutional basis for *all* people being created equal. Despite its origins and original intent, the Equal Protection Clause – no state shall make or enforce any law which shall "deny to any person within its jurisdiction the equal protection of the laws" – is prohibitory. It doesn't create rights or suggest what would affirm our equality, only what would deny it. In other words, it's the first antidiscrimination law. The meaning of racial doctrines in law and politics mostly turn on what you mean by anti- or nondiscrimination.

In conservative hands, antidiscrimination means colorblindness, and colorblindness is a doctrine of radical equality that precludes any use for racial equity. In a colorblind world, we exist in racial equanimity no matter the context, no matter the overwhelming evidence of racial inequality. Since to Federalists there is almost nothing we can do about inequality (but accept it as a reflection of meritocratic ranking), very little in law can be done to produce racially equitable programs that would help us achieve the broader benefits of racial equality – the subject of the next three chapters. Federal courts with Federalist judges have withered away any alternative idea of antidiscrimination, including remedial doctrines like affirmative action. Despite widening inequality and few discernible injuries to white people, the *political* battle over antidiscrimination went nuclear during Trump II.

The ultra-right-wing administration took antidiscrimination on the offensive. What was once racial avoidance transcended racial denial to arouse a wounded racial impatience that morphed into full-blown, retributive victimization. What is conventionally called "reverse discrimination" – that is, discrimination against people from a majority group – has been subverted into the presumptive race discrimination of our time. How? A program created in the name of diversity (e.g., group composition) or equity (e.g., funding assistance to underrepresented small businesses) or inclusion (e.g., a pipeline internship program) violates the colorblind idea of equality in antidiscrimination laws (e.g., Title VI) because maintaining equality is a "zero sum" enterprise. Every racial gain has an equal and opposite racial loss. Not only does this version of equality and discrimination make no room for racial equity, but it also makes racial accountability in the form of remediation measures extremely unlikely. In fact, by vilifying DEI and CRT as euphemisms for a Blackness worthy of punishment, it incentivizes others to distance themselves from racial reckoning and challenges many Blacks into silence. This is a harsh lesson for democracy because it makes an example of the very cause that helped to empower other pro-democratic movements: African-American empowerment. As I discuss further in Chapter 7, the racial reckoning had no collective response to this doctrinal reordering of antidiscrimination except perhaps incredulity.

CYNICAL PENDULATION

Maybe folks are waiting for it to spend itself. The second Trump presidency reminds us that nothing stays the same for long before the pendulum swings back. We should be careful what we hope for. Cynical pendulation is a feature of American racial politics. The predictable swing between a moment of reckoning and a longer moment of backlash has a long history, always implicating the Rules of Avoidance and Denial, always precluding remediation.

Pendulation shaped the stilted path of racial progress in the twentieth century and our expectations. As Derrick Bell observed in 1993, "At best, we can hope for … temporary 'peaks of progress,' short-lived periods of improved conditions that last a few years until white dominance once again reasserts itself."[21] Federal policy to promote, rather than prevent, racial equality was not a significant public interest until the presidency of John F. Kennedy, a Democrat. His successor, Lyndon Johnson, initiated comprehensive program commitments to racial equity with the Great Society and War on Poverty programs during the 1960s. No president before or since took such a serious view of the web of racial inequality in jobs, voting, housing, education and discriminatory practices. Yet nearly every federal policy step forward was followed by a step backward under the succeeding Republican administration of Richard Nixon, whose "Southern strategy" owed its electoral success to the racist sensibilities of Southern members of Congress. Much of what Johnson built Nixon dismantled or diluted. The pendulum swung back only slightly under Jimmy Carter's brief Democratic presidency, then swung radically rightward under President Ronald Reagan. Reagan's hope to abolish affirmative action entirely was stymied. Yet by the early 1980s, the Republican backlash against civil rights had gained strength at most levels of policy, including welfare, housing, aid to cities, equal employment, constitutional law and policing. Much of what we associate with systemic racism today has its roots in Reagan's War on Drugs, his federal financial withdrawal from housing and President Bill Clinton's transformation of welfare. The avoidance was superficial, the denial aggressive.

Yet even if we accept a certain amount of pendulation on federal policy as a fact of bipartisan life, pendulation on race has great consequence for injustice. It produces an unstable middle ground that operates to compromise basic human rights. Cynical pendulation on race issues is not an accident but a feature of systemic racism, a clockwork-like mechanism that sustains it over time.

Beyond policy, there's also the cynical pendulation on race that seems a feature of time itself. We often confuse an epiphany for a moment of structural change. Rodney King's 1994 beating, the acquittal of the cops who mercilessly took turns beating him in the street and the subsequent uprising in Los Angeles in which sixty-three died and $1 billion in damage was done to what was then still called South Central was supposed to be a reckoning on policing and race – especially where accountability failed. The changes did not follow. The race talk at the heart of it all was eventually avoided; that silence meant denial.

Next was Hurricane Katrina in 2005, a perfect storm of wind, flooding, infrastructural neglect and incompetent crisis management that took the lives of 1,800 mostly poor, mostly Black New Orleanians and left homeless many thousands of uninsured households who'd been consigned to live below sea level. The nation couldn't believe the vulnerability of so many Americans languishing in plain sight. It was a racial reckoning. We promised to change. Many never returned and many others never recovered. Awareness was abundant yet transitory while accountability and change ran out in a hurry. That it fell disproportionately on Black people was avoided until it could be denied.

Last was the election of the nation's first Black president. There was a racial reckoning from which the United States would never go back, a signature crossing of a we-shall-overcome threshold. Barack Obama had captured something essential in the best spirit of American voters. His brilliance, charming cool and inclusive vision represented an idea of good governance – and racial pride – for which by 2008, we were somehow ready. Breaking that racial barrier was a momentous achievement for the country and, like the rise of Kamala Harris and others, shouldn't be diminished. The Obama presidency was notable for many important seen and unseen accomplishments. It did not, however, radically reshape racial inequality nor include racial accountability among its political goals. It stabilized a recessionary economy, overhauled health care in equitable ways and offered symbolic hopes to a people always needing it. But it was no racial reckoning unless you include the backlash: Donald Trump and the rise of MAGA.

There is also the pendulation of wishful thinking. Nothing demonstrates the permanence of racism clouding American life more than the almost universal effort to wish it away with inspirational examples. Many believed that Obama was proof of "post-racialism." This wishful thinking is especially powerful for Black and white Americans whose views have long defined the content of race relations. For whites, part of what made sports figures like Muhammad Ali and Michael Jordan so beloved was their symbolic power to unite people in their best wishes for a society done with race hatred. For Blacks, wishful thinking reframed Bill Clinton, a centrist Democratic president whose crime bills finished erecting the mass incarceration complex of millions of Black men, as "the first Black president." Racism is so awful that it creates its own glass-half-full beliefs. Many Americans who are neither white nor Black appreciate enough of the horror and dread of American racism that, for complicated reasons, they too prefer to wish away the worst of it (or to universalize it as inevitable). This is another facet of the Rule of Avoidance. How natural to embrace a colorblind notion of what happens to us. A predictable push on the pendulum that you can set your watch to, wishful thinking about race is peaceful thinking about the society you live in.

All of these social physics – federal policy swings, forgetful memories over time and wishful thinking – can keep the work of white supremacy intact if we don't intentionally and persistently reckon with it. We'd be wise to acknowledge the force of cynical pendulation at the start of this book as we consider what lasting racial reckoning requires.

A WORD

We will have to invent another word or two and perhaps take back a few. The racial reckoning was a critically important but spontaneous outburst based on many quiet years of Black Struggle and a spectacular culmination of economic pain, death and outrage that had been background noise to a young century. It barely made a generational dent. What should have launched a reckoning of accountability for material racial inequality became mired in a reckoning of awareness associated largely with identity. What might have established a more democratic rationale for remedying the cumulative effect of longstanding racial harms never got much beyond the mixture of principles and approaches known generally as DEI. Aided by the compulsion for racial avoidance and denial, the focus on anti-Black marginalization was attached to many other struggles, understandably perhaps, but in the chaotic process, diluted. White supremacy was not taken seriously enough for the transformative change that's overdue.

Before the shortcomings could be addressed, they were attacked by a backlash, followed by a counter-racial reckoning. Pro-Palestinian rights protests of Israel's war in Gaza provided the basis for widespread institutional paralysis over free speech and the pretext for a sweeping right-wing response from the second Trump administration. Into that political void thrust an aggressively retributive executive, who successfully weaponized anti-DEI and antisemitism into a defame-and-defund campaign against hundreds of core US institutions. Then came the ICE raids and mass deportations of immigrants. The naked assertion of so much federal power, unfettered by constitutional law, induced the repudiation of most remaining public promises around inclusion and the abandonment, at least for a time, of the fight for some vague idea of "antiracism." Those who fought back might have waged a battle more for their independent survival than in defense of specific ideals. Few would say. Racial reckoning on behalf of African Americans, at least the kind we might have imagined in the years immediately following the spring of 2020, seemed all but lost.

Consider this grounds for resistance.

CHAPTER 2

How Equality Bred Inequality

If we needed new words to understand what triggered the racial reckoning and its backlash, we may need a new language to understand the inequality on which both are based. Or maybe just our eyes.

There's no reason for racial reckoning if racial disparities don't result from fundamentally unequal opportunities. There should be no reason for a political and legal backlash unless conservatives perceive racial inequality against whites. Both views claim racial injury. I argue that racial reckoning demands remedies, not just awareness. MAGA Republicans seem to demand remedies for racial inequality, too. The racial inequality underlying this conflict shouldn't be so hard to ascertain. This chapter attempts to describe racial inequality in ways a visitor from another world would understand. Key to this understanding is the recognition that unequal resources result mostly from unequal places, and unequal places are significantly determined by race. If the words don't communicate it, the images might.

Racial inequality occurs when important resources for well-being are systematically and substantially unequal in part because of identifiable wrongdoing. It's not simply any situation where things aren't the same. The racial disparity must have a causal connection to racism. When you start from this idea, racial inequality reflects the systematic imposition of excess burdens because of race. The racial injury must be demonstrable, not hypothetical. When we look at rates of unarmed persons killed by police, people suffering from preventable, manageable underlying health conditions or relegated to environments that predictably stymie wealth accumulation, that's unremediated racial inequality at work because those patterns don't recur by accident.

Some people fundamentally disagree. They believe inequality is the mere absence of equality. Equality is ground zero, the status quo. We are all equal. There is not some baseline of racial discrimination to acknowledge. However, when you introduce a racial preference of any kind or take race into account, you disturb the equilibrium with discriminatory treatment. You produce racial inequality. This belief forms the core of the backlash to racial reckoning as well as the reason the Supreme Court majority all but eliminated race-conscious admissions in *SFFA v. Harvard*, explored at the end of the chapter.

Racial reckoning, if it's to happen, must challenge this view of racial inequality, which we'll see in the chapters that document racial inequality in wealth, health and policing. But first we have to settle on what constitutes racial injury. Usually that entails laying out a whole lot of statistics on unequal outcomes, which I'll do later. However, we can start with what's visible. Racial inequality is not an abstract phenomenon. What becomes apparent even from an eye test is that place became the repository of both racial and socioeconomic inequality. Suburbs, in particular, have been very powerful places in producing excess benefits and burdens by race. So has discrimination. It shows that the debate about racial inequality is really a debate about the skewed racial allocation of resources that each of us needs for a stable, productive life.

We don't all have to go to Harvard. Yet whether or not any of us has a legitimate shot at doing so became the crucible of legal debate about racial injury and what contributes to racial inequality. In a case about getting into Harvard, the Supreme Court majority was wrong in 2023 to radically limit the consideration of race in college admissions to an applicant's personal essay. The wrong, as we'll see, went not just to its upside-down reading of race law. In all its colorblind certainty, the Court fundamentally missed the underlying inequality hiding in plain sight, which gives powerful cover to those who distort the whole idea of racial injury.

THE EYE TEST

Racial inequality is visible if you know where to look.

If you go where money is spent – like most airports, in the stands at professional sports arenas during games, along the walkways of luxury shopping malls, at nice hotels and resorts, in above-average restaurants – you'll see a limited number of Black people, far less than their 13 percent of the population. Black absence is acute in coastal enclaves of liberal affluence, like New York City, Boston, Los Angeles, even formally "chocolate cities" like Washington, DC. The purge of Blacks in San Francisco was complete long before the tech industry made it worse. Or take your high schooler on a college tour to the fifty most selective universities in the country or your preschooler to a sought-after private child care center. We're predictably underrepresented in all these places.

Next visit some places where money is not so obviously being spent, like the high school sports leagues that serve as feeders for college programs in soccer, lacrosse, crew, fencing and other scholarships; Congressional staffer internships and STEM apprenticeships;[1] even the leadership offices of DEI programs (76 percent white in 2021);[2] or the racial composition of prison wardens.[3] These are expensive pipelines to power because of their unadvertised price tags. Or they're lucrative positions hidden in less-obvious career ladders. The US spends a lot on prisons and wardens, $80 billion[4] and $150,000 per year, respectively. Whereas 38.6 percent of prisoners are Black, only 3.7 percent of wardens are.[5] The racial composition of these sports fields, marbled hallways, classrooms, even prison executive wings tells you much about unequal access to the means by which opportunities become outcomes.

Then look at the composition of places where serious money is made, like corporate boardrooms, Wall Street firms, Big Law, tech companies, private equity, the US Senate, the fashion industry, accountants or doctors.[6] We know many Black people hold these jobs. Yet most of us don't even *expect* to see Black people represented in these workplaces with more than token numbers. They're not.

Now visit the places where much less money is made: mailrooms, warehouses, nursing homes, electric-bike delivery-worker dispatch areas, fast-food restaurants. No surprises here. There we are, in far more than our 13 percent would predict, in the places we expect Blacks to be overrepresented. African-American workers have swung the farthest into the service economy, not just in low-wage employment, but in many solidly middle-class jobs in administration, transportation, health care and business operations.[7]

Finally, go where most of us never go willingly – the "'hood" sections of cities and inner-ring suburbs. Here a landscape neglected by private investment and public amenity is grounds for struggle. There are few stores or fresh-food retailers, few welcoming public spaces, the open and obvious risks of abandoned properties, a diminished sense of safety; and trees are noticeably absent. However, of course, Black people are not only overrepresented, they are also hyperrepresentative of these very places. For generations, areas of high "concentrated poverty" in the United States (i.e., 30 percent or more of households having incomes below the poverty line) have been associated with African Americans more than any other group – around 45 percent.[8] This is a spatial expression of persistent poverty that isolates residents by both economic and racial segregation. About one in five Blacks lived in concentrated poverty in 2022 whereas only one in twenty whites and Asians did.[9]

Where people show up and in what capacity is good evidence of racial inequality. We're not a colorblind nation unable to detect these differences. What we see is stark. What it means is complicated. Black people lack the disposable income in proportion to their numbers that enables them to partake casually in the upper strata of expensive activities, because fewer hold the jobs in numbers that sustain those lifestyles. Instead, most inhabit more moderate-income spaces, both as consumers and workers. Black poverty rates are still comparable only to Native Americans, and Black poverty is compounded by its geographic isolation. Our little eye test shows that place is so powerful that it signifies not only who achieves in the racial economic hierarchy, but how. Blacks are not in corporate boardrooms in large numbers because they weren't on lacrosse teams where those connections were first forged. Blacks are disproportionately in those minimum-wage jobs because Blacks have disproportionately lived where those are the most available. Place describes *and* determines outcomes. Ample research predicts these outcomes based on place-based opportunities. When we scan the rooms to see who's there, we see the unequal opportunities that led to the unequal outcomes.

Scenes of racial underrepresentation and overrepresentation suggest a working definition: Racial inequality is the race-based denial of the resources necessary to succeed as an individual and a community. Being equal beings has little to do with it. The disproportionality of racial presence in the places above – far too few Blacks where resources are great, far too many where resources are fewer – reflects racial hierarchy in the US. To many African Americans, the scenes depict the fruits of a rigged system that demands reckoning. Research demonstrating how place mediates racial inequality offers some of the most analytically important insights on post–civil rights, post–industrial capitalism in the United States. We explore its cumulative effects on the racial wealth gap in the next chapter and some of the implications for reckoning in the final one. Next, we see its basic mechanics.

THE GEOGRAPHY OF OPPORTUNITY

Simply put, your life chances were helped considerably if you grew up in a stable American suburb, with friendships across class lines and fathers around. This isn't to deny the importance of hardworking parents and other role models who poured love into you and taught you how to be resourceful and committed. That's something most families do for their children. Researchers George Galster and Patrick Sharkey show that, in three ways, we soak up the resources for life through the "spatial opportunity structure" in the immediate neighborhood around us and other formative environments.[10] First we encounter the environment itself, whether it contains a range of elements from positive resources to threats. This is beyond our control, but it conditions many important choices we make. Second, the spatial opportunity structure shapes our perceptions of how to evaluate the "payoffs" from the choices available to us, life decisions that can affect generations. Third, "in the case of children and youth, the spatial opportunity structure indirectly influences their attributes through induced changes in the resources, behaviors, and attitudes of their caregivers."[11] In other words, our life chances are heavily influenced every step of the way by the life choices made available to us and others in our immediate social environments. These environments are often radically unequal in the institutional resources they offer families – safe opportunities for recreation, solid schools with high expectations and supportive teachers, parenting norms and levels of education, the presence of working people and access to job opportunities, healthy food. Spatial opportunity structures may not *cause* racial inequality based on place, but they characterize the relationships between environmental opportunities and life outcomes. They are among the key social determinants of what happens to us, because they strongly influence the probability of what's possible and how to get there.

Looking around, we know this already. Locational choices are baked into every meaningful decision we make. It's like talking about air. Or trees. Most Americans take this reality for granted as the linguistic calculus of a good life. Area median income. School rankings. Tax base per capita. Firearms deaths per square mile. Locally unwanted land uses. Walkability ratings. The worst house in the best neighborhood. A vast literature shows that opportunity starts and often ends with the geography of residency: the character of home.

Viewing place from a strengths perspective, economist Raj Chetty and his colleagues show how place promotes or retards economic mobility – the ability to improve a child's socioeconomic life chances by moving to another place.[12] They too found that children's opportunities are closely connected to what they're exposed to, and the earlier, closer and longer the exposure, the more its impact. They identified five key ingredients of high-mobility neighborhoods: They have less segregation by income and race, lower levels of income inequality, better schools, lower rates of violent crime and a larger share of two-parent households.[13] "On average, moving within one's metro area from a below-average to an above-average neighborhood in terms of upward mobility would increase the lifetime earnings of a child growing up in a low-income family by $200,000. Children who grow up in better areas are also less likely to be incarcerated and are less likely to have teen births."[14] Unfortunately, the same research shows chronic income inequality between Blacks and whites. In fact, intergenerational income gaps between whites and other groups are shrinking except for the two most segregated groups, Blacks and Native Americans.[15] Black men's experiences and outcomes, for better or worse, have the greatest impact on inequality measures like income.

But why do neighborhood resource differences affect societal outcomes *by race*? Two reasons: continuing segregation and discrimination. First, because segregation sorts the quality of available resources, place *overdetermines* Blacks' access to opportunities. Growing up in a resource-rich place with low racial bias tends to produce a lifetime trajectory of benefits or advantages. Growing up in a resource-poor place with high racial bias tends to produce struggle or disadvantages. One would think that the sheer diversity of American communities – 53% growth in non-white populations compared to 1% among whites – would compel more integrated living environments and spread resources more evenly.[16] Yet segregation today stands roughly where it did when the century began, with whites living in mostly white neighborhoods across the country despite the growing diversity of the metro around them. Since most Blacks still grow up in the most segregated neighborhoods (and segregation may be rising for all groups) and tend to have lower incomes,[17] residential segregation by both race and class makes the disadvantages of place more challenging and harder to overcome. This simply doesn't affect other groups as much for reasons I explore in the next chapter.

Second, place-based disadvantages *amplify* the power of other forms of unchecked racial discrimination, especially implicit or covert bias. Anti-Black racism still has more socioeconomic impact than prejudice against other groups. This is why the ability to grow up in stable middle-class suburbs is so important and being white continues to help a lot. Neither fact is an accident nor the result of pure "merit."

The research from Chetty and others may help to explain a distinctly twenty-first-century story that I explore in the final chapter: Nobody knows these findings like the Black people who have moved because of them. There's growing evidence that since at least 2000, Black households are not waiting for structural inequality to have its way with their futures and, more than any other group of Americans, they're moving in pursuit of greater opportunity, though affordability constraints force some very difficult choices.

THE SUBURBS AND EXCLUSION

And then there's trees – how abundant and who gets access to them.

At mid-century the United States created the greatest avenue to household wealth imaginable through access to suburban homeownership.[18] As discussed in the next chapter, those towns and subdivisions beyond city limits were subsidized through a vast network of federal and state programs. These places were built for family success – safety, schools, protection from disturbances, access to nature, plenty of public goods – and they produced it. Historically, subsidization was downplayed and self-sufficiency exalted. We need not linger on these benefits too long, because there's an excellent chance that most readers of this book already know firsthand what I'm talking about. They also know that these places were (and often still are) racially homogeneous, the benefits extended almost exclusively to white people for a very long time. Less well-known perhaps is that what made suburbia so valuable to inequality today is the structure of racial exclusion it institutionalized in both policy and law seventy-five years ago.

The America in which most judges, politicians, industry leaders, lawyers, investment bankers and academics grew up calculated the gains of racial exclusion and made it a systemic artform. Although *Brown v. Board of Education* eventually outlawed *de jure* racial segregation, other facially neutral rules of local self-governance were more effective in recreating segregated environments. First, localism (or local control) as a method of governance proliferated at the state level through Home Rule laws, giving localities great latitude to exercise "police powers" on behalf of their community's welfare. The police power includes local taxation, zoning and land use, education and public safety. It's contained within jurisdictional lines, creating an us-versus-them mindset that formally privileges the voices of insider-homeowners against the interests of outsiders who may be affected by their decisions. These mechanisms of governance and finance promote the idea of self-sufficiency (not outside subsidy) that then entitles these small local democracies to great deference from courts whenever their policies are challenged. If exclusionary mechanisms are ever challenged, municipalities need only offer a court a "rational basis" for their policies in defense. Why? They stopped mentioning race.

Second, local control not only signifies self-determination, but it also relies on a kind of fiscally conservative business model. What's good for tax ratables is good for local democracy. Thus, racially homogeneous localism produced a set of common tools to increase local tax ratables yet keep taxes down, remove "undesirable elements" from the schools and housing and thereby keep property values up. The official tools were exclusionary zoning (typically against multifamily housing, rentals and smaller lots), rejection of public housing and school district policies like neighborhood schools and school choice. The unofficial tools were blatant real estate discrimination, intimidation of nonwhite buyers and unyielding rejection of fair housing rules when they arrived in the late 1960s. Rather than appear racist, towns think of themselves as rational.

Because towns compete with each other for new people who want the same things, there's little incentive to question the practices and the cycles repeat themselves.

The system worked. In tens of thousands of suburban communities across the country, these techniques of governance and racial exclusion were supported by courts and state legislatures, producing the higher property values, solid schools and stable tax bases that most of us identify with the "American Dream."[19] Most importantly, they lay the foundation for what Chetty and others call "neighborhood effects," just as they were intended. The suburb as an institution was designed to agglomerate the opportunity resources necessary for both individual or community success: appreciating home ownership; schools attached to college readiness; safe streets and abundant recreation; effective social networks connecting households to jobs, community support and political voice. Even the Supreme Court weighed in prosaically to defend the value of suburbs:

> A quiet place where yards are wide, people few, and motor vehicles restricted are legitimate guidelines in a land-use project addressed to family needs ... The police power is not confined to elimination of filth, stench, and unhealthy places. It is ample to lay out zones for family values, youth values, and the blessings of quiet seclusion and clean air make the area a sanctuary for people.[20]

The Court failed to mention the benefit of trees, but you don't get the proverbial "leafy 'burb" without them. This no doubt establishes the power of place to affect people's life chances.

Yet here's the catch: *It didn't have to resist integration forever.* The race-neutral model could have become a race-neutral way of life but for the underlying condition of racism. Nothing else, not even the desire for higher property values, compelled continuing patterns of racial exclusion across so many American suburbs. From the standpoint of racial inequality, the techniques of racial exclusion employed in the suburban growth model heightened its gains for whites and compounded losses for Blacks. It was – and in many places still very much is – place-based opportunity built on racism where racism and rationality are in effect deemed synonymous.

Of course, you didn't have to grow up in an affluent white suburb to experience enhanced preferential opportunity relative to Blacks. Nor did you have to be excluded from one to experience racial discrimination. In *The White Bonus*, a carefully researched book about members of her own white family and friends, journalist Tracie McMillan examined the lives of working-class whites in the Midwest to see whether they benefited from racial inequality.[21] At first blush, it seemed improbable that ordinary Midwestern people – union workers, nurses, construction tradespeople – even indirectly benefited from being white compared to their Black coworkers and friends. But in small yet important ways they had. For instance, McMillan describes how Katrina Rectenwald, a likable, hard-working white woman, rose from hourly work in a nursing home to become a nurse, union leader and spouse who owned her own newly renovated home while a similarly situated Black coworker – also likable, also hardworking – struggled to be recognized and rewarded for her talents. McMillan describes the cumulative benefits of being white as falling into two buckets, a social bonus and a family bonus.

> [R]acism is both a direct payment and a form of compounding interest. One person gets paid more, or gets to buy a house, or doesn't get locked up, because they are white. This is their social bonus. They use that bonus to build wealth. Then they pass that wealth on to their children, who experience those resources as a family bonus. As these children enter the world as adults, they accumulate their own social bonuses – which in turn become the family bonus they pass on to *their* children.[22]

In the case of Katrina, McMillan conservatively estimates that her family bonus was about $160,000 by the time she was thirty-eight, her social bonus almost $16,000 (in 2023 dollars). Most of the family bonus is related to place. The ability to pay subsidized rent, the loan for home improvement and the family-subsidized housing in lieu of a costly mortgage are all traceable to being white, according to the author. Even for ordinary people, these things add up.

Or they don't, diminished by discrimination.

RACISM IN THE TREES

Racial discrimination also works alongside place-based resource disparities to sustain racial inequality over time. Racist behavior and implicit bias worsen inequality. Decades of studies, for example, show that hiring managers discriminate against job applicants with Black-sounding names like Shanice or Terrell in favor of white-sounding names like Emily or Adam.[23] Across all fifty states, employers take less time reviewing their resumés and less frequently call them back for interviews.[24] Impatience is one of the characteristics of hiring discrimination of men with criminal records, too: formerly incarcerated white men are hired at much higher rates than Black men and called back for interviews more often.[25] We know that white high-school drop-outs are more readily hired than Black college students.[26] In consumer transactions like car insurance purchases, Blacks are charged higher prices for the same products.[27] When the federal government tested access to bank loans with equally well-qualified Black and white small businesses, Black owners were offered lesser products on worse terms and otherwise given unequal treatment.[28] McMillan ascribes the remainder of the white bonus Katrina Rectenweld received to race discrimination by unions, employers and educational institutions. We can't know in every case how the relative advantages of growing up in one place versus another affects individual outcomes, nor exactly how those experiences condition racist behavior. But we know it creates a feedback loop of consequences.

Those consequences appear as the lopsided numbers of racial inequality in the United States that most analyses start with. Blacks have lower median household income than any racial group – $52,860 compared to $81,060 for non-Hispanic whites, $108,700 for Asians and $62,800 for Latinos.[29] Black median household net worth (measured by assets minus liabilities) is $24,520 – though a quarter of all Black households have either zero or negative wealth. Whites have *ten times* that amount and only 8.6% have zero or negative wealth.[30] Much of this reflects disparate rates of homeownership – Blacks at 45%, whites 74.4%, Asians 61% and Latinos 48.6%.[31] Even if you own that home, its median value (not to mention how much equity versus debt one actually has in it) means everything to financial well-being. The average home value for white homeowners is higher than Black homeowners by a ratio of 2.5, unchanged since about 1970.[32] College attendance boosts lifetime earnings. Four-year college attendance is steeply less for Blacks (23%) than whites (39%) and Asians (59%) while Latinos still lag (18%).[33] College is also the ticket to white-collar or professional employment where again Blacks underperform – 40% for women and 28% for men; whites 48% for women and

39% for men; Asians 57% for women and 59% for men; and Latinos 30% for women and only 20% for men.[34] Black unemployment has for decades been recorded at about twice the national rate.[35] The lifetime gap between the experiences of Blacks at birth – 10.55 deaths per 1,000 births versus 4.3 for whites[36] – and death – Black life expectancy was 70.8 years in 2021 compared to 76.4 for whites – is profound.[37] Black liberty lags others, with incarceration rates twelve times more than whites.[38] And Blacks' poverty rates are second only to that of Native Americans. In each case and many others, the numbers reflect continuing racialized harms not shared by whites. That's not to deny that most Americans experience socioeconomic disadvantage at some point; many struggle. Racial inequality presents a problem for racial reckoning that, I've argued, ultimately demands a democratic reckoning. The needs of racial justice are like oxygen to the canary in the coalmine. Or trees, the abundant presence of which is a defining difference between Black-identified spaces and white as well as a factor recent research says has demonstrable public health benefits. Believe it or not, trees seem to extend your life.[39]

None of this extra burdening is to ignore broad Black gains. One can recognize the racial character of place-based advantages while acknowledging that there are plenty of strong Black and mixed communities. There's no shortage of resilience, hard work and Black excellence. However, it is also true that Black people and Native Americans are the only groups in the US for whom statistical progress over time is questionable. That is, only our children may have *fewer* opportunities to attend elite schools than we did, or live shorter lives, earn and own less wealth, vote less freely or hold fewer positions of leadership. For Black people, ordinary notions of progress are contingent, not expected. The question here is, how is colorblindness consistent with such undeniable racial inequality?

DISPARATE IMPACTS AND THE LAW NOT WITH US

At this point, our imaginary visitor might pipe up to ask why American law couldn't correct such obviously visible racial disparities. She would think that 160 years after emancipation we had solved the problem at its root. A national strategy of ending racial inequality would have required a baseline principle of equality and clear citizenship status that included the right to vote, serve in government and sit on juries. All the fundamental rights in the Constitution would apply. We brag to the visitor that we did all that – formal equality of citizenship – recognized in the Civil Rights Movement's statutory victories of the 1960s and commemorated in Martin Luther King's (unevenly observed) holiday. For about one fraught decade, the nation experimented with affirmative efforts to open up industries and employment practices that excluded Blacks, ensure voting integrity, end institutional barriers to entry, demand fair housing and enforce antidiscrimination rules. Congress passed the immigration law that welcomed diverse millions of nonwhite peoples to the country. Like conservatives today, many civil rights leaders at the time argued that antidiscrimination law was the path to equality regardless of "race, color, religion, sex, and national origin." In the majority of early cases, the race discrimination at issue had occurred under law – *de jure* – and was explicit and intentional, such as segregated schools or all-white unions. At the time of what some historians call the second Reconstruction, racial inequality could be read understandably as the eradication of unmistakable, in-your-face racial discrimination.

But racism and racial inequality are more savvy and profound than that, the effects of white supremacist structures lasting long after vulgar race talk has gone mute in public. To end, not just modify, racial inequality would require a broad theory of remediation that reaches the processes that reproduce systemic disadvantage, even if they spoke in race-neutral terms, not Jim Crow. The theory would view racial injury in a consequential way, asking what rules, norms or practices are responsible for these consistently disparate results? Its idea of discrimination would include the many ways it happens – conscious and unconscious, intentional and negligent, individual and institutional, direct and indirect. Its timeline of racial injury could extend beyond an identifiable moment of transgression. It might even remedy large racial injuries that can be traced only indirectly to large discrimination. Finally, it would see that in a world of racial inequality, causation is not just a matter of causing harm to a victim. It's also causing the advancement of white supremacy, the thing most responsible for racial inequality in the first place, and the main threat to US democracy.

This we didn't do. Instead, the Rule of Denial entails resistance, which took the almost imperceptible form of doctrinal compromises, carve outs and occasional "hell nos" in the law. A few examples suffice to show how judicial chess moves in landmark cases dramatically eroded the potential to remedy racial inequality through litigation.

Take discrimination in public contracting. To integrate infrastructure development beyond the overwhelmingly white private contractors that built public works projects in the former capital of the confederacy, the Richmond, VA city council passed a minority business set-aside ordinance that required 30 percent participation by minority firms. But in the 1989 *Croson* case,[40] the Supreme Court applied the strict scrutiny test and criticized the city's justification for racial inclusion. To the majority of justices, Richmond's all-white contractor class had themselves become victims of a racial classification policy designed to gradually remedy long-standing racial inequality in the construction trades. As a result, states cut back on affirmative action contracting programs, and, six years later, the federal government banned them, too (*Adarand*).[41]

Take school segregation. To remedy a verdict that the Detroit public schools were intentionally segregated, a court ordered the adjacent white suburbs to participate in the desegregation plan. The Supreme Court found that this too victimized innocent white people (parents). In *Miliken v. Bradley*,[42] the Supreme Court acquitted them of any responsibility for the segregated schools many had recently fled for the suburbs. The case not only killed the possibility of regional remedies, but also gave a definitive thumbs up to white flight at a time when cities were hemorrhaging their tax bases.

Or take denial of the right to vote. To ensure compliance with the Voting Rights Act among states with a proven history of suppressing Black votes, Congress created a mechanism whereby those states would have to get pre-clearance for any changes to their voting rules. But in *Shelby County v. Holder*, another five-justice majority of the Supreme Court decided that, by 2013, such racism was a thing of the past and ruled the pre-clearance provision unconstitutional. Immediately after the decision, a spate of voter suppression laws were launched across the South.

These decisions are bound by a staunch refusal to acknowledge the underlying conditions that reproduce inequality. By often slim majorities, the judicial branch read the nation's civil rights protections narrowly, skeptically, always cautious not to impinge on white innocence. Atomizing race discrimination against Blacks as if it had already been overcome, they invented increasingly stringent tests on racial justice advocates to prove its existence. These were rulings of denial.

But what if we wanted to litigate on racial inequality in a big, structural way where the specific discrimination by a specific discriminator was not as obvious as the racial harm to a class of people?

This is the problem of disparate-impact discrimination, one of the hardest structural inequality problems to solve. When we think about racial inequality in structural terms, we use big numbers over large periods of time to point to a harmful imbalance. The income statistics from earlier show unequal results and they *suggest* that each result demonstrated the uneven impact of something that caused extra harm to Blacks. Most arguments about racialized harm – whether reparations for slavery or statistically significant differences – are a version of disparate impact where the cause is indistinct. Something wrongful is causing higher asthma rates among Blacks as well as higher maternal mortality rates and excess deaths. Whatever the probable causes – years of nearby polluters, a warming environment, expensive neonatal care, rogue cops, unhealthy food options – they have a disparate impact on Black lungs, Black moms and Black bodies. Structural inequality can predict these bad results. People don't give themselves asthma or present themselves unarmed to be beaten to death by police or excluded from healthy neighborhoods with excellent schools. The list of racially disparate impacts is long and demands reckoning. Yet it's not always clear what caused the disparity and who or what is responsible for the inequality of outcomes. Again, the causal nature of racial wrongfulness can't just be claimed; it must be proved. In a different legal world, we would recognize that racial discrimination takes many causal paths and that where its harmful effects align with the mode of discriminatory behavior, it raises an inference that the discriminatory conduct, policy or pattern of practices caused the harm. Hence the legal fight over the disparate-impact doctrine. It's been largely lost for now.

Briefly, the doctrine is judge-made, first appearing in a landmark employment discrimination decision in 1971, *Griggs v. Duke Power*.[43] That case involved whether an employer could continue using racially neutral tests that clearly favored white applicants over Black but offered no business justification. The test itself appeared "racially neutral," meaning that it did not say "Black people can't take this test," or "Black people need not apply." But the test itself was not needed for the job and was designed in a way that would either prevent Black people from applying, for fear of failing the test, or fail them. The mechanics of disparate impact require the plaintiff to show a certain amount of disparity that can't be explained by nondiscriminatory means. Specifically, the Department of Justice has defined the burden-shifting architecture of disparate impact this way:

1. Disparate impact. Does the adverse effect of the policy or practice fall disproportionately on a race, color or national origin group?
2. Justification. If so, does the record establish a substantial legitimate justification for the policy or practice?
3. Less discriminatory alternative. Is there an alternative that would achieve the same legitimate objective but with less of a discriminatory effect?[44]

The doctrine expanded to housing, voting and other areas in some form. Agencies promulgated incredibly technical rules to show how much statistical evidence had to be shown at each stage. Legal scholars debated its meaning and merits – was it a proxy for showing intentional discrimination or something less?[45] The Supreme Court narrowed it considerably by demanding that it prove intentional discrimination, but it didn't ban the doctrine outright. Nevertheless, disparate impact as a method of causal proof is not especially popular or successful in US courts[46] – even if it makes a lot of intuitive sense to people who worry about the consistent racial lopsidedness of structural inequality.

Disparate impact may be one of those rare legal doctrines that enjoys more success outside of court because of the fights about it within them. Conservatives have railed against disparate impact for decades as if it were a gift to civil rights plaintiffs. It's not. They've argued that it makes the job of showing discrimination too easy. Results show otherwise.[47] Nevertheless, they've politicized their contempt for disparate impact. In fact, one of the Trump administration's early executive orders attempted to ban the use of disparate-impact proof. We can't know what lasting legal damage Trump's EO will have on the doctrine. But it should rejuvenate nonlegal efforts to show how past and present patterns of race discrimination can manifest as racially disparate harms that we must address as a matter of policy fairness. That is, the public conflict over disparate impact helps to keep the idea alive for other uses, such as teaching about structural inequality. Ironically, revanchism may have so severely weakened legal disparate impact that only political conflict can save it.

SUING FOR PLACE

But what if we just wanted to make a more direct assault on racial inequality that focused on its underlying conditions? Place, I argued, contains most of the relevant benefits and burdens connected to life chances. What if you don't live in a leafy suburb? You live in a low- to moderate-income segregated neighborhood where property values hardly move, rents keep rising, public services are substandard and schools consistently rank among the bottom fifth in the state. Does antidiscrimination law afford you a remedy for the redlining, highway construction and/or urban renewal that determined those economic conditions? What about suing for the generations of direct housing discrimination that limited your parents' or grandparents' residential options in the first place? As we'll see in the next chapter, all of these problems that conditioned the availability of resources in Black-identified places existed at the time of the Civil Rights Movement, yet very little in the civil rights laws addressed remedies for them. None of the problems of place that followed that period are readily susceptible to legal remedy under any theory. Almost seventy-five years after *Brown*, if you can't undo segregation, surely you can undo segregation's disparate impacts and reduce racial inequality? The answer before Trump II was sadly no. The answer afterwards is how dare you ask.

Overall, the single biggest obstacle to straightforward remedial lawsuits against racial inequality is colorblind constitutionalism,[48] which conservative and Federalist judges used to preclude true remediation when the goal of antidiscrimination law was to do just the opposite. Soon racial inequality addressed only intentional discrimination, narrowly defined. Attention to context or history was replaced by an elegant but simplistic principle: radical equality. Far-right conservatives (and some more moderate thinkers) would disagree. They believe the goal is equality, and there's nothing radical about that. Colorblindness is a way to say the goal's already been met, which sets up the claim that race-conscious remediation efforts – even by the milder standards of "diversity" – discriminate against whites (and Asians). They don't really want to argue about material inequality because they can't. The evidence of persistent disparity is all around us. They don't care to engage in the mechanics of structural inequality as we've done in this chapter or to measure its actual racial injuries as we'll do in the next three. They're more interested in nonvisible injuries against often hypothetical whites (and Asians). Ultimately, colorblind constitutionalism effected a full reversal, standing racial equality on its head in a decision on college admissions that made white people the victims of racial discrimination – *Students for Fair Admission v. Harvard* – and gave the second Trump administration everything it thought it legally needed for its racial reckoning.

GETTING INTO HARVARD

At some point we had to expect that our American paroxysms with racial inequality might blow our visitor's mind, but here is where she bows out. Not only do we obfuscate constitutional principles with exceptions and labyrinthine distinctions, but we openly allow line-cutting by the rich and call it meritocracy.

It may seem an odd strategy to argue for a reverse understanding of racial inequality in a case based on the admissions standards for the most elite colleges on Earth, but the wisdom of the top-down approach eventually reveals itself. In the lawsuit, the plaintiff, Students For Fair Admissions (SFFA), claimed that Harvard's holistic evaluation process that includes race as a factor among many, discriminated against Asian (and white) students in violation of equal protection. Giving any weight at all to race not only tends to discriminate against specific racial groups, but it's also an offense to the principle of meritocracy, represented by standardized criteria (e.g., tests and grades), which SFFA argued is the only fair and rational way to make selections in a "zero-sum" contest. A majority of Supreme Court justices agreed. *SFFA v. Harvard,* decided in June 2023, effectively put an official end to the racial reckoning that began in 2020.

I won't repeat the problem with "zero sum" reasoning from the last chapter, but I begin with a question about meritocracy. Raj Chetty, the economist who demonstrated the power of place in conditioning life benefits and burdens, also studied the characteristics of elite college admissions at schools like Harvard.[49] Specifically, he and his colleagues found that "merit" is closely associated with being very rich. Examining socioeconomic diversity at thirty-nine of the most selective universities in the United States (all but nine of them private), the researchers set out to answer a central question: Do highly selective private colleges amplify the persistence of privilege across generations by disproportionately admitting applicants from very high-income families? A secondary question was whether it's true that graduates of these most elite schools go on to lead elite lives – in the money they earn, the graduate schools in which they subsequently enroll and the prestige of the firms for which they work.

The research confirms that both are true. The top 1% have a profound advantage in being admitted to, and enrolling in, the top 1% of colleges, and going to the top 1% of colleges correlates strongly with subsequently living a top 1% life. Privilege begets privilege. Yet the advantages they found are not pegged to innate superiority or perfect scores on standardized criteria. According to Chetty:

> Children from families in the top 1% are twice as likely to attend an Ivy-Plus college (Ivy League, Stanford, MIT, Duke, and Chicago) as those from middle-class families with comparable SAT/ACT scores. Two-thirds of this gap is due to higher admissions rates for students with comparable test scores from high-income families; the remaining third is due to differences in rates of application and matriculation. In contrast, children from high-income families have no admissions advantage at flagship public colleges.[50]

The secret sauce? Three factors account for the advantage: preferences for the children of alumni, donors and faculty; recruitment of athletes; and "weight placed on non-academic ratings," such as attending private schools, cool field trips to faraway lands and other costly "enrichment" programs. Wealthy students who attended flagship public universities received no such "bounce." The study confirms the importance of non-academic factors in elite admissions, and that so many of those determinative factors correlate to socioeconomic status *and race.*

Pause to consider a well-known truth about Chetty's study. Anyone who's raised kids around affluent and even solidly middle-class people know this game. It's a line-cutting adventure that begins at a child's birth and consumes thousands of parental planning (and scheming) hours plus a tremendous amount of money – as in hundreds of thousands of dollars long before a single tuition check is cut. Parents assiduously scour listservs, bulletin boards and any other source of private information to identify the best preschool or nanny, the highest-rated summer camps, tutors, coaches, private trainers, skills programs, extracurricular activities, internships and clubs for their children at every stage. They make calls. They send emails. They donate. They build a utilitarian network so that their child doesn't have to compete cold. Sports are chosen and abandoned based on likelihood of success. Hundreds of hours are spent waking at 5:00 a.m. for swim practices on Saturday and three-day tournaments in Texas or Florida or who knows where. Tennis or golf? Fencing or lacrosse? These highly recruited sports don't even exist at most schools, another reason to either spend five figures on private school or its property tax equivalent to live in certain towns (or both). We know this. It's no secret. The meritocracy of it all depends on who you know and what you can afford. Do these kids work hard? Of course. Are those who get into the most selective schools bright? No doubt. But as President Obama once told business owners who forgot how much the government spends to provide the infrastructure on which their business models depend, "You didn't build this."[51] It took a wealthy village, which had no monopoly on talent but a private map of shortcuts and the means to take them.

Again, we look upon a place – this time, the nation's most elite college campuses – to examine the composition. Again, we see its composition reconstituting itself in a cycle of privilege. Yet this time, we're to understand that the paucity of Black students is (disparate impact) proof of race discrimination against whites (and Asians). Somehow the underrepresentation of Black students among the richest people alive violates the equal protection rights of privileged applicants to be even more overrepresented than they are and always have been. This, the Court admonishes, is a problem of racial inequality only a colorblind constitution can remedy.

Note: This is an inequality problem among the economically privileged, as the research also shows. The vast majority of colleges and universities in the United States have such high acceptance rates that nobody would pretend to call it zero sum.

There are many ways to read the Supreme Court's opinion in the consolidated cases of *Students for Fair Admissions v. Harvard* and *SFFA v. University of North Carolina*, but the dozens of interested amici opinions submitted to the Court as well as the many conservative groups supporting the plaintiffs believed that, through the constitutional issue of using race in elite college admissions, the case would say something profound about the law's role in remedying racial inequality everywhere. And say it did.

The Court's majority, per the opinion by Chief Justice John Roberts, asserted a nearly absolute colorblind standard, ignoring all of the obvious forms of racial discrimination that I discuss above. "Eliminating racial discrimination means eliminating all of it," he wrote. Any exception had to survive strict scrutiny's two-level test, which neither school had done. Their use of race for the once-compelling interest of advancing classroom diversity was insufficiently measurable to be reviewed by courts any longer. The schools failed to articulate how their use of race connected to their goal of educational benefit. Further, race had become a negative factor for some Asian applicants, proof of a zero-sum competition where race, used mainly in stereotypical fashion, was ultimately determinative. Finally, nothing in the schools' admissions practices suggested there would ever be an end in sight, the Court concluded. Whites (and Asians) had become victims of a racial inequality scheme designed to help Black and Hispanic applicants.

Two dissenting justices and countless scholars and court watchers have opined in detail about the problems with Roberts's analysis.[52] I won't recanvass them here or go point by point the way others have, except to note that Justice Sotomayor spent seventy pages describing the majority's alternative racial universe in which the history of the equal protection clause was rewritten to protect whites, the value of fact-finding by trial courts ignored, court precedent was thrown out and colorblindness triumphed as a camouflage for racial equality. "[T]he Court cements a superficial rule of colorblindness as a constitutional principle in an endemically segregated society where race has always mattered and continues to matter," she wrote. "The Court subverts the constitutional guarantee of equal protection by further entrenching racial inequality in education, the very foundation of our democratic government and pluralistic society."[53] Justice Jackson was even less interested in wrestling with the majority's foreign logic on race. She refocused the analysis on the schools' defense of diversity's benefits, including substantial evidence of favorable student perspectives that had been persuasive to both trial courts yet all but ignored by the Court majority. Yet she too framed the core issue around the problem colorblindness won't see: the need to create remedies for ongoing racial inequality.

> Our country has never been colorblind. Given the lengthy history of state-sponsored race-based preferences in America, to say that anyone is now victimized if a college considers whether that legacy of discrimination has unequally advantaged its applicants fails to acknowledge the well-documented "intergenerational transmission of inequality" that still plagues our citizenry.
>
> It is *that* inequality that admissions programs such as [the defendant universities'] help to address, to the benefit of us all.[54]

Undoubtedly, the use of race in selection criteria is a very challenging subject, either as an affirmative action remedy or to advance an interest in diverse environments. There are legitimate fairness concerns on both sides. Everyone wants their efforts to receive equal consideration, to have equal value and to get equal treatment. Few of us want undue preference, our individual attributes and identities objectified into something not seen but imagined. It gets complicated when we factor in the divergent conditions that underlie our efforts, however, and a system of radical equality – one free of context, ignorant of race, blind to economic resource differences – treats all efforts the same no matter the often obvious advantages. As a method, holistic review tries to embrace that difficult work where race is one among many factors to consider. However, opinions like *SFFA* demonstrate how conservative reasoning has taken over the discourse on racial inequality, forcing strict scrutiny tests onto defenders of racial justice that none can hope to pass, check-mating with exceptions, fact distortions or legislative history that didn't happen. They hypothesize an equality at odds with empirical inequality. Yet the Roberts court beholds a magician's mastery of racial misdirection; it never asks us to focus on racial inequality unless the victim is white. Only when we blink twice and take the full measure of reality do we realize something is wrong.

For the sake of racial reckoning, what if we could start the argument anew? If we could argue afresh for the limited use of race in any competitive selection criteria, without resort to unwinnable colorblind frameworks, what would we say?

We might start by saying the Equal Protection Clause was passed after emancipation not only to protect the rights of African Americans to equal treatment but also to overcome the most profound inequality imaginable, slavery. This hasn't happened yet despite significant, sometimes momentous progress. Perhaps what's missing is an equity norm that modifies how we understand equality. Or a more explicit command to remedy enslavement status. The evidence of racial inequality against Blacks (and other minorities) is still visible, complicated and problematic in its persistence. The dearth of Black presence in resource-rich environments, such as Harvard, and the stubborn overrepresentation of Blacks in under-resourced places represent the continuing effects of discriminatory structures that, if left untouched, will go on to reproduce unequal opportunities. Fortunately, Black excellence is evergreen and there are multiple kinds of greatness, which *all* institutions responsible for developing resourceful people have an obligation to welcome through objective criteria. If Harvard is relieved of the obligation to reduce inequality, it will go back to being yet another institutional purveyor of racial inequality, as it was for much of its almost 400-year history. Others will no doubt follow its lead.

And the offense to meritocracy is a red herring – another problem altogether, and not one created or solved by ending the use of race in admissions. Our current standards of meritocracy perpetuate the unfair cumulative advantages of people who have the resources and incentive to cut the line as often as they can. It's understandable that they do, but selection criteria shouldn't blatantly reward it. This too is a problem of socioeconomic and racial inequality. The institutions' selection methods are not perfect, and better means should be discovered that take the benefits and burdens of place into account. For instance, Chetty's research recommended selective schools stop giving advantages for legacies, athletes and donor's kids. Even when the plaintiffs themselves suggested this, the Supreme Court majority looked the other way.[55]

The problem with my argument is that its remedial logic sounds more like a justification for affirmative action, which is unpopular (though empirically justifiable), and less like diversity, which is legally disfavored but popular among people. Both are currently disallowed by far-right colorblindness. As we've seen, those who embrace colorblindness would probably have renamed the title of this chapter "How Inequality Finally

Bred Equality," not the other way around. Since Trump's second term, that view has taken the essential logic of *SFFA* and other cases into white supremacy overdrive. The lawsuit seemed to begin as another in the long history of legal attacks on affirmative action. Then it merged with a cultural movement (MAGA) and an autocratic executive branch (Trump) to attempt the radical remaking of nearly every facet of American life under the pretextual claim of white victimhood. Proponents offer scant proof. What started from the top – elite university admissions for the 1 percent – soon reached pipeline programs for disadvantaged Black high school kids and research grants for genetic diseases primarily affecting Black women and other disfavored groups[56] – anything and everything vaguely associated with "woke ideology." This argument is still being tested in federal courts. Yet by starting at the top of the resource pyramid, the argument threatening all things identified as Black gained fuel from the *SFFA* decision, which was instrumental to the claim that race as a consideration in conferring benefits constitutes "illegal DEI" and can be defunded or worse. The Supreme Court did not go that far. The Trump administration acted as if it did.

Yet this is a racial inequality analysis under accountability reckoning. Currently, the judicial voices that concur in these arguments are buried in dissents. I hope they'll rise again. Until then, the work continues. Racial inequality is, as I've asserted, the race-based denial of resources necessary for the opportunity to succeed/flourish as an individual and a community. This chapter offered a conceptual take on how key resource disparities persist. Keep in mind that most of those resources are bound by place – local places governed by mostly local institutions, norms and practices. Local power and policy will become a theme as the next three chapters demonstrate in detail how racial inequality has worked to create so much struggle in wealth, health and policing. A federal racial reckoning was always going to be a challenge and that challenge is even more difficult now. But facts on the ground may yield a different hope.

CHAPTER 3

Displacement, Urban Renewal and Racial Bargaining

Because all needs go back to housing, residency is at the root of racial reckoning for systemic racism. The risk of being displaced from home is the mother of most anxieties. Lack of affordability in both rents and sales prices has become a defining twenty-first-century American dilemma. About half the country is cost-burdened, meaning they pay more than a third of their incomes on housing costs, with steep differences by race and place.[1] Cost burdens of up to one-half of monthly income are not uncommon, and they increase the insecurity of being displaced into tight, expensive housing markets. In 2020, however, the Covid pandemic requirement to shelter in place inflamed a raft of housing insecurity issues already common to African Americans, especially poorer ones – overcrowding, interior pollution, exposure to trauma, the risk of eviction and rental arrears – that were only temporarily postponed by eviction moratoria and emergency rental assistance programs. Before the pandemic, African Americans faced distinct displacement anxieties fueled by gentrification, predatory lending and the foreclosure crisis that followed the Great Recession. The recession alone evaporated hundreds of millions of dollars of Black wealth. These phenomena are related. For instance, foreclosures in Black neighborhoods stimulated a new asset class for large investors – the buy-to-rent market of one-to-four unit homes – which in turn have produced passive income returns while reducing the supply of homes for owner-occupancy purchases and dramatically pushing up rents.[2] Whole blocks and even neighborhoods in predominantly Black areas are being bought up and rented out by private equity. The trend is the latest feature of an affordability crisis that disproportionately destabilizes – and targets – Black households and the neighborhoods they live in. The crisis is a primary driver of homelessness, perhaps the ultimate condition of housing vulnerability, which again disproportionately affects Black children, households and individuals.[3]

Yet what we see today are iterations of past policies experienced by our great-grandparents. The destabilizing aspects of systemic racism around housing and housing wealth have been related for a long time. All are connected to place. All have profound implications for the ways Americans generate household wealth. When we seek racial reckoning for material wealth gaps, then, we have to begin with the government's race-conscious housing policies that set the present course *for all racial groups* since about the middle of the last century.

Other than slavery itself, no system of racism has done more to harm the material well-being of African Americans than racial segregation. The scarcity and instability we know today as a wealth and resource gap is the direct result of a federal–local interest in racial segregation. It was instituted on the eve of what became the American Dream for millions of other Americans. It involved another instance of American history's grand racial bargains and installed a system of oppressive transactional norms I call racial bargaining. It began with the Great Migration of Southern Black migrants to cities across the North, Midwest and West. The grand racial bargain, as we'll see, was the sacrifice of those migrants' possessory interests in their homes, businesses and institutions, deliberately destroyed by the 1949 National Housing Act's urban renewal program in order to rescue cities from decline. Racial bargaining was then, and is now, the lopsided, unfair terms of ordinary deals in segregated Black neighborhoods that arose from the grand bargain over Black migrant residency. Because of our nationalized policy of segregation during our grand- and great-grandparents' time, transactions over property, consumer products and services, even the value of public goods like education and sanitation, were discounted to much less than their worth for the same things in non-Black neighborhoods. This asymmetrical devaluation is clear to anyone who tries to sell a house, buy insurance or find fresh produce in Black-identified areas compared to others. It didn't come out of nowhere, and the design of housing policies since a little before mid-century guarantees that it's not going anywhere until we take accountability reckoning for it. That reckoning dates back to about the second wave of the Great Migration, the movement that turned Black folks into urban folks and white folks into suburbanites.

The devastating effects of the national program of urban renewal on Black migrant communities in mid-century cities has been hidden beneath a colorblind history that mostly chronicles it as a well-meaning mistake of city planning. However, the grand racial bargain that persisted for almost twenty-five years was much more than a miscalculation. At the urging of local officials in response to the swelling presence of Black migrants, the federal government would finance the redevelopment of cities primarily through the expropriation of Black interests in land.[4] Between 1949 and 1974, an estimated 4 million people were displaced from segregated neighborhoods across the country, about three-quarters of them Black.[5] In many industrial cities, the racial targeting of Black migrants averaged about 10 to 15 percent of all Black residents.[6] Forcibly evicted from their homes, most displacees would go without relocation assistance or compensation into what historian Arnold Hirsch called a "second ghetto." The impact on local businesses was often fatal, especially the small ones. Almost no displaced business could recover their actual business losses, which also affected their employees.[7]

The costly immediate outcomes for Blacks were not unintended or unexpected. For example, in Baltimore by the late 1960s, urban renewal projects displaced 8,678 families – 74% of them Black. In fact, *9% of all Black families experienced displacement, compared to 1% for whites.* This while Blacks made up only 35% of the city's population. In Cleveland, urban renewal family displacements took disproportionate racial impact to the extreme. While Blacks made up only about 29% of the city's population, *88% of displaced families were Black* – a total of 5,572 by the late 1960s, or about 9% of all Black families. The experience was far less familiar for white families, whose 716 displacements amounted to only 12% of all and a rate of just 0.4%. Despite the participation of over 1,200 cities in hundreds of neighborhood-sized projects, each spanning an average of eight years and altogether costing US taxpayers over $13 billion (worth about $135 billion in today's dollars),[8] the urban renewal program was largely deemed a failed experiment to revitalize cities as white people fled them. What it did accomplish, however, was catastrophic to the existing and continuing interests of newly urbanized African Americans, conditioning the economic realities of urban life for decades to come. Through systematic segregation, displacement and exclusion, it contributed substantially to the impoverishment of ghettoization for many Blacks and the diminished wealth opportunities for many others. Not simply historical, planning policy by its nature is always intended to become the future. When we talk today about the causes of the racial wealth gap and point to excellent studies about the importance of place, racial stratification, even redlining, the template was written in race-conscious government policies about seventy-five years ago. Succeeding generations of wealth-diminishing policies would follow its lead to the present day. This is that story.

BECOMING THE URBAN

Americans do not customarily think of American descendants of enslaved Southern Blacks as immigrants, but in every relevant sense except language they were. Until the first wave of Black migrants starting in about 1915, most American cities were the province of the industrial labor of mostly European immigrants. World War I curtailed European immigration and created needs that fueled labor and housing shortages. Urban industrial employers actively sought Black immigrants to brave the journey to work in a promised refuge from the economic exploitation, peonage, sharecropping and raw violence of the Jim Crow South. As captured by Isabel Wilkerson in her Pulitzer Prize winning *The Warmth of Other Suns*:

> Their migration was a response to an economic and social structure not of their making. They did what humans have done for centuries when life became untenable – what the pilgrims did under the tyranny of British rule, what the Scots-Irish did in Oklahoma when the land turned to dust, what the Irish did when there was nothing to eat, what the European Jews did during the spread of Nazism, what the landless in Russia, Italy, China and elsewhere did when something better across the ocean called to them. What binds these stories together was the back-against-the-wall, reluctant yet hopeful search for something better, any place but where they were. They did what humans looking for freedom, throughout history, have often done.
>
> They left.[9]

Like all migrants, African Americans migrating north from Jim Crow states took an unfathomable chance that America could produce more than its most virulent practices of racial exploitation and degradation; they trusted its values despite what they knew and what little they could foresee. In this sense, theirs too was the classic immigrant story with one exception: Northern cities offered no real promised land so different from where they'd come. It was the same federal system, the same constitution and the same caste system in which Blacks were the bottom. Trust and race made them uniquely vulnerable.

What they found after migrating was residential segregation and the rough end of exploitive racial bargains. Although Black migrants lived briefly in biracial neighborhoods, most were forced to settle into patterns of urban residential isolation that were still new outside of the South: "Black belts," "darkietowns," "Bronzevilles" and other sobriquets of racially segregated enclaves. They laid down roots in these communities, acclimated to new social norms, built businesses and institutions, raised children and left for industrial and domestic work. The presence of Black people in cities north or south was limited until about 1910. Most remained on farms in the rural South until labor needs during World War I pulled them north.[10] This and other push factors down South produced a second wave of the Great Migration by the mid-1940s, exponentially swelling Black enclaves.

As their numbers increased, Blacks encountered a "dual housing market" based on the emerging norms of northern segregation in which Blacks were constrained to compete with others for the same housing.[11] One study of racial dissimilarity[12] (a quantitative measure of segregation) between Blacks and native whites in ten US cities shows that racial segregation tended to increase steadily between 1910 and 1950.[13] The dual housing market configured a growing set of segregation norms that affected Black migrants' social and economic interactions in nearly all aspects of life in the promised land.

In Chicago, for example, historians St. Clair Drake and Horace Cayton described what Black migrants faced in the city's "Black Metropolis." Before the first wave, Chicago had a Black population of around 50,000 scattered across the city. Between 1915 and 1920, 50,000 more Blacks arrived.[14] They were directed into what the authors call the "Black Belt." While ethnic enclaves for newly arrived foreign immigrants were common, their members assimilated through education and employment opportunities, often relocating beyond the boundaries of their original enclaves. This was the pattern for all but Black migrants despite the education many brought with them.[15] Instead, as their numbers increased, the borders of their enclaves were policed by restrictive covenants and random violence against "spread." They would occupy the places at the core of the city abandoned by other groups.[16]

This was the basis for two aspects of racial bargaining, both ultimately conditioning the prospects for wealth accumulation among Black migrants. The first was a racially segmented labor force in which they were offered only the worst, most dangerous jobs available, often beneath their skills, for wages less than what white workers – native and foreign born – were paid.[17] The second was the racially segmented housing market whose boundaries inevitably expanded with their growing numbers. Both conditions supported the invention of dynamic segregationist techniques to prevent "invasion" and to exploit Black consumer vulnerability. This vulnerability was symbolized by the notorious "kitchenette" apartment – an apartment that had once housed European immigrants but had been cut up into multiple units and rented to Blacks. As the novelist Richard Wright explained, "The kitchenette is the author of the glad tidings that new suckers are in town, ready to be cheated, plundered and put in their places."[18] Both the underpaid Black worker and the kitchenette in which they lived were exemplars of racial bargaining – systemic devaluations in the markets for labor and housing knowingly exploited by those with racial leverage.

As segregation created artificial scarcity on top of an existing housing shortage, underpaid Black migrants overpaid dramatically for aging and dilapidated housing, which also diminished their prospects for wealth accumulation.[19] In 1944, for instance, the Illinois Inter-Racial Commission found that rents in Black areas were 15–50 percent higher than the same housing for whites.[20] In Chicago, rents in Black neighborhoods actually rose during the Depression.[21] While owners repeatedly subdivided the houses and buildings in neighborhoods where Blacks were allowed to rent or own, these structures became more unhealthful, dilapidated and lethal. Overcrowding caused fatal fires. Limited housing options invited scams and cons, such as "vampire" rental agencies collecting fees upfront for nonexistent apartments or buying tax-delinquent lots at city auction and reselling them to unsuspecting Black buyers.[22] Speculator landlords – many of them immigrants – extracted high rents without repairing structures.[23] With poorer, Black residents carrying increased rent burdens, some cities reduced street cleaning and sewage maintenance.[24] These enclaves became identified as "Black spaces" to be contained within established racial boundaries,[25] vilified as blight, exploited economically and eventually destroyed.

Black people were often negatively associated with the neighborhoods in which they were trapped, which reinforced support for policies that trapped them. Increasing numbers of Blacks in expanding but declining slum neighborhoods fed whites' racial fear about Black presence. Demographic change was substantial and relatively sudden. Dozens of American cities went from housing small enclaves of Blacks to significant populations in a few years. In Baltimore, for example, Black presence was about 142,000 in 1930 (17.7 percent of total population) and jumped to about 225,000 (23.7 percent) in 1950.[26] By 1960, the Black population was 325,589 and over a third of Baltimore's total population. This was the pattern in city after city, as a race of people long identified with the rural South became a symbol of the urban and its blight.[27]

BLACKNESS AS BLIGHT

The idea of Blackness as blight had a powerful influence on the way policymakers addressed two related problems – the city problem and the city-suburb problem. The city problem was slums, housing shortages and capital flight. American cities had confronted these challenges for decades (and would for decades more). But cities were not just declining; they were losing to new suburbs. In the years leading up to passage of the 1949 Housing Act, business elites, major downtown commercial property owners and local government officials of large US cities began to recognize a city-suburb dilemma. In fact, cities were losing to suburbs that federal government policymaking and local real estate interests made increasingly attractive for white families. The increasing migration of Black people, who were excluded from both suburbs and nonblighted neighborhoods, made things acutely worse. Black-identified spaces turned both the city and city-suburb problems into a race problem. The solution would entail race-conscious policymaking, with – ironically – substantial federal assistance. Federal money would subsidize both ends of the problem, city redevelopment and suburban development.

Slums, like public housing, had not always been identified with Black people. The Great Depression revealed how badly tenements built for immigrants were deteriorating with time, and local landlords, many of them less-poor immigrants, were strained to keep up with building maintenance. The housing shortage that characterized the years between the 1930s through the 1950s[28] magnified public and moral health concerns about slums. Thus began a decades-long legal struggle to define slum clearance as a public purpose, sufficient to justify condemnation. The Emergency Relief and Construction Act of 1932[29] funded land purchases for the sake of building low-cost housing.[30] The next year, the Public Works Administration was created in part to clear slums and build the first million units of public housing.[31] According to thought leaders at the time, slums were corrupting influences, breeders of crime, delinquency, moral decay and disease.[32] Beyond the consequences for people who lived there, slums were also bad for economic development, property values and the tax base of cities.[33] They exacerbated cities' growing debt, a consequence of the municipal debt taken on during the land boom crushed by the Depression.[34]

Although the 1937 National Housing Act spoke directly to the need for decent, safe and sanitary dwellings for families of low income,[35] the public housing program that it launched hardly reached the Black migrants most identified with them. Several factors excluded Blacks from the new public housing. First, public housing was initially designed for working- and lower-middle-class white families, who needed housing based on a lack of availability, not affordability.[36] Financial rules required that tenants' rents cover public housing expenses, a further incentive to bar tenants whose limited incomes made them "bad financial risks."[37] Public housing selection criteria screened many people out for cultural reasons, too.[38] Second, public housing was one of the first federal programs to actively support (and in some cases introduce) racial segregation into its rules.[39] The financial selection criteria would eventually cede in the late 1950s and 60s to admit more low-income families, who would dominate public housing "projects" for decades afterward.[40] Yet racially segregated public housing would remain the rule throughout. Blacks were given lesser quality units at rates well below demand. This meant that during World War II, Blacks continued to occupy overcrowded slums in cities, or the least desirable public housing.

Meanwhile, the New Deal was opening up homeownership opportunities to working- and lower-middle-class whites, accelerating the competition between cities and suburbs that would worsen in the next decades.

Federal Housing Administration (FHA) mortgage rules directed most federal support to suburbs. (The Federal Interstate Highway Act of 1956[41] would accelerate this trend with billions of dollars of construction projects.) The agency maintained strong policy preferences for insuring new construction of single-family homes over multifamily homes.[42] Its loan guarantees required "neighborhood evaluations" based on eight criteria that included such vague references to racial homogeneity as "stability," the absence of "adverse influences" and "appeal."[43] The policy commitment amounted to huge disparities in city–suburb funding. For example, St. Louis County received $1.1 billion in FHA guarantees through 1976 while the City of St. Louis received just $314 million. In Chicago, 270,000 whites moved to the suburbs between 1950 and 1956 alone.[44] A building boom in the 1950s concentrated 77 percent of new homes in all-white suburbs. The combination of racially segregated program preferences, outright discrimination against Blacks and huge disparities in funding for white-identified property interests fueled the competition for whites between cities and suburbs. By the 1950s, it was simply more expensive for white families to stay in cities and pay rent than it was to move to the suburbs and own a new home.[45]

The dilemma that cities faced – losing the competition for federal resources and white families to the suburbs on the one hand and needing to revitalize decaying slums increasingly overcrowded with Black migrants from the South on the other – was the basis for a grander racial compromise in law and policy. Local elites hoped it would be resolved with a turn to "redevelopment" laws, governed by planning principles. These purported to be race blind, but in fact would regularly and deliberately sacrifice the interests of Black people to root out the race problem at the heart of the city problem. The inversion of terminology – from race conscious to race neutral – is something many of us probably associate with our own era, not mid-century. Yet the trend may have begun with "redevelopment" and "slum clearance," a camouflaging language for systemic racism.

"REDEVELOPMENT" AND REMOVAL UNDER THE 1949 HOUSING ACT

The varied financial, political and public health pressures that led to passage of the National Housing Act of 1949[46] were loosely translated – minus the explicit racism – in a set of legislative goals. The first was a "decent home and a suitable living environment for every American family."[47] The second was the elimination of substandard housing through slum clearance of blight. Third was to stimulate housing production and community development. The goals included significant appropriations for local grants and loans, with the federal share starting at about two-thirds of the "net project costs" and the local government paying the remainder.[48] The new urban renewal program in Title I replicated many of the pro-local preferences of the first New Deal housing acts, which would guarantee that local priorities and prejudices controlled execution with little federal oversight. It invited local governments to partner with the federal government by taking two main steps: creating a local public agency (LPA)[49] that, in turn, would develop a "workable program."[50] The workable program was to be a blueprint with seven planning elements, including a comprehensive community plan, codes and ordinances for adequacy standards, housing for displaced families and citizen participation.[51] The latter two critical elements of the program's scope were consistently ignored in the racial bargain between legislative goals and program execution. A powerful "blight" designation framework harnessed the growing government power to take, displace, demolish and transform.[52] This power only expanded over time as amendments to the Act in 1954, 1956, 1959 and 1961 made more entities eligible to take ever more land and pay grudging attention to the relocation crisis urban renewal was creating for the very populations it was nominally passed to assist.[53] Congress by 1954 understood that clearance was not bringing investment into the downtowns of the big cities that first joined the program, despite the high costs to taxpayers. In response, Congress increased the scope of the program even further, making eligible the areas surrounding the original project areas, then to whole neighborhoods,[54] and subsequently to combinations of neighborhoods.[55] In 1959, Congress enacted section 112, adding universities and hospitals to the list of entities eligible to make claims on redevelopment areas. This led to massive clearance projects in cities like Newark and Chicago where whole (Black) neighborhoods were razed for university and medical facility expansion projects and buffer zones.[56] Meanwhile, various rules or practices ensured the lowest values were paid for taken property while assuring significant windfalls to future investors, such as "write downs."[57] Land was typically sold at a 50 percent discount from the cost paid to acquire and improve it, with disposition for cleared land sold at one dollar a square foot compared to acquisition and improvement costs at over two dollars a square foot.[58] The potential profits were substantial. According to Urban Renewal Administrator William Slayton, "[I]t appears that after redevelopment assessed values are averaging between four to five times the values prior to slum clearance."[59]

Why did a purely local interest like the redevelopment of individual cities became a national priority, particularly when the most obvious need, decent housing, was made secondary? The answer is partly that the high costs of slum clearance and the extraordinary scale of redevelopment required federal financial support. The increasing housing shortage brought on by World War II helped nationalize the concern.[60] Rational planning theory offered a way to bridge these disparate threads, incorporating nonracialized racism with nonhousing slum clearance in ways capable of bringing national compromise in Congress and deference in both state and federal courts.

Planning, according to Wendell Pritchett, "provided a common language that joined real-estate interests, housing reformers, and local government … [T]hey sought to rationalize the city through the development of strict standards for city growth."[61] As early as 1932, President Hoover's Conference on Home Building and Homeownership had detailed the idea of "district replanning" to address declining property values in downtown areas.[62] Transformation was propelled by the business and real estate interests that stood to gain from slum clearance. Joint real estate and business groups like the National Association of Real Estate Brokers, using their research arm, the Urban Land Institute, lobbied for a framework that turned the eradication of slums into the creation of housing and commercial amenities for affluent whites.[63] In this sense, redevelopment represented a spatial transfer of future value.[64] "To the planners, housing was secondary – to be clearly distinguished from the basic function, the planned redevelopment of cities."[65]

It also needed judicial support for the idea that all this taking of private property satisfied the Fifth Amendment's Public Use Clause, which it received in 1954. Missing from the labyrinth of political interests negotiating the quandary of cities was any serious consideration of racial impact despite race being a guiding force all along. Such was the grand but unspoken racial bargain at mid-century, undisturbed by the Supreme Court's first review of its constitutionality.

BERMAN V. PARKER. The Court's landmark decision in *Berman v. Parker*[66] in 1954 is significant in two respects. First, *Berman* upheld with maximum deference the wisdom of local planning decisions – specifically urban renewal–financed comprehensive plans – against a property owner's Fifth Amendment takings claims and confirmed that the definition of "public use" in eminent domain cases was consistent with slum clearance. However, *Berman* also affirmed the effectiveness of planning decisions to strike a racial bargain without constitutional constraint. Decided just six months after *Brown v. Board of Education*,[67] by eight of the same justices, the Court could have questioned blanket support for a takings rule that could divide the possessory interests of two different publics – majority and minority – the minority's ignored. Yet it didn't. Instead, it affirmed how in the grand bargain of public land-use undertakings, negative externalities like displacement that foreseeably, if not intentionally, affected Black people, were not part of the constitutional calculus of governmental power.[68] In eminent domain cases as in all of urban renewal, African-American interests were collateral to the contest between private property and public power.

The results for Black people were catastrophic. A few years after *Berman*, Washington, DC's Redevelopment Land Authority (RLA) entirely dropped the requirement of building low-cost relocation housing.[69] Whatever relocation assistance was given is uncertain, as accounts have been questioned.[70] A 1966 study showed that most Black Southwest DC residents found housing outside of the quadrant – 43% went to Southeast, 21% to Northeast, 15% to Northwest and only 13% returned.[71] The numbers exclude those who moved on their own – the disappeared – and were not tracked by the RLA. One of the study's most powerful findings was the extent of psychological depression and social isolation experienced by Black displacees. Only 30 percent were "content" to have moved. Five years after moving, over a quarter reported not having made a single friend in their new neighborhoods. The results for Black businesses were similarly scattered, with untold wealth lost.[72] At a time of historic housing production, homeowner wealth creation and the city's economic growth, thousands of Black Southwest residents were instead displaced and replaced by the white beneficiaries of their absence.

RECOGNIZING MASS TAKING

Racial reckoning requires a step back to comprehend as best we can the harms from such mass takings by a federally empowered local government. Americans have never been open to government taking away anything they hold dear – rights, automatic weapons, votes, income – and we are especially sensitive about these things today. Urban renewal compounded layers of harm on a still-migrant population that must be acknowledged and accounted for decades later. The program's systematic mass takings diminished its targets' dignity, impoverished their material wealth and undermined their trust in the very institutions Americans look to for protection.

First was the harm of not knowing where you're going to go, how you're going to get there and what awaits you. Forcible removal was more complicated than eviction. Black people displaced by urban renewal projects learned only indirectly, but never in a timely manner, that their block or neighborhood had been designated an area for redevelopment. Instead, they would experience the designation through signs of decline – the further degradation of an already slum neighborhood as investments would stop, landlords would halt what little maintenance they did and buildings would go vacant, inviting crime. This pattern would drag out for years. Over time, the poorest families would be the last ones left, often given just a month's notice to find alternative housing. This meant that before people were physically displaced, the basic institutions of a familiar place dwindled away, stripped by a drawn-out process of atrophy and neglect. As a result, displacees experienced a loss of safety, a deterioration of health, and a loss of what social and organizational roots they'd developed to sustain them in a large city. Psychiatrist Mindy Fulilove describes this process of intense psychic and physical dislocation as "root shock." These are dignitary harms arising from the involuntary loss of relationship between person and place when the neighborhood goes dark.

As one renter expressed, "I sorrow all the time."[73]

A business owner told an interviewer how the loss affected his family's wealth. "It was home. It was memories. The place could have taken care of us for the rest of our years."[74]

Second was the material loss of property – often severely undercompensated in the case of owners and without rental assistance or costs to renters. By 1964, fifteen years into the program, studies began to show the overwhelming evidence of increased costs, emotional hardship and business losses inflicted upon displaced Black people. Despite amendments that were meant to ameliorate the harsh local effects of the original Act, nearly every study of urban renewal found that about two-thirds to one-half of displacees received nothing in the way of payments or assistance finding new housing.[75] Martin Anderson, for example, found that for contracts executed before August 1956, 9,192 families received an average of $60 each in relocation payments; 3,286 individuals received an average of $54. Despite the statutory increases allowed after 1956 and 1959, families received an average of $71 while individuals received only $48.[76] There is some evidence that support was lower in bigger cities where only 26 percent of displacees received some amount of assistance.[77] While their costs skyrocketed, their housing quality remained substandard. For those who received nothing, 90 percent moved into substandard housing – itself sometimes slated for future demolition – at significantly higher rents.[78] These housing dynamics were consistent across cities, and often made the conditions for hundreds of thousands of Black migrants more expensive, unhealthful and more tenuous than the slums from which they'd been evicted. After his exhaustive 1964 critique, Anderson concluded:

> In essence, the federal urban renewal program eliminated 126,000 low-rent homes, of which 80 percent were considered to be substandard, and replaced them with about 28,000 homes, most of them in a much higher rent bracket. Thus, the net effect of the program has been to aggravate the housing problem for low-income groups and to alleviate it for high-income groups.[79]

Third, was the loss of trust in government at all levels, from courts to congressmen, reinforced by the futility of legal resistance. Courageous displacees sometimes fought the legal and financial obstacles of displacement with lawsuits targeting either unlawful eviction or the relocation assistance promised in the Housing Act itself. Most cases were dismissed on standing grounds. An influential decision was *Hunter v. New York* in 1953. Tenants who were to be displaced by four contracts to demolish their homes under urban renewal projects that were negotiated between the federal Housing and Home Finance Agency (HHFA) brought suit in the state court.[80] The HHFA administrator's decision, plaintiffs argued, deprived them of their statutory "relocation rights." The court rejected the arguments on several grounds. First, the plaintiffs had no such rights to challenge discretion of the HHFA administrator, because Congress had provided no private right of action. Second, even as intended beneficiaries of the Act, the plaintiffs had no legal property interest that superseded the larger interest in redevelopment. Finally, they sued in the wrong court. *Hunter*'s logic on standing and the discretionary power of a federal agency was followed closely by state and federal courts for many years.[81] Plaintiff-friendly outcomes would not occur until about 1968, a generation after urban renewal began.

If trust in law is a hallmark of accountability, the *Hunter* case is noteworthy in racial reckoning because it shows the difficulty of distinguishing between policy racism at different levels of government. The plaintiffs in the case needed to show who or what was responsible for the abject displacement they faced. Was it Congress in passing a statute with neutral terms but the clear racial impact of displacing of Blacks into known segregated housing markets? This questions the urban renewal program's constitutionality. Or was the racism really the work of local agencies that targeted Black neighborhoods for demolition and denied Black residents equal protection in relocating them? This questions the constitutionality of the program's administration at the local level. Or, did the federal government act unconstitutionally in failing to monitor its local partners under the Housing Act? *Hunter* ignored all three questions and dismissed the claims. Similar cases left displacees without a remedy and the program without accountability.

The wholesale rejection of displacees' possessory rights by local and federal courts is striking not only because they denied standing to the very people most directly injured by displacement, but also because these judges, along with local officials, simply ignored the limited relocation assistance required by the Act itself. Relocation was overwhelmingly a problem for renters. Studies from the era consistently showed that about two-thirds of all displacees and three-quarters of nonwhite displacees were renters.[82] Although Title I section 105(c) provided that there must be a "feasible plan" for the relocation of families,[83] the federal HHFA allowed LPAs to provide assistance out of project funding only where it was deemed "necessary for the undertaking of the project," and only after the LPA determined that all means of obtaining possession of the premises, other than eviction, had been exhausted.[84] Not only did the rules put redevelopment costs over the interests of individual and family tenants, but they made eviction the precondition to any meager assistance displacees might get.[85] The consensus among commentators was that providing for the relocation needs of tens of thousands of displaced migrants was an inconvenient burden most LPAs, with some variation, willfully ignored.[86] Participating cities were also obligated to keep records of the displaced immediately after displacement and two years later, but multiple studies showed that this too was often ignored. For instance, one study of 3,700 displaced Black migrant households in San Francisco found that 1,600 had disappeared without a record or assistance from the LPA.[87] Such provisions were often optional, and LPAs refused to offer the services. In 1964, Congress made both relocation payments and assistance mandatory conditions for federal reimbursement yet research shows that even then many LPAs regularly submitted fraudulent proof of compliance while federal officials kept the funding and the projects going.[88] It would not be officially remedied until passage in 1970 of the Uniform Relocation Assistance and Real Properties Acquisition Policies Act,[89] which, for the first time, also obligated governments to pay relocation assistance to the hundreds of thousands of entities displaced by federal highway construction projects. Even then, neither past nor contemporaneous displacees were fully compensated.[90]

These were serial instances of mistrust, creating a pattern of government behavior at all levels that signaled to Black people in the hundreds of cities with urban renewal projects that your home and neighborhood are not safe, your institutions can be uprooted without your input, your routines may be disrupted in a heartbeat and not only will you have no recourse among elected officials or courts of law, but you will have to bear the cost yourself. In this way, the racial bargaining institutionalized by urban renewal on Black property and Black spaces impacted more than just the financial aspects of the bargains Blacks struck. It sapped their faith in the system in which they occurred.

URBAN RENEWAL DIDN'T ACT ALONE

The federal urban renewal program acted as a system of racial disadvantage, coordinated between Congress and federal agencies, local planning authorities and elected officials, protected by vested capital interests and the courts. However, that system acted along with other systems of discrimination to demarcate racial lines in the asphalt between those that got and those that didn't. In the 1950s and early 1960s, when the program was doing most of its immediate damage, the same federal and local governments were offering white workers a bounty in suburban homeownership, building an interstate highway system that also targeted Black areas for destruction, helping to secure segregated wealth paths with racially restrictive covenants and, to ensure lasting detriment to markets, federalizing redlining. By the time President Johnson launched the Great Society programs of the mid-1960s, public housing had become the primary federal approach to the city problem (another process of ghettoization that would be rejected and implode twenty years later). Here's a brief reminder of how the policies of suburbanization, highway construction, racial covenants, redlining and public housing interacted with urban renewal to compound its discriminatory effects.

SUBURBANIZATION

Mid-century suburbanization was the basis for the household wealth that tens of millions of white Americans have relied on for three generations. Racial exclusivity in the suburbs was first achieved by racial covenants and openly racist discrimination in real estate practices, but, as I discussed in the last chapter, it was sustained by racially neutral police powers, mostly involving land use and zoning regulation, that would survive legal challenges up to the present.[91] The most important programs were the Social Security Act, the Federal Housing Administration and the GI Bill. Beginning in 1938, the FHA introduced federal underwriting of mortgages, which welcomed millions of new borrowers with lower downpayments, longer periods of amortization and a government guarantee that, in turn, created a secondary mortgage market.[92] It fueled suburban homebuilding on a massive scale. Federally secured mortgages were responsible for 44 percent of all private mortgage originations between 1949 and 1957 alone – or 2.4 million homes.[93] Blatant mortgage discrimination, naked racism and restrictive covenants prevented Black workers from taking advantage of homeownership opportunities that would become the bedrock of household wealth for their white counterparts.

Often, however, it was local program administrative rules rather than federal ones that blocked Blacks' access.[94] The single most important program in subsidizing suburban homeownership during World War II and its immediate aftermath was the GI Bill. Total federal spending on its programs equaled $95 billion between 1944 and 1971. By 1948, the GI Bill consumed 15 percent of the federal budget.[95] The beneficiaries of each of these programs were overwhelmingly white. It was a time of great hope for a generation of young families, who were overwhelmingly native white or European immigrants who achieved "white" status by virtue of the sudden accessibility of whites-only benefits.[96] Segregated cities became segregated from suburbs, and the racial branding of each bred white hostility. The identification of Blacks with the declining city was matched with the reward of the suburb. As historian David Roediger noted, "Suburban subdivisions could profit from being seen as raceless, as well as planned and stable."[97] "Raceless" meant white. As a result, homes purchased in 1950 by whites in American suburbs have appreciated in value by hundreds of percentage points,[98] contributing to, if not defining, America's racial wealth gap.

INTERSTATE HIGHWAY CONSTRUCTION

The largesse that built the American Dream for so many mid-century whites also included billions spent on the construction of interstate highways that often – and purposefully – destroyed segregated Black urban neighborhoods. For some big city mayors, that destruction was a condition of the law's passage and worked in tandem with urban renewal plans.[99] The Federal-Aid Highway Act of 1956[100] advanced the twin goals of transportation organization and reordering urban space. With limitless budgets, planners realized the simultaneous goals of connecting highways, reclaiming downtown business districts and relocating Blacks.[101] Displacement records for federal highway programs were notoriously (and negligently) scant compared to urban renewal, but the totals are staggering. Bernard Frieden and Lynne Sagalyn describe efforts by local planners in Nashville to reroute a highway from an area of white-owned businesses to one that destroyed the center of a Black community, including the campus of a Black college.[102] Los Angeles officials did the same to predominantly Latino Boyle Heights, running five freeways through the same neighborhood.[103] Urban renewal and the Federal Aid Highway Act could leverage each other, as Frieden and Sagalyn describe the convergence in Baltimore:

> From 1951 through 1964 public programs including highways and urban renewal tore down the homes of about 10,000 Baltimore families, of whom 90 percent were black. By the time the dust had settled, low-income blacks had lost the equivalent of one of every five houses they lived in.[104]

RACIALLY RESTRICTIVE COVENANTS

Racial covenants were among the earliest tools used to dictate the boundaries of segregation in response to the first wave of Black Southern migrants in 1910 and the overturning of racial zoning ordinances in 1917.[105] These contractual promises were contained in a home's deed, keeping real-property ownership or possession out of Black (and other groups') hands on pain of judicial enforcement, even by neighbors. Racial covenants performed double duty, first as a privatized legal norm enforceable in court, second as a public signaling social norm that standardized real estate practices.[106] New suburban subdivisions were designed for and marketed to middle-class white buyers during the wartime housing boom.[107] This standardization, among others in the real estate industry, helped to secure all-white suburban housing opportunities and the seeds of intergenerational wealth. Whole subdivisions, like Levittown, contained racial covenants in their deeds before the first sale.[108] Such standardization also illustrated the competition between cities and suburbs for white homeowners that contributed to the passage of urban renewal in the first place. In effect, racial covenants and urban renewal were contemporaneous tools in enforcing the racial borders between cities and suburbs.

REDLINING

The relationship between redlining and urban renewal is more complicated. The practice of drawing colored lines around a map of city neighborhoods based on their demographics and assigning values to them for the sake of guiding or preventing investment started in the early 1930s with the Chicago Board of Realtors and would be adopted by the FHA (even before their use by the Home Owners Loan Corporation).[109] Both practices originated with the Great Migration's tipping points. In 1900 Chicago, for example, there were only 30,000 Blacks or 1.9% of the population compared to 63.7% native white and 34.4% foreign-born white.[110] By 1944, when each program was gaining momentum, there were 337,000 Blacks, representing 9.3% of the population compared to 73.1% native whites and 17.1% foreign-born.[111] They worked in tandem to address a perceived demographic threat to white people. Their cumulative effects on Black economic, psychological and social interests are still being studied.[112] Further, redlining and urban renewal probably started out at cross-purposes in many cases, only to converge years later. One program designation discouraged economic development while the other cleared land to subsidize it. If urban renewal had been more successful as a tool of redevelopment and white retention, red lines would have had to be redrawn to attract, not repel, investment. But most projects did not succeed, and urban renewal areas simply extended or overlapped the boundaries of redlined neighborhoods in larger swaths of declining cities.[113]

THE LEGACY OF DISPLACEMENT AND RACIAL BARGAINING

I've tried to show that federal interest in national segregation codified by the urban renewal program was bad enough at the time, but from the standpoint of racial reckoning it also inflicted lasting damage to the wealth of African Americans in two characteristic ways: housing displacement and racial bargaining. Both reinforce the significance of place for life chances. Regarding displacement, we've seen how tens of thousands of Black migrants were forcibly displaced from homes and businesses into often substandard housing or neighborhoods bound for a second round of condemnation. These moves lacked forethought, adequate relocation assistance and were economically devastating to a mostly poor and working-class population that had few choices. Yet still we live in a time of immense displacement pressures and costs where the stresses of housing insecurity, mismatches between the location of jobs and affordable housing, gentrification, foreclosure and homelessness have disproportionately destabilized Black households. In the final chapter, I'll discuss findings of a study my research center conducted that show how Black mobility patterns of the last twenty-five years continue in the mode of the Great Migration – that is, they reflect a fundamental need for places that offer economic stability *but especially housing stability.* The through line that connects the mass housing displacements of urban renewal to the housing displacement risks of the twenty-first century isn't perfectly straight, but it's not unbroken. Displacement retards wealth accumulation. It's more harmful than limited mobility because displacement not only precludes the wealth gains of appreciating property ownership, but it also frustrates all the other efforts by which wealth is built – from stable education to employment mobility to healthy environments – and replaces them with struggle.

Racial bargaining is another continuing feature of urban renewal's segregative effects on Black-identified places. Racial bargaining is the term I use to describe the institutionalized norms of transactional devaluation in Black-identified neighborhoods. It's another form of racial inequality. Since the vast majority of African Americans of whatever class then, as now, live in predominantly Black neighborhoods, many aspects of racial bargaining apply. In 1949, racial bargaining was represented by the inflated rents of slum apartments cut up into overcrowded kitchenettes. But mortgage discrimination at the time as well as redlining of Black neighborhoods meant Black homebuyers paid more through unscrupulous land sale contracts with realtor-sellers, who could and did take back properties based on a single default and raise the price for the next buyer. Segregated housing markets set the asymmetrical conditions for price exploitation. 'You'll pay more for this because there's no place else that will take your money.' I also showed how renters and business owners displaced by urban renewal often paid more for substandard housing and commercial space where they could find it. Racial bargaining, especially related to housing transactions and formal lending, drained incalculable wealth.

Because the US has not reckoned with its federal interest in segregation, racial bargaining has continued to drain Black wealth in and beyond housing for decades. Perhaps the best example is racial bargains in lending terms. Black homebuyers faced a variety of discriminatory challenges to obtaining traditional bank mortgages long after passage of the Fair Housing Act in 1968 (and also the Home Mortgage

Disclosure Act of 1975[114] and the Community Reinvestment Act of 1977[115]). The banking and lending vacuum in Black neighborhoods invited fraud and expensive, onerous lending terms – racial bargaining – known throughout the 1980s and 90s as predatory lending. Like extraordinarily high insurance rates in Black neighborhoods, these transactional fees greatly inflated the cost of housing in markets that did not appraise anywhere near the equivalent of the same home in a predominantly white area. (Appraisal disparities and outright discrimination continue today.) Even practices meant to counter the ill effects of predatory lending became predatory, as the reverse redlining of the late 1990s and early 2000s created a poorly regulated bonanza of subprime lending in Black-identified areas that led to the housing bust and subsequent Great Recession. In turn, the Great Recession precipitated the foreclosure crisis, which again disproportionately affected Blacks and wiped out decades of Black wealth.

Less known is how government support for foreclosure sales to private equity would mean a targeting of homes in predominantly Black homeowner communities. These corporate buyers of single-family homes buy low and rent high, often in cash, capturing entire blocks and neighborhoods as if they were asset classes to be exploited rather than "spatial opportunity structures" where valuable wealth and social networks are nurtured. All of this represents racial bargaining where the thing in the Black neighborhood can be had for less in order to earn more because asymmetry has been built into the place. It's a history of racial dominos, falling decade by decade and accumulating Black wealth loss along the way.

Racial bargaining also shows how segregation created a permanent dual housing market that in turn creates dual markets for all sorts of things affecting household wealth. Middle-class Black homeowners see racial bargaining devalue their homes in part because their schools are devalued, though they often pay more in property taxes than middle-class whites. The result is fewer resources for public goods like parks and education as a return on neighborhood investment. Even middle-class Black parents who decide to forego neighborhood schools in favor of expensive private schools are making a racial bargain. Racial bargaining for poorer Blacks is rarely far away, since a characteristic of racial segregation is that the Black middle class tends to live adjacent to the

Black poor.[116] In the latter neighborhoods, the poor typically pay more for some necessities like groceries and fresh produce, if you can find them. There are costs to all these bargains, and they're as high as they are unnecessary.

RECKONING LOST VALUE

Understanding racial bargaining helps us consider aspects of accountability reckoning for wealth loss. For twenty-five years, urban renewal was the primary means by which hundreds of the nation's cities used federal monies to reimagine themselves in a prosperous postwar America. It's the period when cities assumed metropolitan identities and presidential administrations contemplated comprehensive urban policies.[117] The methods of rational planning popularized by urban renewal still govern city planning principles today. They are no longer so race conscious as to deliberately inflict harm on citizens. We expect a government that did inflict harm to be accountable for those losses.

Let's start with the character of the wrongs. Urban renewal consisted of both intentional and negligent harms; that is, as government policy, it constituted both intentional racism as well as disparate-impact racial harm from facially neutral rules and practices. Local governments knew they were affirmatively targeting Black slums and neighborhoods for clearance and redevelopment, because the disparate impact upon those tracts was overwhelming. Also intentional was the withholding of relocation assistance and fair compensation when local governments knew displacees were generally poorer and already restricted by their race to live and open businesses only in certain segregated areas of most cities. Even when the Act was amended to ensure relocation help for displacees, many local governments submitted false claims of compliance, an intentional act, while federal officials looked the other way, another intentional act.[118] Both levels of government were responsible for codifying the long delays between project designation and project completion that sapped the value out of displaced homes and businesses, draining what limited wealth the migrants had accrued. Urban renewal involved intentional affirmative racial targeting, while simultaneous government policies were categorically excluding Black people from the benefits of suburban homeownership. Affirmative targeting and categorical excluding by race constitute traceable racial harms inflicted upon identifiable Black people and their communities. There is some evidence (from Boston, for example) that white people displaced by urban renewal were not as badly mistreated.

Both levels of government were also responsible for negligent wrongdoing. The state cannot simply plan the forcible removal of vast groups of people and property without a corresponding plan for their welfare. The federal and local governments shared duties to extend relocation assistance and relief to the displaced that were frequently breached. They had a duty to foresee the consequential harms that displacees would face as they struggled to find replacement housing on their own in segregated housing markets. This amounted to a combination of negligent and intentional conduct, as the court in *Norwalk CORE v. Norwalk Redevelopment Agency* recognized in 1968:

> What plaintiffs' complaint alleges, in substance, is that in planning and implementing the Project, the local defendants did not assure, or even attempt to assure, relocation for Negro and Puerto Rican displacees in compliance with the Contract to the same extent as they did for whites; indeed, they intended through the combination of the Project and the rampant discrimination in rentals in the Norwalk housing market to drive many Negroes and Puerto Ricans out of the City of Norwalk. The argument is that proof of these allegations would make out a case of violation of the equal protection clause. We agree.[119]

And both levels of government failed to foresee urban renewal's long-term harms to people and communities, simply discounting them instead.

There are many ways to value what was lost by these wrongs, each with their own causal complexity. A simplified analysis might create three categories – urban renewal's direct and indirect costs to Black displacees and urban renewal's more lasting segregative effects on Black wealth. Directly, urban renewal produced legions of Black (and other) people who were denied the full value of their possessory interests (e.g., leases, homes and businesses prior to blight designations). This would include some portion of the future value of those properties and any foregone gains as a result of having to leave to make way for others to profit. They are due a percentage of the land whose value was increased by their removal. Finally, millions failed to receive adequate relocation expenses.

Urban renewal's contemporaneous indirect costs on Blacks might be comprised of lost opportunity costs – the price of exclusion from homeownership offers their white coworkers received. While many of those real estate actors were private companies, one could calculate the value of government-subsidized mortgages, schools and some portion of home value appreciation. After all, Blacks too would have enjoyed these household wealth accumulations if only they'd been allowed into the market. Another indirect cost is the access to social capital that came with suburban homeownership.

Then there are the peculiar indirect effects that urban renewal's plan of segregation set in motion. These arise from norms as well as place, but they are no less traceable to what both the federal and local governments conditioned for the lives of Black people beginning at mid-century. For instance, the field of environmental justice (banned by the Trump administration) is based on the study of locally unwanted land uses (LULUs) and NIMBYism (Not In My Backyard). Yet many barriers to putting hazardous things in neighborhoods where people live simply arise from zoning protections. Black neighborhoods have traditionally been denied these protections, another feature of segregated land management, devaluing them with respect to environmental risk. These risks have resulted in so many well-documented harms over the generations that calculating their cost is challenging but not impossible. And that's just one example, to which we could add others like inadequate public safety resources and recreational disparities.

Finally, consider the myriad costs of racial bargaining. While causation dynamics might be hard to overcome conceptually, we could certainly do a lot more to protect existing Black wealth from the waves of predatory economic activity to which it's been periodically vulnerable. Consumer fraud enforcement, real estate regulation and equitable local taxation rules could do a lot to lower costs and increase certainty. Racial bargaining is a set of economic norms. We change norms all the time.

The pushback to all of this is expected. First, critics would argue that all policies have unintended consequences, especially those involving large, comprehensive bureaucracies. If urban renewal required reparative remedies for Blacks, wouldn't a dozen other policies of the last 100 years require it too, for millions of Americans? Second, causation is problematic. Even if you could identify the victims of the program's direct harms, attributing predatory harms of the 1990s and beyond to a program that had petered out before its official end in 1974 is a causal stretch. Numerous other factors intervened along the way to cause, for example, the foreclosure crisis of 2008–11. Third, many conservatives would blame culture for the racial wealth gap and consider structural arguments mere excuses for Black failure.

The rejoinder is that the unintended consequences of a prolonged *race-conscious* policy can't be dismissed at this scale. Federal and local policymakers doubled down on the financial waste of urban renewal despite clear evidence that it wasn't achieving its stated goals. By the time fiscal crises hit US cities in the 1970s, the impoverished ghettoes that policymakers had created were as unmistakable as the race of the people struggling there. The results were completely foreseeable. Black people had been telling policymakers for years. Lawsuits had detailed the damage and sought to mitigate it through injunctions. The consequences can't be called unintended when they're ignored.

As for causation, calibrating causal nexus is a normative exercise; we see the relationships we want to see, often depending on the interest at stake. As the last chapter showed, courts make increasingly stringent demands on, say, fair-housing plaintiffs to show causally connected disparate impact. But the same courts are often willing to second-guess holistic admissions processes as "zero sum" (as in *per se*) discriminatory treatment without proof that an actual white or Asian applicant had been denied admission on the basis of their race. Ultimately, where we draw the line reflects our commitment to the demands of racial justice. The trend now is to narrow while the truth is often more expansive.

Culture has mostly been an argument built less on empirical fact than anecdote. Critics somehow know a lack of commitment to Black excellence when they see it. Yet the many attempts to prove this claim have failed to account for any significant cultural shift. For instance, Daniel Moynihan's account of Black matriarchy and the supposed problems of "fatherless" households were neither proven nor addressed by policy. Like racial backlash, conservatives hurl culture of poverty arguments at Black people every few years to no particular effect but policy name-calling. During the Reagan years, safety net policies were overhauled and aid halted on the ground that it fostered a culture of dependency among Blacks. Female-headed households, pregnant teens, gangsta rappers and hip-hop culture were to blame.[120] Plenty of scholarship said otherwise but was ignored.[121] Bill Clinton in the 1990s pledged to "end welfare as we know it" in response to that round of cultural accusation. Again, the empirical support was lacking. These policy retrenchments did demonstrably nothing to improve "culture." To this day, we know that most poor people work hard, often at multiple jobs, family formation has limited effect on options, and economic forces like wages and housing affordability (i.e., structural factors) better explain limited incomes. Place has cultural influence based on the kinds of resources available to the people there, not their character. As urban renewal demonstrated, starve a place of resources and a culture of hardship and scarcity ensues. Investing in a place with resources creates a cradle of opportunity.

This chapter has shown that a mid-century race-conscious policy camouflaged by planning language created a system of displacement and racial bargaining that would condition the segregated economic life chances for large numbers of the country's Black population for decades to come. In reaction to the Great Migration, urban renewal's racially disproportionate harms were both intentional and negligent. Because it established a federal interest in segregation, the system urban renewal set off interacted with several others – contemporaneous and subsequent, public and private – that produced norms of racial bargaining that define key aspects of the racial wealth gap. These warrant remediation in a racial reckoning. Note, however, that despite the indispensable role of the federal government in joining many systems of systemic racism, many ideas about reckoning rely on place. Place is often governed locally. Federal help is essential for a full accounting, but the second Trump administration has so far expressed a keen hostility to fair-housing rights, gutting the Department of Housing and Urban Development's resources and retreating on enforcement activity.[122] Nevertheless, we can start at the state and local level without federal cooperation.

Accountability reckoning entails a greater focus not only on why Black folks' wealth opportunities have been stymied, but on their health outcomes and interactions with police. Like urban renewal and the wealth gap, each of those has a close relationship to where people live, subjects we explore next.

CHAPTER 4

Colored by Covid and the Comorbidities of Race

The sudden onset of the Covid pandemic put African Americans in a special bind. Like all Americans, they were scared of the virus invading them like an invisible monster. Everyone had to do daily cost–benefit analyses about when to mask, where not to go, what risks to take. For some, certain costs couldn't be avoided. In those early months, the virus seemed to be targeting Blacks with a vengeance. By the late summer of 2020, talk of a possible vaccine was to dream in miracles. But not necessarily for Black people. African Americans were split roughly 50-50 on whether we would get "pricked" once one became available.[1] The split bitterly divided families. Disagreements were heated, often generational. "You take multiple pills *every day*," younger Blacks asked older family members. "Why wouldn't you trust science this time if you know it can save you?"

Maybe because, when it comes to the Black body and doctors, knowing and trusting can be separated by rational fears about how racism can make you sick. Science has discriminated before. Public health is a vast graveyard of structural inequality.

The transactional debasement of Black bodies is as old as the Middle Passage during which infectious diseases went untreated on slave ships. Later, the horrors of sharecropping, peonage, convict leasing and lynching all rested on distinct social norms of exhausting, defiling, confining, threatening and destroying Black bodies. We haven't completely overcome this past. Segregation policies of modern life, as we saw in the last chapter, were more prepared to remove blight than to treat its public health consequences among Black migrants. Residential segregation would perpetuate racial differentiation in housing conditions and condition Black access to the quality of care, the availability of treatments and even to medical testing.[2] Black illness, pain and suffering are still sometimes treated as if they had a separate etiology. For instance, nephrologists until recently used debunked racial theories about supposed Black muscle mass to misread Black kidney transplant patients' bloodwork and delay their eligibility, demanding they be sicker than white patients in order to qualify.[3] The practice may first have been questioned by Naomi Nkinsi, a courageous Black first-year medical student at the University of Washington.[4] Even when biological race matters, like in dermatology where a shortage of Black doctors results in skewed research priorities and uneven competency around African-American skin conditions, racial bias can determine the efforts of the profession to bridge gaps.[5] Black interests in medical care can be devalued, manipulated and bargained away. African Americans have ample cause for suspicion. From birth to death, Black people have the highest rates of infant mortality, the lowest life expectancy and the highest age-adjusted death rate from all causes among all groups.[6] Like police brutality, these are patterns as old as the republic. They play out in complicated data we know by its awkward name: "racial health disparities." They contributed mightily to the special bind Covid vaccines raised in African-American communities during the reckoning.

Research interest in racial health disparities began in the 1980s and has expanded ever since. In 2003, an authoritative report by the Institute for Medicine called *Unequal Treatment* collected a wide body of research on disparities, pointed to racism as a causal agent and helped to spawn decades more research.[7] A follow-up study released in 2023 confirmed that many of the same issues persist decades later.[8] Yet few phenomena brought racial health disparities to light like the sudden appearance of the Covid virus that seemed particularly suited to hunting and killing Black people. In April 2020, for instance, Black (and Native) people were three times more likely to be infected and two and a half times more likely to die. The ratio of vulnerability would change over the course of the pandemic, as the number of whites dying from the variants increased and the political dynamics of vaccination took hold. African-American deaths from Covid again acted as a canary in a coalmine, the disease targeting people who were vulnerable because they had to go out, they lived in cities and they already had health problems that weakened their immune systems.[9]

The confusion was as palpable as the fear. We were left to weigh information against rumor, mixed with politics, wrapped in geography, soaked in speculation. We knew little about the early victims of this confusion except, as data trickled in, that some neighborhoods were hit hardest, some occupations, some ages and, of course, some races. It was an unprecedented public health disparate-impact nightmare scenario of rampant rumor and unimaginable grief. Yet amid all the confusion, suffering and death, a racial reckoning that began with the airing of George Floyd's violent death brought people outside to protest. From the standpoint of a public health crisis, the reckoning seemed to want a coherent answer to two obvious questions: Why were so many more Black people getting sick and why did so many who got sick succumb to the disease?

There were two primary answers. The first was that the virus was opportunistic; it found people who could be most easily found. These people became known as "essential workers." By definition, essential workers held jobs that did not allow them to shelter in place and work remotely. Workers in public transportation, sanitation, Amazon warehouses, food delivery, health care, custodial services and poultry slaughterhouses were members of the often working-class to blue-collar labor force on which a homebound public relied to keep the crippled economy moving. These exposed people were disproportionately Black and Latino.[10] Many essential workers were *required* to keep working despite the risk, often without adequate personal protective equipment, which racialized the threat of death.[11] One reason Covid had a disparate impact on Black people is because their socioeconomic status exposed them to the virus.

The other reason we were told was that research was beginning to show that Black people disproportionately experienced "underlying health conditions" that made them especially vulnerable to the most devastating effects of the virus on the body. This reason didn't receive nearly the reckoning it deserved. Specifically, public health officials were discovering that there were four to five preexisting health conditions whose coexistence – comorbidities – put people at much greater risk of dying from Covid if they were infected: heart disease, diabetes, chronic kidney disease and obesity.[12] The fifth, hypertension, seemed to act as a gateway to the others, since its presence in patients was highly correlated with extreme or lethal outcomes. These just seemed to be unfortunate problems a lot of Black people had, which made them unlucky in a global pandemic.

Covid was uniquely capable of exploiting the layered prevalence of these health conditions, turning chronic illnesses into sudden deaths or extended hospitalizations. It became increasingly clear that Covid attacks organs throughout the body, not just the lungs, particularly the heart and kidneys.[13] A recent large-scale study found that almost two-thirds (64 percent) of hospitalizations due to Covid in the United States could have been avoided if Americans did not suffer from the four preexisting cardiometabolic conditions – obesity, hypertension, diabetes and heart failure – in that order.[14] Patients with multiple comorbidities have been found to be at the most elevated risk for Covid hospitalization and death. According to the Centers for Disease Control, those patients with two underlying conditions are four and a half times more likely to be hospitalized for Covid, and those with three or more conditions are five times more likely.[15] The research on comorbidities consistently shows chronic conditions are interconnected and affect one another. For example, the two leading causes of chronic kidney disease are obesity and hypertension. And chronic kidney disease, in turn, is associated with the onset of chronic heart disease and type 2 diabetes. Patients with end-stage renal disease, an advanced form of kidney disease, were found to be eleven times more likely to be hospitalized with Covid.[16] Adults with diabetes are three times more likely to develop a severe case of Covid, and two to three times more likely to die of Covid, particularly those who also have hypertension.[17] The CDC reports that having obesity may triple the risk of hospitalization from severe Covid infection.[18] Covid directly damages the respiratory system, forcing the heart to work faster and harder to supply oxygen-rich blood to major organs. Patients with weak or compromised hearts are therefore at increased risk. In one study, 50 percent of patients with heart disease died from Covid.[19]

These conditions stalk the lives of African Americans and their family members. Chronic health conditions render the average Black American substantially sicker than the average white person, even though the care provided to Black people cost $1,800 less per year than the average care given to a white person with the same number of chronic health conditions.[20] As common as it is among Americans generally, hypertension affects 54% of Black adults, but 46% of whites.[21] As too many dialysis centers attest, 16.4% of Blacks suffer from diabetes while less than 12% of whites do.[22] Obesity is the same: 38.4% of Black adults meet the criteria, ten percentage points beyond the rate for whites.[23] All of these conditions contribute to the risk of heart disease. Going from prevalence of condition to mortality, in 2020 Blacks died of cardiovascular disease at much higher rates than all racial groups, 1,783.7 per million (compared to 1,234.2 for whites, 968.5 for Hispanics and 685.7 for Asians), already a significant jump from the year before the pandemic (1,503.8).[24] Blacks aren't alone in facing disproportionate chronic conditions, however, the disparity in death rates is telling. Many Americans live with underlying conditions that don't kill them or put them at as great a risk during a pandemic. Research indicates that the prevalence of underlying conditions is very high among Blacks, but also that many of the conditions are not adequately controlled. The issue of racial health disparities is not just a question of who has what illness at the highest rates, but also who can manage a condition before it overcomes them when an inflammatory disease attacks.

In this light, dying from Covid means something more. Cause of death can be more complicated than even an autopsy can reveal. "He died of Covid." Did he? Or did he die because he was a bus driver and was exposed to hundreds of times the risk people who worked remotely faced? And did he die of his poorly treated high blood pressure, which, together with his not fully controlled diabetes, were two too many underlying conditions when Covid entered his lungs, becoming "comorbidities" when he succumbed to a cytokine storm that someone his age without those conditions and working from home and under the appropriate medical care would not likely have died from? Despite reams of data, the racial reckoning did not dwell on this complication long enough.

A more complete racial reckoning should ask, just why do Black people suffer so many underlying health conditions and what makes them so disproportionately lethal?

The answers to these questions are not straightforward, but a useful way to get at them is to recognize that what makes one person sicker than another comes down to four major factors. The first two, genes and behavior, are internal. One is out of your control and the other can only be controlled by you. In fact, the behavior question was often asked and answered during the pandemic, with assumptions about Black people's unwillingness to eat well, exercise regularly, refrain from high-risk behaviors – all issues of personal irresponsibility.[25] (This assumption ran so deep that researchers hypothesized that one reason white mortality took so long to catch up to Black mortality was many whites' erroneous belief that the virus targeted only Blacks and other people of color.)[26] The other two reasons are external: environment and treatment. These have fewer factors within your control because they involve questions of access to institutional resources that are not equally available to all of us. For racial reckoning, we explore these two, acknowledging that genes and personal agency nevertheless play a significant role in why one has underlying conditions that are associated with higher mortality rates from Covid.

Environment and treatment appear in the public health literature on racial health disparities in two broad ways. Scholars often speak of environment as the "social determinants of health" – or SDOH. Once again, place – the resources around you – plays a pivotal role in life chances. Treatment, on the other hand, often comes down to the caregiver–patient relationship – how the interaction goes, where and how often, the diagnosis, the treatment plan and any interventions along the way. Treatment disparities by race often come down to implicit bias. The effects of implicit bias are magnified by socioeconomic class, so that poverty and race often compound it.[27]

The causal pathway that joins environment and treatment looks something like this: An unhealthy environment creates or exacerbates health risks, like toxins, or stressors, violence or eviction anxiety. Managing these issues requires access to resources, either to reduce the threats or to provide effective countermeasures. The main nonpreventive countermeasure is medical treatment. Where medical treatment is the main intervention, it must be competent and it must inspire trust. Competent care is possible without trust. Even biased doctors can deliver competent care. Yet trust is key to the patient–caregiver relationship, because anyone affecting our bodies directly encounters our dignity. They do so with our consent, which, as a legal and social matter, should be informed. Any nonconsensual trespass against our inviolate body is an offense to our dignity, and we react. When the treatment is either substandard or is so infected with the perception of racial bias, it breeds mistrust. People avoid visiting or cooperating with doctors and caregivers they distrust, which can make them sicker. Add in scarcity of available, affordable options near you. If you already can't afford the time or expense of getting help, untrustworthy care makes it even costlier. So, you put it off. Meanwhile, problems get worse.

This pathway to poorly managed underlying health conditions led to Covid's disparate impact on Black people and should have fueled a racial reckoning around health disparities. Let's examine environment and treatment more closely.

THE SOCIAL DETERMINANTS OF POORER HEALTH

Take the social determinants of health first. Many of the factors associated with poor socially determined health outcomes – such as lead in the walls or water, mold, indoor pollutants, inadequate heat, pest infestation, fear of violence – sound like another way of describing structural inequality. Whether it's housing, neighborhoods, social dislocation, crime or climate risks, these are the health-related dimensions of having little choice but to live in substandard, unwanted, devalued places. They lead to a greater incidence of certain kinds of cancers, infant mortality, inflammatory illnesses and autoimmune diseases. We associate these environmental negatives as things that people without power have to live with, people on the wrong end of NIMBYism. For instance, Americans may have been shocked to learn that residents of Flint, MI were ingesting and bathing in water contaminated with high amounts of lead, but we weren't surprised to learn that the residents were overwhelmingly Black.

The social determinants of underlying conditions and illnesses could have been anticipated by federal and local officials at mid-century when they passed the 1949 Housing Act to clear slums. Recall that for decades leading up to World War II, cities were concerned with the public health consequences of slums. They spoke of them in epidemiological terms, like preventing the spread of contagious disease. The facts bore them out. Yet, as we saw in the last chapter, segregationist government policymaking did little to address the public health needs of Black people living in substandard housing. Urban renewal forced many to move to even more blighted housing than the slums they cleared. Meanwhile, federal–local policies supported one of the great public health initiatives in American history: suburban living. The commensurate exclusion of Black people for decades of wealth-building also produced social determinants of poorer health in the ghetto neighborhoods where so many lived during the 1950s to the 1980s.

The public health effects of ghettoization, urban residency and hypersegregation are not only the bygone antecedents of our parents' and grandparents' underlying conditions. Poor and working-class neighborhoods remain to this day teeming with social determinants that heighten the risk of chronic disease and debilitating illness. "[N]eighborhood of residence explains substantial amounts of the race–mortality association even after health behaviors and other demographic and socioeconomic characteristics are already accounted for."[28] Housing in low-income city neighborhoods is on average much older and poorly maintained.[29] Arson is more frequent.[30] The siting of environmental hazards, such as waste facilities and bus depots is many times more common.[31] Crime is higher as are car and pedestrian accidents.[32] All of these disproportionately impact the health of Black people, based solely on their housing market options. Risk is not only what may happen to you, but is also what may not be available to *prevent* health risks. Poor air quality in segregated urban neighborhoods is not only a factor that contributes to higher asthma rates, but a reason not to go for a jog after work. Exclusion from the Belle Terre neighborhoods does not just inhibit access to wealth; it traps people in areas where recreational opportunities in open space are few. Jogging and exercising outdoors are common prevention recommendations for people at risk of hypertension, heart disease and diabetes. Suburban municipalities routinely devote significant tax dollars to ensuring that these public amenities are inviting and well-maintained. It's not just aesthetics. Having them extends lives.

Finally, racism itself is another socially determined factor in Black people's health. Several studies have compared health outcomes among Black and non-Black subjects and found, for similarly situated people where race was the only material distinguishing factor, Blacks' experience of racism explained the results.[33] One explanation is "weathering," the physiological effects over time of coping with the uncertain stressors of racism.[34] Interestingly, the results are more pronounced for professional Blacks, who typically spend more time in predominantly white settings.[35]

Evidence about heart disease, for instance, suggests Blacks experience fewer health-related benefits of increased income and education levels compared to whites.[36]

THE TRAUMAS OF INSECURE LIVES

Psychological trauma represents a related category of harm that is mostly determined by our social environments. Again, the pandemic was a force multiplier, especially for Blacks. In 2020, Covid presided over a 30 percent spike in murders despite falling street crime, most perpetrated with guns, many inside the home.[37] That's a lot of violence, especially for children. Gunshots and other psychologically traumatic experiences reveal a lot about the structure of inequality in the United States. In economically marginalized environments, a single gunshot can live on indefinitely, beginning with the flesh it tears, the memories it traumatizes and the stereotypes it confirms in the minds of distant others. That lone traumatic event can travel from barrel to bone and beyond over the space of generations, marking and defining the places where opportunity dies or thrives. Violence often begets violence and also efforts to ensure its absence. Thus, the child witness who fears, sees and relives violence may react to the experience with post-traumatic stress disorder (PTSD) or other conditions that potentially rewire her brain, impair cognitive abilities, imperil learning and condition her body for an array of life-threatening addictions and illnesses over time. Many of those illnesses are the very underlying conditions that became comorbidities in a pandemic.

Since research on trauma found a public audience in the early 2010s, the word "trauma" has become so overused as to risk meaning anything especially nasty and hurtful to a person. Although clinical trauma is hard to define – "an emotional response to a terrible event like an accident, rape or natural disaster"[38] – I prefer to reserve the term for the extraordinary occurrence. Traumas represent the unspeakable, and our reactions the very human, yet adaptive, responses to atrocities.[39] They are inflicted on us from the outside. Anyone may experience trauma; all of us face potentially traumatic experiences (PTE). However, there is evidence that Black children, especially in low-income environments, face a disproportionate number of such events.[40]

I focus on childhood complex trauma – the "poly-victimization" by multiple traumas, sometimes multiple types – because it has the greatest power to negatively affect both mental and physical health. Research indicates that the most debilitating traumas to overcome are the chronic, often unavoidable complex traumas that may accumulate.[41] Nonetheless, the consensus is that about 25 percent of American children have had at least one significant exposure to a traumatic experience before reaching adulthood.[42] For low-income children, however, estimates of exposure to *multiple* traumatic events range between 40 and 80 percent. One of the standard diagnostic tools is the Adverse Childhood Experiences Study (ACE).[43] This approach uses a seventeen-question (sometimes reduced to ten) questionnaire. Adverse childhood experiences are correlated with psychological and physiological health issues among adults, such as depression, heart disease, diabetes, emphysema, alcohol and drug dependency and sexually transmitted disease. Children scoring at least four ACEs are considered to have been exposed to complex trauma. By that definition, one study estimated that nationally, almost a quarter (22 percent) of children are exposed to complex trauma in a one-year period.[44]

The major sources of complex trauma in children occur in their home, school and neighborhood environments: domestic or intimate partner violence, maltreatment (abuse and neglect), death or serious illness/ injury of a loved one, separation from family members due to incarceration or other child welfare removals, car accidents, fires, terrorism and, very significantly, community violence.[45] These trauma sources tend to cluster socio-demographically. Children living in isolated, concentrated poverty are at highest risk for exposure to complex trauma.[46] As poverty increases the risks of a child being exposed to traumatic events, it also tends to increase the severity of the traumas themselves. For instance, a longitudinal study of children found that "vulnerability factors" such as poverty are associated with a greater prevalence of exposure to "high magnitude events" like sexual abuse or death of a loved one.[47] Since poorer children may also lack access to therapeutic services for a variety of reasons, their heightened risks for trauma exposure are compounded by fewer resources to cope with post-traumatic effects.[48]

Exposure to traumatic events can have devastating effects on neurobiological development, psychological makeup and cognitive, socio-emotional development. Consider exposure to, or victimization by, violence. Neuroscientists have developed a rich body of research that shows how traumatic events can alter the brain's architecture, sometimes in ways that reach the gene pool and live on in our descendants. This array of disturbing findings includes several categories of post-traumatic harm, studied through distinct biomarkers of stress from the neuroendocrine, immunological, metabolic and cardiovascular systems. As children's brains react to traumatic stressors, processes are triggered that affect different systems in the body. The effects range from behavioral self-regulation problems and mental illness, predisposition to certain diseases,[49] risk of alcohol or substance abuse and accelerated biological aging.[50] According to Bruce Perry, "[E]xposure to violence activates a set of threat-responses in the child's developing brain; in turn excess activation of the neural systems involved in the threat responses can alter the developing brain; finally, these alterations manifest as functional changes in emotional, behavioral and cognitive functioning."[51] This interaction between external experience, neurobiology and behavior typically occurs across a spectrum with hyperarousal at one end and dissociation at the other.[52] Psychological impacts may be profound. Using ACE scores, considerable research suggests that cumulative childhood PTEs are significantly related to increased risk of lifetime psychiatric illness, such as Major Depressive Disorder, PTSD and anxiety disorders.[53] Other research shows that childhood exposure to traumatic events can profoundly disturb cognitive functioning, especially academic performance. For instance, Theodore Thompson and Carol Massat studied 110 eleven to thirteen-year-old African-American students from four Chicago neighborhoods. The authors demonstrated that exposure to family violence, community violence and witnessing violence were each significantly related to lower academic achievement. Each type of violence exposure was also closely related to higher PTSD symptoms, and in turn, higher PTSD symptoms were closely related to lower academic achievement.[54] These findings suggest that children's PTE exposure directly and indirectly (through PTSD symptoms) places them at disparate risk for academic underachievement and later socioeconomic disadvantage. These are among the burdens of place.

Most of the sources of trauma increased in the concentrated confines of Covid shelter-in-place policies, with demonstrably higher risks for Black children who live in neighborhoods of the most concentrated poverty from which there's limited escape.[55] It's safe to infer that the pandemic both increased exposure to trauma and exacerbated existing clinical and sub-clinical traumatic conditions. Things got worse, and psychological factors can have bodily consequences.

Why draw such an inference, and why connect that to racial reckoning? Covid separated tens of thousands of Black people from their family members, thousands of them permanently. Beyond the sudden deaths of loved ones was the added stress of having incarcerated loved ones in less-protected prisons, an emotional burden disproportionately borne by African Americans. Then there was the pandemic's increased violence – both domestic and community. In other words, just as a preexisting set of cardiometabolic underlying conditions awaited the death blow of a virus peculiarly suited to attack those vulnerabilities, so did preexisting exposure to complex psychological traumas expose disproportionate numbers of Black children to the radical compounding of trauma brought on by the virus. It was, like Hurricane Katrina, the perfect storm. Again. For months.

Also like Katrina, the convergence of these factors by a chance event reveals structural inequalities that demand reckoning. These are not race-based risks. These are terrible things that can happen to everybody and do. Rather these are place-based risks that happen disproportionately to African-American children, who, *because of their race*, live in the places most at risk for producing traumatic events. Covid was an accelerant. Its impact on neurobiological development, socio-emotional learning and the association with underlying inflammatory conditions like chronic heart and kidney disease, diabetes, obesity and hypertension will be fully revealed years from now.

The trauma from hurricanes, like the trauma from other sources, may continue to shorten lives long after the clean-up. A fascinating study of tropical cyclones is among the first of its kind to demonstrate the complex relationship between traumatic climate events and their deadly long-term impact on humans – especially Black people. Rachel Young and Solomon Hsiang looked at more than 500 hurricanes that struck the continental United States between 1930 and 2015 to see how much "indirect excess death burden" they produced.[56] They found that each event was attributed with killing an average of 24 people immediately, but cumulatively, each event killed or was responsible for an earlier death of 7,000 to 11,400 people over fifteen years since landfall. Black people were three times as likely as whites to suffer indirect excess deaths. Because subsequent hurricanes strike within that time frame, the researchers used a process called deconvolution – "an established signal-processing technique used to analyze time-series data in many contexts" – to stack the cumulative impacts. The factors that they hypothesize cause these excess deaths include economic disruption, social network changes, fiscal adjustments in state and local programs and heightened mental and physical stress. We are, in many ways, what happens to us.

IMPLICIT BIAS AND HEALTH-CARE TREATMENT

Seeing doctors regularly may be critical to our health, especially as we age, but the formal hierarchy between doctor and patient sometimes obscures the fact that even the briefest visit involves an intensely private, emotionally fraught relationship between two human beings. It's both the relationship and the sense of hierarchy that enables racism to enter in decisive, if not explicit, ways. For some this seems as unfair as questioning the motives of cops. Doctors (and other health-care workers) are highly trained, extraordinarily skilled professionals whose duty is to preserve life. They are also extremely busy, conducting a variety of complex tasks, often under urgent circumstances. They should be the last people we worry about bringing bias into a relationship of care. Because this is probably true, the disparities literature is almost silent on explicit bias. What it shows is the myriad ways that *unconscious* bias permeates these medical encounters. In a society still trained on the simplistic idea of intentional racism, implicit bias often goes unacknowledged, where it can travel throughout institutions, affecting doctor and medical staff perceptions, the treatment of classes of patients with certain kinds of conditions, the degree of care in an entire hospital or health-care system and the accuracy of diagnosis and treatment. Its most immediate consequence is distrust. For many Black patients, it may be a substantial factor in death – sudden or sooner than expected – because of its effect on the management and treatment of underlying conditions.

As an initial matter, available research shows that Black folks who complain about experiencing disrespect, dismissiveness, condescension, negative assumptions and second-class status in health-care settings know what they're talking about. In a qualitative study of patient–doctor communication, physicians' implicit pro-white bias on the Implicit Association Test (IAT) confirmed Black patients' perceptions of poorer communication and lower quality care.[57] Focus group studies reveal many deeply felt misgivings about doctor encounters. One African-American participant said, "I felt that because of my race that I wasn't serviced as well as a Caucasian person was. The attitude that you would get. Information wasn't given to me as it would have [been given to] a Caucasian. The attitude made me feel like I was less important."[58] A twenty-eight-year-old, low-income Black patient wished doctors would "take physical pain more seriously without me having to … get out of character … I should not have to contemplate having to take it to that level of rage in order for you to get something done."[59] A third described the problem of trying to give informed consent without being perceived as uncooperative.

> I don't have a problem with taking more time to be able to understand each other, but they get really annoyed when you don't understand them. Basically, they get really annoyed if you talk too much because they know they don't understand your language. When I go to the doctor I ask a lot of questions, so they can get really aggravated with me. I don't know if they would do the same thing to a white person.[60]

These sentiments are widely supported by research. A 2020 survey exploring African Americans' views and experiences of being Black in America, including within the health-care system, found that seven in ten Black adults believe race-based discrimination in health care happens at least somewhat often, and one in five say they have personally experienced it in the past year. "Black women – particularly mothers – report experiencing even higher rates of discrimination in health care settings."[61] In a nationally representative cross-sectional survey study, 21 percent of 2,137 US adult survey respondents indicated that they had experienced discrimination in the health-care system, and 72 percent of those who had experienced discrimination reported experiencing it more than once. Racial/ethnic discrimination was the most frequently reported type of discrimination respondents experienced.[62] This can be especially pronounced for lower-income patients, particularly those on Medicaid[63] or Medicare.[64] Yet the tragic story of Kira Johnson, a young lawyer in Los Angeles who died following untreated complications from a botched caesarean section, show that the same indignities follow Black patients across income groups.[65]

What's going on? Racial stereotypes and other flawed perceptions are making their way from many health-care providers' assumptions to the care they deliver. White doctor–Black patient interactions may be characterized by verbally dominant doctors, less patient-centered communication and lower levels of positive affect.[66] Studies of physician attitudes from the late 1990s and 2000s found that physicians view their black patients more negatively than white patients.[67] For example, van Ryn and Burke found that, even after "adjusting for patient age, sex, socioeconomic status, sickness or frailty and overall health, and patient availability of social support – physicians viewed black patients, compared with whites, as less kind, congenial, intelligent, and educated, less likely to adhere to medical advice, and more likely to lack social support and to abuse alcohol and drugs."[68] A Black patient in his thirties or forties at the time of these studies would have been in the highest-risk age group when Covid struck decades later. However, more recent research suggests implicit bias remains an unconscious factor in treatment.[69] In fact, Black doctors observe it too. Despite their sympathy for the constraints on doctors, studies record Black doctors witnessing mistreatment by their non-Black peers. According to one Black doctor interviewed, "Most doctors who are very good doctors, and otherwise nice people, are simply doing less for the Black patient because they have this unconscious racism."[70] The *Unequal Treatment* report found Black doctors quietly advocating for their Black patients by avoiding referrals to specialists known for their racial bias or, in some fields where stereotypes have long established disparate care based on race, such as psychiatry and gynecology, overruling inaccurate diagnoses.[71]

Although it's hard to know with confidence just how often Black patients encounter implicit bias in health-care settings, it's clear that these negative interactions matter to Black health. Unconscious racism follows from a tradition of explicit racism in medicine that many Blacks have not forgotten. Forced experimentation in gene testing and syphilis in the mid-twentieth century as well as the Arkansas prison blood plasma scandal that ended in 1994[72] linger in vernacular memory as official policies to degrade Black bodies. Further, the chronic underrepresentation of Black doctors makes bridging the gap between doctor and patient more difficult. Even the stark power differential between non-Black doctors and Black health-care workers demarks a hierarchy across the medical profession that's persisted for generations. The ultimate loss is trust. Throughout the United States only 60% of black adults trust doctors to do what is right most of the time, compared to 80% of white adults. Only 56% of Black citizens trust their local hospitals compared to 70% of white adults. The numbers only worsened during the Covid pandemic as 70% of African Americans said the health-care system treats people unfairly based on race very often or somewhat often, an increase from 56% in a 1999 poll.[73] Where dignity is central, trust is a dependent variable.

Lack of trust may impact different patient populations in different ways. Take Black women whose health issues illustrate the relationship between higher incidence, poorer treatment and resulting mistrust. They are twice as likely to be overweight, have heart attacks, develop diabetes (high blood sugar), lupus (an autoimmune disease) and hepatitis C (a liver disease). They also have a significantly higher risk of asthma, arthritis, cancer and the sexually transmitted disease chlamydia. Experts say these disparities start when black women don't get adequate health screenings. Only 75% of African-American women seek prenatal care, compared to 89% of white women. Only 7% of Black women with depression get treatment, compared to 20% of other patients with depression. Even when they do get medical care, African-American women still often get short shrift. A 1994 study published in the *Journal of the American Medical Association* found that Medicare patients who are African-American, poor and seriously ill receive worse care than other gravely ill Medicare patients in every type of hospital in America.[74] In a 1999 *New England Journal of Medicine* study, actors pretending to have heart problems described their symptoms to 720 physicians. Black female actors received the fewest referrals for specialized treatment – even though they related symptoms identical to those of white men, white women and black men.[75]

Finally, lack of trust may be mutually reinforcing. The less you trust doctors to see you, the sicker you may become. The less doctors trust you, the sicker you'll need to be to get the same help a white patient is likely to receive.[76]

RECKONING

In this chapter, which has shown how Covid made black the color of viral risk and excess death, we asked why, if so much boils down to "underlying conditions," do Black people suffer from so many that imperil their health? The answers came from two areas of research – environment and medical treatment. Social determinants of health and disparate treatment by the medical profession structure the inequality of health outcomes, or "racial health disparities." The mechanisms are as complex as hurricanes, with cumulative effects that last long after the emergency has abated. For these reasons, public health is extremely complicated. This chapter has shown that there are many causes of disparate care, incidence of illness and poor, often preventable, outcomes. They vary by place, region, insurance status, state policies, the medical marketplace, genetics, behavior and chance – to name a few, each a policy world of its own. Behind each is a curable lack of distrust. Distrust contributes to diabetes and obesity complications, taxes resiliency in the face of another trauma and makes the miraculous availability of a vaccine seem not so miraculous.

Three racial reckoning goals follow, especially since the backlash and Trump II. First, the neighborhood must keep the score. Because Black-identified areas carry greater health risks for the people who live there, those risks should be standardized, regularly assessed, publicized and made part of a treatment plan that governs how public health dollars are spent. (Scorecards, like those created by an organization like the Commonwealth Fund, may be produced for local areas on a periodic basis by local public health agencies of government, nonprofit groups or university centers.) It's imperative that the numbers improve – on diabetes control, neonatal visits, blood pressure compliance, etc. If they don't, there must be accountability imposed from state agencies, with funding implications and provider contracts put at risk until *neighborhoods* meet adequacy standards. The structure of care for Black patients has to meet equality metrics or change. The metrics must be sensitive to neighborhood change, too, so that, for instance, providers in gentrifying areas do not benefit from improved numbers associated mainly with a changing patient population, not the improved lives of Black patients.

Second, make those responsible defend against the evidence. Professional accountability in the United States usually results from one of three sources – the stringent oversight of professional licensing organizations like the American Medical Association, the market or lawsuits for malpractice. The first two have not done enough to challenge the position of doctors and medical organizations to overcome patterns of substandard care, often as a result of implicit bias. (The same is true for police officers, who also enjoy great deference from a system unwilling to impose deterrents to save Black lives.) This leaves lawsuits. Successful malpractice suits for implicit bias against doctors causing avoidable harm to Black patients – while currently infrequent – would open up a new line of liability exposure that would lead to new institutional treatment norms and the greater caregiver–patient trust so critical to health maintenance. Medical malpractice laws are creatures of the states, but few states have incorporated claims for implicit bias in health-care treatment or outcomes.[77] The medical profession opposes it. Even if a clearer legal path existed, patients would probably need to pursue it privately through expensive litigation. A state attorney general's office, however, could investigate implicit bias like those presented in this chapter and either recommend legislative changes to ease the way for lawsuits or bring claims itself. A few successful cases would establish a clear record of unlawful conduct and legally binding standards while encouraging the insurance industry to impose change on medical treatment norms. Malpractice by implicit bias should become rare.

Third, the Trump II era of radical cuts to Medicaid, denial of research funding for racial health disparities and the appointment to public health leadership positions of people untrained in science and medicine cannot be allowed to normalize over time. Because not all public health is state and local, the nation will need to rebuild the federal infrastructure supporting public health that the Trump administration has dismantled or undermined. Voters in 2024 seemed to have forgotten the first Trump administration's botched response to the Covid pandemic. In early 2020, the administration was slow to acknowledge the spread of the virus and lost valuable time in which to require contact tracing, order PPE and implement mandatory testing, all while ginning up racist invective ("the China virus") and promoting unserious cures (injecting bleach, hydroxychloroquine).[78] Not only did the overall response damage the country's economy far more than that of other developed nations,[79] but the losses were compounded by a variety of the administration's cuts to various public health programs before the pandemic struck.[80] The Biden administration reversed many of those changes, but a hallmark of the current era is attempts to make ideological changes permanent. Back in office four years later, the second Trump administration resumed targeting public health infrastructure for cuts – again, with a special focus on any research or programming deemed "DEI" or "woke." For instance, severe spending cuts and clawbacks for National Institutes of Health–supported projects on racially concentrated health risks or "health equity" and "environmental justice" targeted just those preventive interventions that value and save Black lives, among others. At the universities where critical discoveries are made, public health schools are uniquely dependent on federal research grants to survive; before Trump's defunding of the university, Harvard's T.H. Chan School of Public Health received over half of its budget from the competitive federal grants it won in 2024 compared to just 3 percent federal grants at Harvard Law School.[81] The administration that discounted the lethal effects on Black essential workers came back with a vengeance to dismantle the knowledge infrastructure that enables progress on health outcomes. Billions of dollars of cuts to Medicaid will have a generational impact on recipients and those who receive care at centers with large Medicaid populations, cutting off access to health care through a combination of defunding, imposing onerous administrative hurdles and the official distrust of patients now required to work in exchange for health care. This is federalized racism, designed to harden statistical health disparities long known to exist. It will compromise Black lives with an accumulation of untreated but gradually worsening underlying conditions. It must be reversed in order for more local initiatives to regain ground. Like all racism, it also breeds systemic distrust, which in the case of health care can result in sicker lives for generations to come. Local actors must be more responsible caregivers for patient lives despite what federal decisionmakers do far from people's lived experiences.

Thus far, we've seen the material effects of systems that breed distrust of the government and distrust of health-care institutions. We turn next to the distrust that started the 2020 reckoning: the police.

CHAPTER 5

Police Brutality and the Disappearance of Things Past

Finally, police brutality, the original reckoning.

Ronald Greene's violent death at the hands of Louisiana state troopers occurred just before, and was resolved well after, the period of racial reckoning yet it illustrates how systemic racism structures policing. Several officers pulled Greene from his car after he refused to stop. As he pleaded "I'm sorry" and "I'm scared," they tasered the forty-nine-year-old multiple times, beat him about the head and face and handcuffed him in a pool of his own blood beside his car where he died. That day, May 10, 2019, the five troopers said Greene died when he crashed his car. This was a lie. The Union Parish coroner wrote that Greene died of a cardiac arrest, not a homicide. This too was a lie. Not until two years later when the Associated Press obtained the forty-six minutes of body camera footage did we learn the truth. Three years after Greene's death, only one officer – Kory York, a "Master Trooper" – was charged with negligent homicide and counts of malfeasance in office. The other four officers were charged with malfeasance in office. Four years after Greene's death, York pleaded no contest in exchange for one year of probation. The judge approved the plea.[1] There is no record of consequences for the coroner who lied about the cause of death, a critical assist in the cover-up and, unfortunately, a common occurrence in police use-of-force cases.[2]

Except for a lynch mob, there may be no more frightening expression of racial violence, or reminder of powerfully organized oppression, than the surrender enforced by the unprovoked hand, stick or bullet of a police officer. George Floyd's death embodied scenes of horrific regularity, many thousands of times. It was unique only in the gravity of its public performance. Yet whatever form of accountability victims' families and protesters demanded – indictments, convictions, terminations, personal liability – the structure of law enforcement would almost certainly never allow it.[3] Without accountability, the disparity in the number of Black people killed by police since Floyd died didn't even go down; it actually went up.[4] True reckoning will require a redesign of consequences.

Reckoning will be as complicated as the fundamental relationship between cops and Black people. It's rooted in mutual distrust. Because police distrust Black people, Black people seem destined to distrust the police.[5] Yet Black people need public safety more than anyone else. Fear of violence is a common aspect of psychological trauma, we saw in the last chapter; violence in some segregated communities is pervasive enough to become a public health issue.[6] Thoughtful, strategic policing could help change that. Instead, policing is often another source of traumatic violence. From an early age, Black children, especially boys, learn that police are dangerous to their bodies and their self-image. Chronic police suspicion criminalizes Black innocence. As Kristin Henning has shown, police encounters often adultify young men of color, teach them that they are no better than threats and rob them of other ways of being.[7] Police assumptions about Black adolescents may go on to become presumptions adopted by judges, school disciplinary officers, principals, bystanders. Police effectively become the voice and the presence of government, often antagonistic, engaged in surveillance and harassment, negatively defining Black citizenship against its will. When Black children most need protection, they often face suspicion instead. This is a failure, bound for disaster in certain situations. The dangerous level of police distrust accumulates in moments, reinforcing itself through unnecessarily hostile encounters. It was present in the troopers' reaction to Ronald Greene and the Minneapolis cops' collective treatment of George Floyd. The accumulation of suspicion has been policy. It must be deterred. Reckoning is deterrence.

Critics point out that accounts like this overstate the extent of abuse. They argue that brutality is rare, often under murky circumstances that demonstrate the incredibly difficult, often exigent decisions the police have to make. I don't always disagree, and I'm not anti-police. However, I am pro-accountability. Statistical proof is challenging in a field in which law enforcement routinely refuses to document its own conduct while arguing for the right to discipline itself. But what we can learn demonstrates that negative encounters between Black people and police are undercounted, affect vastly disproportionate numbers of Black and other young men of color. These encounters include being beaten, shot or killed at rates that are at least twice the number for similarly situated whites, and that most of this aggressive policing (and prosecuting) occurs in predominantly Black, low-income, segregated neighborhoods. Accountability of any kind – criminal, civil or administrative – is exceedingly rare because of three aspects of system design.

First, the very idea of police criminality is preempted by prosecutorial discretion, the police "code of silence" and arbitration rules. Second, exculpation of police misconduct is part of the structural design of federal civil rights laws despite their origins in protecting freed slaves during Reconstruction. Last, whatever accountability remains is undermined by contract provisions in collective bargaining agreements, such as indemnification and police union authority. Before examining these system features, I start with a little background, followed by what is known about how much brutality actually occurs.

A BRIEF HISTORY

"The police are the king's men," writes historian Jill Lepore,[8] to describe the original role of police to protect the polity, the landed and, once institutionalized in this country, the white power structure from the mischief of Black lives. That lineage began with slave codes in the seventeenth century and slave patrols throughout the eighteenth and well into the nineteenth. The militarization of police forces today has roots in the dual role of militias and slave patrols, where the same men who learned military strategy exterminating native Indian tribes captured, whipped and sometimes killed enslaved Africans.[9] (This link between military service and violent policing remains true to this day; many cops, especially the most likely to use force, are military veterans.[10]) The Industrial Revolution brought immigration and new types of crime, which hastened the modern era in policing.[11] Historians have noted the wide use of urban police forces against union organizers, strikers and socialists in the early twentieth century.[12]

Yet the criminalization of blackness is one of the organizational tenets of policing,[13] a key social construct in the interests of a racialized social order. For instance, the exception in the Thirteenth Amendment for "punishment for crime whereof the party shall have been duly convicted"[14] was a legal and conceptual loophole to continue the exploitation of Black labor while linking servitude to state-sanctioned punishment.[15] The Civil Rights Acts of 1871 – 42 U.S.C. 241 and 242, the criminal Acts; and Section 1983, the civil – were Reconstruction-era statutes specifically designed to protect the right to life and liberty of freed African Americans (and Union sympathizers) against serial violence by the Ku Klux Klan, white mobs and local police.[16] They were passed amid great political conflict.[17] Yet they never served their purpose. Few prosecutions were ever brought against police acting violently under color of authority.[18] The civil statute was hardly utilized to deter police misconduct until the Supreme Court decided *Monroe v. Pape* in 1960, almost a century after the law's passage.[19] Even this structural attempt to impose federal constraints on local abuses failed to institute new norms of justice and safety from official brutality. Later, we'll see the more contemporary judge-made impediments to Section 1983's effectiveness that evolved after those inauspicious beginnings to produce the same outcomes: a predictable lack of accountability. It's not that these laws are incapable of treating races equally. It's that their very structure facilitates racial intent – the criminalization of blackness – to produce racially unequal results, the often-unseen acts of abuse. Structure is what makes things go as they do. It means that even in an ambivalent system of laws and practices, where pro-Black and anti-Black forces have been in active opposition since before the Revolution, the process by which accountability is supposed to be secured fails. Something – the rule, its interpretation or its disregard – consistently and predictably gets in the way of enforcement.[20] And deterrence is lost.

INCIDENCE OF VIOLENCE

The systemic prevention of accountability might begin with the impossibility of defining and measuring the thing itself. Every year approximately 1,000 people are fatally shot by police.[21] Their deaths occur under myriad circumstances, armed and unarmed, suspicious and clearly justified.[22] These people are disproportionately Black.[23] An NPR investigation found that at least 135 *unarmed* Black men and women – mostly teenage boys – have been killed since 2015; 75 percent of the officers involved were white.[24] Thirteen were charged with murder; two were convicted.[25] Police misconduct encompasses illegal or unethical actions or the violation of individuals' constitutional rights by police officers in the conduct of their duties. Examples include police brutality (unjustified violence), dishonesty, fraud, coercion, torture, abuse of authority and sexual assault, including the demand for sexual favors in exchange for leniency.[26] There is no universally agreed definition of police brutality. I focus here on the unreasonable use of force, particularly in circumstances where facts suggest that it was excessive, such as shooting unarmed persons. Even with such a narrow definition, there is currently no national system for calculating police misconduct.[27]

Instead, data on police misconduct are produced by journalists, researchers or political activists, not the federal government.[28] In 2015, *The Washington Post* began to log every fatal shooting by an on-duty police officer in the United States.[29] Since 2015, there have been more than 5,000 such shootings recorded by *The Post* that show a racially disparate *rate* of fatal shootings – Blacks 34 per million (1,428 total); Hispanic 26 per million (1,003 total) and white 14 per million (2,741 total).[30] According to *The Post,* most victims are male (95 percent).[31] In 2018, New Jersey released The Force Report, which created the first comprehensive statewide database of police force ever created. The sixteen-month investigation by NJ Advance Media for NJ.com, found that New Jersey's system for tracking police force is broken, with no statewide collection or analysis of the data, little oversight by state officials and no standard practices among local departments. It also found that just 10 percent of officers accounted for 38 percent of all uses of force; a total of 252 officers used force more than five times the state average.[32] Nonlethal force is substantial. At least 9,281 people were injured by police from 2012 through 2016; 4,382 of those were serious enough to require hospitalization. At least 156 officers put at least one person in hospital in *each* of the five years reviewed. Again, the use of force was used disproportionately against Black suspects, who overall were more than three times as likely to face police force than white people. The Force Report also found that brutality, especially against Blacks, was much greater in certain municipalities than others.[33] Finally, the system for reporting use of force by police is confusingly disorganized, with different departments using different forms, making tracking difficult. Officers self-reported incidents, but thousands of reports were incomplete, illegible, lacking supervisory review or missing altogether. In at least sixty-two instances, forms were so sloppy the officers accidentally marked themselves as dead.[34]

The empirical evidence about who gets abused and where most of the abuse occurs raises strong inferences about the dynamic interaction between racial animus and racialized place. It suggests a convergence between racist policies of residential organization, like what we saw in Chapter 3, and racist beliefs among individual officers. But the issue with which we're most concerned is what accounts for the lack of accountability. The empirical studies show that whatever the motivations, police officers clearly believe they can act more brutally against Black bodies in Black-identified spaces and get away with it. The moment of violent encounter begins the causal chain. The brutality ends with the injustice of unaccountability. What confers immunity is cumulative, making its way through various legal checkpoints ordinarily meant to punish and deter misconduct. But not here. This is how causation works to show systemic racism in policing.

HOW POLICE CANNOT BE CRIMINALS

It begins with the idea that police officers cannot be criminals. Notwithstanding the criminal prosecution of Derek Chauvin, the Minneapolis police officer sentenced to twenty-two and a half years by a state court in the killing of George Floyd, and over twenty years in a federal plea bargain for violating the constitutional rights of Floyd and a fourteen-year-old victim, police officers are almost never charged with crimes or suffer criminal penalties.[35] Of the 1,000 fatal shootings of civilians each year, only 110 law enforcement officers nationwide have been charged with murder or manslaughter for on-duty shootings.[36] Noted policing expert Phillip Stinson observes that: "To charge an officer in a fatal shooting, it takes something so egregious, so over the top that it cannot be explained in any rational way ... It also has to be a case that prosecutors are willing to hang their reputation on."[37] But even in the extreme instances where prosecution occurs, the majority of the officers have not been convicted.[38] In *The End of Policing*, Alex Vitale notes the significant legal, institutional, and social impediments to prosecuting police:

> While hard numbers are difficult to come by, a successful prosecution of a police officer for killing someone in the line of duty, where no corruption is alleged, is extremely rare ... From the moment an investigation into a police shooting begins, there are structural barriers to indictment and prosecution ... Police officers at the scene are sometimes the only witnesses to the event. The close working relationship between police and prosecutors, normally an asset in homicide investigations, becomes a fundamental conflict of interest in all but the most straightforward cases. As a result, prosecutors are often reluctant to pursue such cases aggressively.[39]

At the state court level, there are three tiers of structural obstacles to bringing criminal indictments of police violence even against unarmed suspects. In the first tier are institutional norms affecting prosecutors, the public, police union and administrative rules. There's a tradition of close working relationships between local police departments and districts attorneys' offices. There's also common sympathy among jurors for the on-the-job judgments of officers they view as public protectors. Large disparities exist between public perceptions of police violence and how it is treated in criminal courts.[40] Other factors, including union protections that shield police officers from timely investigations,[41] legal standards that give them the benefit of the doubt[42] and a tendency to take officers at their word, add up to few convictions and little prison time for accused officers.[43]

A second structural tier is the relationship of the police to each other – the unwritten code of silence among police officers ("the blue wall") by which corroborating testimony from other officer-witnesses at the scene of the misconduct is systematically withheld, hindering investigations and prosecutions.[44] In 2000, a conference paper by the International Association of Chiefs of Police studied the phenomenon using survey research from over 3,700 officers across forty-two states and reported several troubling conclusions. The authors found that the code of silence exists and "is prompted by excessive force incidents more than for any other specific circumstance."[45] A majority of officers expressed no problem with the code; many described pressure from the officer who committed the misconduct, from senior officers and from uninvolved officers.[46]

The final impediment to accountability for criminal misconduct is arbitration. Even when police officers are disciplined or terminated for serious violations of departmental policy such as use of force, police union contracts (and some constitutional precedent)[47] allow for an appeal to arbitration. The idea is that officer discipline should be subject to due process in order to overcome the possibility of departmental partiality. The result, however, has been a pattern of disciplinary actions that are reduced or overturned more often than not, and a culture of accountability replaced by a culture of compromise, as officers disciplined for even the most egregious misconduct are reinstated, sometimes on procedural technicalities.[48] One constraint is the "past precedent" rule of equal treatment for the same transgressions, a rule with origins in racial equality that has since been used to bar discipline where past offenses have gone unpunished, thus institutionalizing leniency based on prior failures to discipline misconduct.[49]

CHALLENGES TO USING FEDERAL CIVIL RIGHTS LAW

Police misconduct rarely makes it to a criminal court, and even then results in little accountability or deterrence. The vast majority of police misconduct cases are private civil actions. Private plaintiffs may hire their own lawyers and bring suits under state tort law for claims such as false arrest, and assault and battery, including wrongful death.[50] The federal alternative is 42 U.S.C. Section 1983,[51] that allows private plaintiffs to bring suit directly against a police officer or department acting pursuant to an allegedly unconstitutional policy or violating a person's constitutional rights. Without an onerous state-of-mind requirement, Section 1983 requires plaintiffs to show:

- state action by an official acting under color of state law
- to violate plaintiff's federally protected rights.[52]

The rights protected include constitutional claims for life and liberty, and follow the Fourth Amendment prohibition against the state committing unlawful searches and seizures of the person.[53] Force used by an officer acting under color of law must rise to the level of a seizure, according to the Supreme Court in *Tennessee v. Garner.*[54] A seizure constitutes "an intentional acquisition of physical control," occurring "only when there is a governmental termination of freedom of movement through means intentionally applied."[55] It must also be deliberate, purposeful or knowing, not merely negligent.[56] Thus, the seizure may start when the officer stops a suspect or at the point when force is used.

Yet for use of force, including lethal force, to be actionable, it must be objectively unreasonable. This standard often poses a significant hurdle for plaintiffs. *Garner* was a lethal force case in which a police officer shot and killed a fleeing felon. The Supreme Court held that a cop may use deadly force to prevent escape only where he has probable cause to believe that the suspect poses a threat of death or serious harm to the officer or others. The shooting was the seizure. Its reasonableness would be measured by a balancing of interests – the nature and quality of the intrusion on personal liberty vs. the government interests justifying force. In *Graham v. O'Connor*,[57] the Supreme Court said the reasonableness of the officer's action was subject to a "totality of the circumstances" approach "from the perspective of a reasonable officer on the scene."[58] This entails "careful attention to the facts and circumstances of each particular case, including the severity of the crime at issue, whether the suspect poses an immediate threat to the safety of officers or others, and whether he is actively resisting arrest or attempting to evade arrest by flight."[59]

Pause to consider how Section 1983's reasonableness standard for finding whether a constitutional violation occurred divides those who believe police misconduct is rampant from those who view it with deep skepticism. The language of the standard itself suggests how rare misconduct is, that its interpretation is highly contextualized yet starts from the perspective of the officer, who is "often forced to make split-second judgments about the amount of force used in a particular situation,"[60] and that the officer's perception is typically accurate enough to be trustworthy. In order to do their jobs effectively, police officers certainly deserve some level of deference that they act reasonably; legal standards should be designed to insulate them from constant second-guessing of their conduct at the risk of liability.

Yet this notion of reasonableness often defers too much to officer judgment. It frequently allows for too much supposition while interrogating too little about the reasonableness of actual police perception. Police defendants often claim to suspect murderous intentions on the part of people they kill, including the probability of reaching for a weapon or fleeing to escape arrest for a recent felony when the limited research about these claims indicates that most people who flee traffic stops fear only a misdemeanor violation, such as a suspended registration, being beaten by police or were driving under the influence.[61] The officer reasonableness standard allows officers to exploit beliefs unrelated to the evidence of particular encounters in order to facilitate doubt. This opening creates a tension with the Constitution itself, which is supposed to protect people against government abuse, and not the government (here the police) against the public. The officer's version of events is often believed no matter what.[62] Police officers commonly overstate the threat, especially during traffic stops – they simply guess wrong.[63] Or they fabricate. "Behind closed doors, we call it testilying," one New York policeman told *The New York Times.* "You take the truth and stretch it out a little bit."[64] And bad conduct goes unchecked.

The popular deference to police judgment is also strengthened by a judicial narrowing of relevant context. The "totality of the circumstances" standard suggests a wide breadth of evidence admissible to show reasonableness/unreasonableness in relevant context. Yet the evidence considered is often one-sided. Plaintiffs commonly attempt to portray the officer's initial aggressiveness, such as getting too close too soon, drawing a weapon when simple de-escalation techniques might be used or misreading an ordinary situation as unusually dangerous, to show how the officer's unreasonable conduct *before* the use of force created the circumstances that led to the moment force was used. Police officers typically defend on the opposite grounds, that only the moments directly before and during the use of force are relevant to an estimation of reasonableness.[65] By rejecting officer provocation as grounds to show unreasonable police conduct, the Supreme Court has declined to address the full scope of circumstances surrounding police violence.[66] "Before the final frame" analyses by researchers and journalists increasingly reveal the extent to which officer behavior itself – often in violation of training protocols – contributes to or creates the occasion to use deadly force that is later exculpated by the *Graham v. O'Connor* standard of split-second decision-making.[67] The lack of a clear standard indicating that the totality of relevant circumstances includes *all* the contextual facts that influence behavior in a conflict between cops and civilians runs counter to how tort law typically interprets that standard[68] and further supports arguments that the law itself is simply not designed to hold police officers accountable. Deterrence is again diminished by deference.

Qualified Immunity and "Clearly Established" Law. Judge-made modifications to qualified immunity doctrine have created formidable Section 1983 barriers to police officer discipline, undercutting the deterrent purpose of Section 1983 as a means for protecting civil rights.[69] Qualified immunity arose in a 1967 Supreme Court[70] decision and has gained so much strength in immunizing the police and other public officials from liability that even many conservative writers have called for its abolition.[71] Qualified immunity offers additional insulation from external judgments of police use of force, traveling a complicated, sometimes convoluted, jurisprudential path to a pretrial determination that a plaintiff cannot bring suit at all. In essence, "qualified immunity will be available when a reasonable official would not have known that his actions would violate a right that was 'clearly established' at the time of the incident."[72] However, as Justice Sonia Sotomayor has cautioned, "Police officers are not entitled to qualified immunity if (1) they violated a federal statutory or constitutional right, and (2) the unlawfulness of their conduct was 'clearly established at the time.'"[73] In the abstract, the doctrine makes a certain sense, shielding police officers from liability for on-the-job conduct they couldn't know was constitutionally unlawful because the applicable law was unclear.[74] But the application is flawed. Instead of applying a broad reading of what is "clearly established law," courts apply a very narrow lens and usually examine only appellate law from the same circuit as the case arose. Additionally, although the Supreme Court has stated that lower federal courts should not be too literal in their analysis of whether a law was clearly established, some courts still mainly examine whether the *precise* misconduct an officer is accused of committing was found to be a constitutional violation.[75] This generous expansion of qualified immunity to require factual sameness contradicts earlier Supreme Court precedent holding only that officers must have "fair warning" that their conduct invaded a constitutional right.[76]

On its face, the doctrine presents significant hurdles for plaintiffs. Is the law regarding the constitutional right at issue relevant here, or the law regarding the officer's conduct?[77] How clearly must the *particular* conduct by the officer be established – e.g., punching with a fist yes, but jabbing with a found object no?[78] What level of agreement among courts clearly establishes illegal conduct?[79] Determinations often rely on whether specific police conduct was ever litigated to a reported decision – which excludes the majority of cases that settle – not common sense.

As if these obstacles aren't sufficiently burdensome for plaintiffs in Section 1983 cases, the Supreme Court has created more procedural hurdles that harm plaintiffs and protect abusive police officers. Police officers can raise qualified immunity immediately after a complaint is filed, often before any discovery has occurred.[80] At this point, all litigation literally stops so that the court can consider the qualified immunity claim. If the police officer loses, he or she gets an automatic interlocutory appeal.[81] The litigation is at a standstill during this time. No discovery is allowed. The process can take years, particularly if the Supreme Court agrees to hear the case. This disadvantages plaintiffs.[82] Key evidence may be lost or inadvertently destroyed while federal courts sort out the legal issue of whether the law was clearly established. The procedure invites abuse by defendants and puts plaintiffs at severe risk.

Both the very architecture of qualified immunity and the interpretive means by which courts have expanded it have worked a reversal of deterrence, preventing lawsuits rather than misconduct. As one commentator put it:

> The barriers raised by qualified immunity, as currently administered, far exceed the rationales that support limiting damages liability. The result is an inversion of sensible policy. Damages liability for constitutional torts should be the rule, from which exceptions are created only for good reasons, and only to the extent justified by those reasons. The reality today for excessive-force claims is the reverse. Immunity is the general policy, and liability exception. This should change.[83]

INDEMNIFICATION. Should a police officer found liable for violating a person's civil rights or otherwise intentionally inflicting harm have to pay a damage award out of their own pocket? This is the question of indemnification. Legally and philosophically, we might expect the answer to be yes. Nothing in the Section 1983 legislative history or case law compels a municipality to pay for the misdeeds of the police officers they train and employ, unless the misconduct was committed as part of an official policy or custom.[84] The Supreme Court long ago held that cities may be sued for violations of civil rights, but they are not responsible under *respondeat superior* for judgments against their officers.[85] Certainly, forcing bad actors to internalize the costs of their own misconduct has been a feature of basic deterrence in American law since its beginnings. Having to take personal responsibility for legal judgments against you is a fundamental aspect of accountability.

Yet police officers almost never pay the judgments against them, because of generous, universally recognized norms of indemnification. Judicial doctrines such as qualified immunity arose, in part, from the erroneous assumption that the harsh financial effects of judgments against police should be ameliorated.[86] The public often assumes the opposite is true, or if indemnification occurs it must be compelled by law. Neither is the case.[87] An analysis by Professor Joanna Schwartz reveals that police officers are virtually always indemnified: she found that governments paid approximately 99.98 percent of the dollars that plaintiffs recovered in lawsuits alleging civil rights violations by law enforcement.[88]

Schwartz's findings show that law enforcement officers never satisfy a punitive damages award entered against them[89] and almost never contribute anything to settlements or judgments – even when indemnification was prohibited by law or policy, and even when officers were disciplined, terminated, or prosecuted for their conduct.[90] Many cases of police brutality settle.[91] For example, from 2011 to 2017, New York City spent a total of $630 million on police misconduct settlements, including paying more than $100 million each fiscal year from 2015 to 2018.[92] Similarly, from 2011 to 2018, the city of Chicago spent $389 million on police misconduct settlements.[93] Yet taxpayers – or the insurance premiums they pay on behalf of municipal government – paid for all of it.[94]

Indeed, widespread indemnification of police officers by municipalities – often a term in the collective bargaining agreement with police unions – is a direct repudiation of the Supreme Court's guidance on Section 1983 liability in *Monell v. Department of Social Services.*

Of the many suggested ways to reform indemnification, all argue for a system with more deterrence for actual officers, their departments or both. Some would disallow indemnification completely[95] while others would impose a sliding scale of partial responsibility by the officer in proportion to the seriousness of the violation.[96] Still others would shoulder the entire departmental budget – not its insurers – with the costs of its members' misconduct.[97]

THE DESIGN OF POLICE UNION AUTHORITY

Police unions represent one of the most important but least understood sources of resistance to public accountability for misconduct, especially excessive force.[98] This resistance comes in the form of union protections against local and state regulation (a problem primarily of state labor law), collective bargaining and local politics, rather than the constitutional rights of aggrieved citizens.[99] Since 1962 when municipal unions were granted federal rights to bargain collectively with municipalities,[100] police contracts have typically included numerous disciplinary protections that work together with state labor laws, civil service rules and Law Enforcement Officers Bills of Rights (LEOBORs) to frustrate discipline and undermine deterrence. Justified on due process grounds and concerns that police will be the target of arbitrary discipline, police union contracts afford police greater procedural safeguards than citizens suspected of a crime, and offer employment assurances that are not available to other public servants.[101] A 2016 report written by Campaign Zero outlines seven ways in which police contracts and bills of rights contribute to making it more difficult to hold police accountable for misconduct:

1. They can disqualify misconduct complaints that are submitted too many days after an incident occurs or if an investigation takes too long to complete.
2. They can prevent police officers from being interrogated immediately after being involved in an incident or otherwise restricting how, when, or where they can be interrogated.
3. They can give officers access to information that civilians do not get prior to being interrogated.
4. They can limit disciplinary consequences for officers or limit the capacity of civilian oversight structures and/or the media to hold police accountable.

5. They can require cities to pay costs related to police misconduct including by giving officers paid leave while under investigation, paying legal fees, and/or the cost of settlements.
6. They can prevent information on past misconduct investigations from being recorded or retained in an officer's personnel file.[102]
7. They can expunge violations from the record of the guilty officer after little or no time.[103]

There are even studies showing that the existence of police union collective-bargaining rights are associated with an increase in misconduct and killings by police.[104]

William Finnegan notes that police unions operate in a unique social and political space that differs from traditional unions. "Police unions enjoy a political paradox. Conservatives traditionally abhor labor unions but support the police. The left is critical of aggressive policing yet has often muted its criticism of police unions – which are, after all, public-sector unions, an endangered and mostly progressive species."[105] Police unions derive from a different tradition, too. Before the New Deal created the National Labor Relations Board, police departments were often private (e.g., Pinkertons) and called into labor conflicts by industry leaders to clash physically with union members and break up strikes.[106] As police began to form their own unions, the Great Migration dramatically increased the Black population of northern cities, heralding the era of urban policing. Along with rising crime rates came a more concentrated police presence in ghetto communities, leading to the routinely abusive practices that eventually set off riots in places like Watts, Detroit and Newark in the 1960s.[107] Especially in the Northeast, police unions grew politically stronger as a useful symbol of law and order, their ranks consistently filled with working-class white ethnic conservatives.[108] These attitudes could be explicitly racist, as they were when 10,000 police officers in New York City rioted in 1992 against the city's first Black mayor David Dinkins, some waving signs like "Dump the Washroom Attendant," after he called for the creation of a civilian review board.[109] In 2015, the International Union of Police Associations endorsed Donald Trump for president. Yet union power changed what had been in most places a job with weak pay into a prized status, where, in cities like New York, cops often retire after twenty years with full pensions that average $74,500 a year.[110]

The use of police union power to control officer discipline and frustrate accountability is classically structural. The point of collective bargaining is to contract for the applicable rules and practices that will guide the institution according to agreed-upon norms. Since the rise of police union power in the aftermath of Detroit's 1967 riot – a riot, ironically, brought about in part because of a police incident that inflamed a long history of outrageous police misconduct, a riot in which police officers executed three Black male students at the Algiers Motel[111] – police unions understood that they needed to formalize their institutional power.[112] In fact, the union bargaining approach was reduced to an influential playbook that teaches negotiators to be unyielding and to "throw out all those traditional notions of right and wrong."[113] The campaigns go beyond the bargaining table to raising union funds for selective political donations, distributing pamphlets to smear elected officials negotiating on behalf of the public and blatant fear-mongering about public safety lapses if police do not get the pay, pension, overtime, health benefits and control over discipline they seek.[114] The approach has been so successful and police unions across the country have used it to such effect that the playbook's author, Ron DeLord, now believes police unions have gone too far and "need to be prepared to bargain over things that their community thinks are fair."[115]

Though structural, police union power is also political. For instance, after protracted years of struggle, New York City eventually created a Civilian Complaint Review Board. However, the city's police commissioner possesses the discretionary power to override a validated complaint against an officer when he or she determines "retention" is appropriate. This amounts to a final say over whether any discipline occurs. Different police commissioners exercise this discretion differently, depending in part on who's mayor. Under Mayor Eric Adams, a former police captain himself, the police commissioner used his discretion dozens of times and, according to ProPublica, overturned discipline in multiple cases, including ones in which the officer pled guilty to the charges. Yet none of it is known to the public. "[T]he department does not publish the commissioner's decisions to retain cases, and the civilian oversight committee makes those details public only months after the fact. Civilians are not told that the Police Department ended their cases."[116]

RECKONING

This chapter revealed an unsettling array of doctrinal and administrative obstacles to deterring police misconduct and promoting accountability, only to remind us of another problem: cynical pendulation. No sooner had a national protest against police brutality engendered serious discussions about defunding or abolishing the police than crime rates started to rise. Like clockwork, increases in crime became political issues, seized relentlessly by Republican officeholders in particular, who campaigned for *more* police authority, *more* police funding and, of course, less criticism of law enforcement. (That these political emergencies often originate in communities that have not actually experienced much increase in crime doesn't seem to matter.) Whatever headway was made was lost in the hysteria to vilify whichever group was accused of threatening public safety. This describes the fate of one of the most sensible bills ever presented on the issue to Congress, the George Floyd Justice in Policing Act. Police accountability is clearly within the purview of local control; adjacent police departments can have radically different use-of-force cultures. However, the Act, along with other federal incentive programs, would have significantly advanced the sort of consistent local reforms that accountability reckoning demands.

The George Floyd Justice in Policing Act of 2021 passed the House of Representatives on June 17, 2020. In its current state, H.R. 1280 would address multiple aspects of police accountability, record-keeping and transparency, training, racial profiling and a separate section on body cameras.[117] As structuralist national legislation, the proposed law would centralize through federal oversight (principally by the Civil Rights Division of the Department of Justice) what is mostly local decision-making and would standardize the practice of policing in key respects. Specifically, the Act would mandate state data collection, increase investigatory powers of independent bodies, create a national police misconduct registry, ban no-knock warrants in drug cases, incentivize a ban on chokeholds, require body cameras, prohibit racial profiling, improve training and hiring of diverse law enforcement departments, study ways to change the culture of law enforcement and significantly increase funding for federal enforcement of the Act itself. Some of this would follow enhancement of traditional powers of the Attorney General's office, such as the more comprehensive pattern-and-practice investigations of departments by the Department of Justice (DOJ).[118] Still more would occur through substantive changes in the law – for instance, the elimination of qualified immunity as a defense[119] and replacement of Section 242's virtually unattainable "willfulness" standard with a "knowingly or recklessly"[120] standard for depriving a person of their constitutional rights. The proposed statute uses significant incentives and penalties to reach areas of local control, such as whether a municipality can collectively bargain certain disciplinary measures with police unions. Section 103(d) of the Act would deny significant federal grants to government units that entered into or renewed any agreement with a labor organization that would hinder pattern-and-practice relief or conflicts with the terms of a consent decree. Unfortunately however, the proposed Act remains bottled in committee, the victim of a divided Congress and a predictable pendular swing to the right on policing and race.

The currently doomed fate of the George Floyd bill is devastating to the prospects of racial reckoning over police brutality for several reasons. First, it's a sensible, minimalist law, which makes a basic first step in seriously addressing an issue that divides the country. For rule-of-law conservatives, it expects no less from police than compliance with rules as a condition of wearing the badge. Most Americans work in jobs subject to performance metrics. For progressives, it is a foundation for federal action, even if much more may be necessary (and even if local experiments in policing prove more effective). Relatedly, the bill's provisions are so reasonable that it illuminates the scope of partisan disagreement. If you recognize that Black lives really matter and police are accountable *whenever* they use their state authority to take one, then you must have measurable and uniform standards for the use of such force. That means accurate reporting and data. If you're against that, then you believe law enforcement can make its own laws – an implicit attack on our constitutional system. To do nothing after the racial reckoning brought this singular issue to the world supports the most pessimistic, cynical and hopeless characterizations of the republic.

Although the bill is imperfect and there may be other kinds of remedies for immunized police abuse, it is better than some racial reckoning alternatives like defunding and abolishing the police. Initially, I supported defunding the police as an idea to end the enrichment of police forces that rewarded their members for resisting public governance. If the police are the government, then the government is responsible to the taxpayer-voters. That relationship is mainly expressed in funding. Both deterrence and more effective policing (e.g., limiting police roles to police expertise) are served by reconfiguring police budgets. But the nuances of rebudgeting sometimes got lost in the political debates over defunding, where defunding seemed strictly punitive. Some debates need to start over. I would recenter the funding issue in two ways: as a reallocation of existing police funding for specific nonpolice expertise (e.g., mental health intervenors, campus protests, traffic stops, violence interrupters) and as liability for certain misconduct violations in order to compensate victims and to deter wrongdoing. Some defunding might be the practical result, but it's not the policy goal.

Abolition as a path to reckoning involves different problems. Police and prison abolition has inspired a movement of serious advocates who seek radical change in the basic idea of public safety and how it's achieved. Those discussions are fundamental, encompassing myriad aspects of well-being, with direct application for local organizing. Abolition doesn't imagine policing in a victim–perpetrator prism, where the innocent calls the protector to vanquish the bad. "Instead," according to Mariame Kaba, "abolition challenges us to ask 'Why do we have no other well-resourced options?' and pushes us to creatively consider how we can grow, build, and try other avenues to reduce harm."[121] Abolition embraces violence as a public health issue, which is overdue, and shares many of the critiques about racism underlying American policing that I make here. The key difference is transformation versus reform. Abolitionists put their faith in the former whereas I retain faith in the latter. For abolitionists, transformation in policing corresponds to much broader transformations of the safety net. To me, that expects public safety to carry an undue freight in solving related but extremely complex problems. Nor is it clear what transformation would look like community by community. Local variation may have benefits, but there are also critical national norms and federal laws that must be common to local approaches. Even state-level abolition wouldn't change the existence of federal laws, law enforcement and prisons. Mine, therefore, is a bet on reform efforts abolitionists wouldn't make.

Beyond the George Floyd Justice in Policing Act, a willing executive branch has the funding authority to incentivize a culture of accountability in local police departments and district attorneys' offices that is also consistent with broader criminal justice reforms. Since the Reagan Administration, federal funding originally meant to encourage community-based criminal justice programs that promoted trust between police and the communities they serve was redirected to increasing police hiring. This "war on drugs," then "war on terrorism" funding relationship between local departments and federal programs like Justice Assistance Grants (JAG) and Community-Oriented Policing Services (COPs) coincided with carceral reforms like "three strikes" penalties responsible for the mass incarceration of the 1980s through the present. However, the policy origins were philosophically distinct and arose from the racial unrest of the 1960s. Presidents Kennedy and Johnson presided over the intense poverty, civil rights protests and police brutality that would yield mass rioting across US cities. Johnson in particular believed that crime resulted from inadequate housing conditions, economic inequality and mental health issues and endorsed a series of federal statutes that focused on rehabilitation.[122] Also envisioned was a different role for police – trust-inducing community collaboration paid for with federal funds. Johnson created a lasting federal police funding bureaucracy with the Omnibus Crime and Safe Streets Act of 1968, which created the Law Enforcement Assistant Administration (LEAA). The LEAA paid for several categories of local police aid, including community policing and increased numbers of officers.[123] Thanks to cynical pendulation, the executive largesse proved problematic.

Federal funding was administered mostly by the DOJ, which meant that its priorities would change dramatically from administration to administration. The notion of trust-building and community policing gave way to war on crime policing during the Reagan and Bush years, took a hiatus for Clinton between 1994 and 2000, only to fund more militarization and the war on terror during George Walker Bush's presidency. Community-based criminal justice programs paid for with federal JAG and COPS funding can produce reductions both in incidences of crime and of police brutality.[124] For instance, Camden, NJ's police department was notorious until it was dismantled, recreated as a county-wide office of public safety and launched successful programs. Boston's police department created "Safe Street Teams" that reduced crime and complaints against police. Newark, NJ, acting under a consent decree with the DOJ, following a long pattern-and-practice investigation into a history of racially disparate police mistreatment, created a Trauma to Trust initiative that resulted in lower crime and a 50 percent reduction in civilian complaints. We can build trust, respect people's constitutional rights *and* create safety.

But what the federal government gives, the federal government can take away. While these represent successful structural reforms coordinated between Washington, DC and local police departments and prosecutors, the second Trump administration quickly demonstrated how quickly they can be undone. Within the first months of taking office, Trump issued an executive order questioning police investigations and pledging uncritical support for law enforcement.[125] His DOJ withdrew, unwound or canceled multiple consent decrees and pattern-and-practice investigations of police departments around the country.[126] Federal investigations launched by Biden's DOJ into deadly practices like the massacre of Breonna Taylor by the Louisville police, the fatal gang beatdown of Tyre Nichols by Memphis police and the Minneapolis police asphyxiation of George Floyd were repudiated by Trump's DOJ just days before the fifth anniversary of Floyd's death. Trump even extracted deals from some of the country's most powerful law firms to expend pro bono hours to represent accused cops for free.[127]

These moves invoke the president's enormous power to reinforce the notion that I've argued underwrites our laws and procedures: Law enforcement can do no wrong and is unfairly accused. That fundamental idea is a major factor in the preclusion of police accountability for brutality against African Americans and others. The facts as shown in bodycam and eyewitness video, the testimony of witnesses and other police, the results of lengthy professional investigations by DOJ staff and the common sense of human beings be damned. Behind the idea of police impunity is the suggestion of colorblindness, that what we think we see as an age-old hostility by many state officers to Black lives is not as we see it, because it's no longer there. Yet what remains a mobilizing force, as Trump and dozens of elected officials and legislatures have shown since the racial reckoning, is that Black criminality never abates. It's a chronic threat to be suppressed. Colorblindness thus preserves police impunity while racist stereotypes sustain Black suspiciousness, both to maintain an undemocratic status quo. The insidious danger that follows is *more* brutality in those very conservative places where restraints on racialized policing have been officially repudiated – up by as much as 23 percent compared to areas where racial accountability measures have held.[128] And Ronald Greene's death in Louisiana? Here's what the Justice Department found on January 16, 2025:

> Mr. Greene's death and its aftermath demonstrated serious failures at [Louisiana State Police] – excessive force, improper supervision, ineffective training, and breakdowns in accountability. As our civil pattern or practice investigation revealed, these failures were not isolated, but part of a larger pattern or practice of law enforcement conduct that deprives people in Louisiana of their rights under the Constitution.[129]

This too Trump's DOJ repudiated only a few weeks later.

CHAPTER 6

DEI and the End of Blackness as We Knew It

The great untruth about diversity, equity and inclusion (DEI) programming is that it's meant to benefit African Americans and was therefore central to racial reckoning. It wasn't. However, the ambiguity around DEI is as understandable as it is exploitable. By 2022, the backlash to racial reckoning specifically included many legislative repudiations of DEI, like banning Critical Race Theory (CRT) from curricula and removing books on the country's racial history from libraries and K-12 classrooms. Coupled with anti-immigrant initiatives, anti-DEI backlash was synonymous with the backlash to racial reckoning. Even opposition to pro-Palestinian protests at Harvard or to the Democratic presidential candidate conveniently joined race, gender and DEI by denigrating Harvard's Black woman former president Claudine Gay and the Black US Vice President Kamala Harris as "DEI hires." To oppose racial reckoning was to oppose DEI, as if the two were the same thing.

The most aggressive strategy of race conflation arrived with Trump II when the administration revived a dormant backlash to mount a counter-racial reckoning on the fragile shoulders of what it called "illegal, discriminatory DEI." Suddenly, everything was DEI again, and everything DEI was unlawful or about to be declared so – local governments, nearly entire federal agencies, private sector hiring, Big Law pro bono dockets, STEM research funding, graduation celebrations, even decisions to publish books like this one. The meaning of "DEI" was deliberately vague, a strategy that made the list of prohibitions self-perpetuating, fueled by the threat of federal defunding (and sometimes by tacit endorsement) that would follow a formal Title VI investigation whose sequence was suddenly reversed. Unsurprisingly, this threat coupled with a loss of process guarantees led to self-censorship which had and will continue to have real consequences. More than website references were scrubbed, and more than job titles were changed. Jobs were eliminated, pensions were disrupted and lives were destroyed. The job cuts in particular seemed surgically targeted to do disparate harm to Black middle-class public sector workers or the DEI divisions of HR departments that only a few years earlier had attracted Black professional talent.[1] By June 2025, Black women had lost over 100,000 jobs, their unemployment rate up a full percentage point, more than any other group.[2] Meanwhile, Black college student admissions were taking the expected hit in the first full cycle since the Supreme Court's anti-diversity opinion in SFFA.[3] Any outcry was muted at best. DEI as a popular mindset proved incapable of carrying the fight against racial injustice.

Whatever DEI really is, it's been effectively weaponized against its own power, redefined by opponents so that it could be eviscerated. Arising from the diversity rationale in the 1977 *Bakke* case, diversity, equity and inclusion policies have proliferated across institutional life, changing the language, norms, procedures and expectations we use in our daily work. As the Supreme Court recognized in *Bakke*, diversity benefits everyone. Although DEI's individual beneficiaries are rarely identified, the message is some version of "it's all of us" – the team, the organization, the classroom environment, the boardroom – who benefit.

Perhaps this was a mistake. Or perhaps the implementation of DEI's utopian message of equality was the failure. Stripped to its elements, DEI national and global policies typically involve recruitment of disadvantaged group members, training and mentoring opportunities for underrepresented groups, preferential selection criteria in close cases and anti-bias training.[4] This emphasis on overcoming patterns of unequal participation among underrepresented groups – women, the disabled, LGBTQ people, people of color – suggests a commitment to racial equality. Yet DEI clearly has two strains, one committed to corporate pluralism that offends no one and the other committed to securing incremental racial justice within constitutional bounds. That commitment is borrowed from DEI's civil rights roots yet buried under appeals to universality. The confusion between the two is a source of frustration for many, who, like me, believed that over the last few decades the corporatization of DEI led to the deliberate omission of racial justice, objectified people of color as merely "diverse individuals" and invited cosmetic virtue signaling by for-profit firms.

During the racial reckoning, the corporatized, more prominent strain of DEI offered the infrastructure for awareness – sharing, teaching, learning – and problems associated with its vague racial moorings recurred. Specifically, a lot of DEI programming focused on awareness of identity differences and implicit biases. For instance, a typical review of trainings based on the popular *White Fragility* book showed that participants concentrated on discovering white privilege.[5] Another difficult problem is measuring DEI benefits and beneficiaries, especially for the African Americans at the heart of the reckoning moment. Exactly who is the "underrepresented minority" in a particular setting, why are they considered underrepresented, or to which "people of color" do you refer? There are plenty of ways to measure African-American progress, as earlier chapters show, but DEI as an organizational mindset shied away. In fact, evidence indicates that material gains to Blacks from DEI are not negligible but are hardly substantial.[6] It suggests instead that DEI has most benefited white people, especially women.[7] Whoever it is, the primary beneficiaries of DEI programs are almost certainly not African Americans.

To be fair, that's not their purpose. DEI supplants a direct interest in remedying racial inequality against Blacks for an interest variously described as belonging, business necessity and organizational efficiency. This explains its widespread adoption in an unmistakably diverse world. From birthrates to enrollment projections, to labor pools, to customer bases, people across the Western world occupy diverse places in which full participation is no longer a choice but a core value. The African-American interest, once the heart of racial justice, has been subsumed into economic pluralism.

Yet that doesn't alter the zero-sum perception held by the well-organized resistance to DEI, which seemed to see both opportunity to attack the corporatized signaling character of one DEI strain as well as the Black-identified racial justice remnants of the other. The resistance followed what social scientists describe as a range of defensive reactions to DEI among advantaged groups that include "resource threat," "symbolic threat" and "in-group morality threat."[8] All three threats are consistent with MAGA-identified DEI opponents, for instance, who argue that DEI reallocates benefits to nonwhites, changes the meritocratic rules of the game and imputes racial guilt for unearned privileges. The fear of Others – especially Black people – is usually central to the threats. The second Trump administration shows how this can become an institutionalized belief system with its own rules, language and enforcement mechanisms. Now the attacks on Blacks have become casually vicious. They've emboldened an old-fashioned sense of white superiority, justifying the self-serving presumption that a white (or Asian) candidate/hire/person is highly competent while a Black (or Hispanic) in the same role could not be. Years after the so-called reckoning, a lot of American culture actively traffics in vulgar racial stereotype and dehumanizing racial tropes, like the president's son calling Blacks "monkeys" and "animals."[9] As support for a besieged DEI has slackened while its association with Blacks remains strong,[10] we risk raising a new generation of Americans who, because of their non-Black status, tend to believe in the intellectual inferiority of Black classmates, Black coworkers, Black service workers, doctors, teachers and thought leaders. Because this casual hostility often comes from the most powerful voices in society, the risk of generational harm is acute, especially for young Black people. At best, this is more cynical pendulation; at worst, it's what Derrick Bell called the permanence of racism.

Against this background, I've been arguing that racial reckoning requires accountability. I discounted awareness because it's not structural and clearly not durable. The second Trump administration's counter-reckoning hardens all the challenges we've examined so far. Now the ultimate question for the DEI/anti-DEI era is whether the principles and practices associated with one of its strains can have a remedial impact on racial inequality in areas like wealth, health and policing. I'm skeptically optimistic. Before we can imagine that defense, however, we should recall how we reached this point of exploitable confusion.

DEI can be negatively associated with Black people because it's presumed to be synonymous with affirmative action. That association, however, is almost entirely untrue, and the journey distinguishing them is worth taking. Affirmative action is premised on the remedial idea of racial equity, triggered by evidence of cumulative racial injuries, for which some compensatory action is due. Affirmative action promised substantive results to overcome demonstrable inequality. We rarely ever discuss affirmative action today just as we rarely discuss racial remedies. Diversity, on the other hand, was born to do something else. Its connection to racial inequality is more tenuous, suggestive. Yet both confusingly come from the same legal idea, antidiscrimination, which makes them vulnerable to capture.

Because of the age-old ambiguity over the Fourteenth Amendment antidiscrimination principle, antidiscrimination can mean three things with very different implications for racial justice. One is that equality requires a bar on all discrimination in order to ensure a just society in which individuals are judged only on their own merit. This is the civil rights idea that repelled explicit Jim Crow racism. It acknowledges that discrimination has been the instrument of inequality, so ending its invidious forms against minorities restores our basic race neutrality. A second idea of antidiscrimination is more active in overcoming that history of discrimination and recognizes that equality sometimes requires equity. Equity guides efforts to compensate for any continuing legacy of racial disadvantages in order to make true fairness possible. This is a civil rights–plus idea, a necessity when formal equality isn't enough to produce change. The third idea of antidiscrimination, what I call radical colorblindness, was described by Chief Justice John Roberts, when he declared that "the way to stop discrimination on the basis of race is to stop discriminating on the basis of race."[11] This idea of antidiscrimination is abstract and a-historical and pretends that we are already at equality because we are all theoretically equal. *Any* attempt to modify this equilibrium is discrimination no matter for whom or for what. Colorblindness is radical, I say, because it prohibits progress on racial inequality. This current idea of antidiscrimination commits us to a cynical pendularity in which we must keep proving and disproving what's obviously racially unequal.

Overall, this chapter explains how laws meant to liberate and protect can be made to contain and constrain, little by little, until substantive justice escapes through the cracks. The journey from affirmative action to diversity, to vilification of DEI and the triumph of colorblindness has altered my own views of DEI's potential value. My goal is not to defend DEI in all its iterations, but instead to show that some of the possibility of remediation that was lost to colorblindness and opposition to affirmative action can be won back through some DEI principles and a clearer articulation of their goals. From the standpoint of racial reckoning, that entails protecting DEI as bodies of thought and as expressive identity. Courts have already begun to read the First Amendment to protect DEI thinking. The explicit protection against Black erasure is still to come.

A SHORT HISTORY OF AFFIRMATIVE ACTION THROUGH "ANTIDISCRIMINATION"

Even before the term "affirmative action" was used, the nation struggled with a contest over some kind of compensatory justice for formerly enslaved Black people as a prerequisite to full equality. Then, as now, there was little interest in reparations for enslavement,[12] despite brief calls by abolitionists like Thaddeus Stevens to confiscate 400 million acres of Confederate plantations and distribute "40 acres and a mule" to Blacks.[13] One of the enduring hallmarks of American racism is that since the end of its most oppressive institution, fairness toward African Americans has never compelled formal restitution to sacrifice any of the wealth their bondage created. Even in the immediate aftermath of a bloody civil war and the reconstruction of our constitutional system, material accountability for stolen Black labor was only made to former slave owners, not to the enslaved.[14] During the debates over the Fourteenth Amendment and the civil rights statutes of the Reconstruction period, members of Congress argued over the extent to which the activation of equality and the extension of rights enjoyed by white men entailed race-conscious remedies for inequality. It took 100 years, which included lynchings, bombings of cities like Tulsa, and other acts of anti-Black violence, for proponents of the idea that equality for Blacks also entailed some limited form of equitable compensation or preference as a guarantee of opportunity to prevail. To do otherwise would continue to detach emancipation from citizenship, they argued. Some kind of racial preferences for Black people were due to repair clear racial injury. As Justice Thurgood Marshall wrote in his dissent to the *Bakke* decision: "Such a result would pervert the intent of the Framers by substituting abstract equality for the genuine equality the Amendment was intended to achieve."[15] Opponents of compensatory justice for Blacks had long couched their arguments against racial preferences for the newly freed people as racial preferences and "reverse racism." On that basis, President Andrew Johnson vetoed the civil rights act of 1866 at a time when Black people in Texas were still enslaved. His veto was overridden, but his argument and the racial impatience behind it has persisted ever since. Today, the claim that antidiscrimination, as embodied in the text of the Equal Protection Clause, means a strict race neutral, noncompensatory view of racial equality has gained considerable ground in federal courts. We arrived here through the exploitation of compromises over dual interpretations of what equality requires.

Fights over the meaning of equal protection were purely academic for generations after slavery ended. Resistance to compensatory justice and impatience with equal rights for Blacks dominated the country's laws and norms for roughly the next 100 years in the form of abject, often violent racial discrimination. Racism was the law of the land. Because of this, ending race discrimination was the central organizing motive of the Civil Rights Movement that began in the 1940s and 1950s. The "equality of all men" was a powerful idea that lost no resonance just because it applied only to white men for generations. To the early architects of racial justice – from Frederick Douglass to A. Phillip Randolph, to Bayard Rustin – nondiscrimination, or antidiscrimination, was a radical formulation of equality, a legal demand *not* to tolerate discrimination on the basis of race. The principle was there in the text of the Fourteenth Amendment: "[N]or shall any State deprive any person of life, liberty, or property, without due process of law; nor deny to any person within its jurisdiction the equal protection of the law." It had been argued a century before, but never realized. For a country raised on anti-Black racism, race-neutral equality would be an almost revolutionary return to first principles.

A few significant cracks in the Jim Crow edifice offered hope at the federal level. To avert a huge march on Washington organized by A. Philip Randolph, president of the Pullman Porters Union, President Franklin Delano Roosevelt signed Executive Order 8802, creating the Fair Employment Practices Committee (FEPC).[16] The FEPC required the federal government and government defense contractors "to provide for the full and equitable participation of all workers in defense industries, without discrimination because of race, creed, color or national origin."[17] In 1943, Roosevelt signed Executive Order 9346, expanding 8802's breadth by applying the antidiscrimination requirement to all government contractors.[18] Hoping to overcome resistance by Southern segregationists in Congress, President Truman in 1948 signed Executive Order 9981 "abolishing segregation in the armed forces and ordering full integration of all branches," and establishing the President's Committee on Equality of Treatment and Opportunity in the Armed Services.[19]

In 1951, Truman signed Executive Order 10308, creating the Committee on Government Contract Compliance.[20] This oversight power was further emphasized by President Eisenhower's 1953 Executive Order 10479, which reorganized the Committee so that all government agencies contracting with private companies individually ensured that contractors comply with its antidiscrimination terms. Each of these were limited, but important, steps made possible by a strategy that called attention to blatant contradictions between textual equality and racist reality when fascism and other world events spotlighted American democracy. Each crack came about as a result of organized Black protest, not random white beneficence. Black protest worked as organized awareness reckoning to illuminate discriminatory business-as-usual practices. The antidiscrimination principle offered an incontrovertible moral power over the long-held racist beliefs that guided institutional policy and race relations. Seeking nondiscrimination could mean "fair employment," "open housing" and other terms of inclusion without regard to race. These policy concepts were embodied in an umbrella term – equal opportunity – that became the foundation for national civil rights legislation and a variety of voluntary practices.

Yet conflict over reliance on nondiscrimination and equal opportunity arose during the 1960s when two critical executive orders preceded passage of the modern civil rights statutes. In Congress, nondiscrimination rather than compensatory justice proved pivotal to Southern votes for enactment of civil rights laws. We tend to think of these accomplishments today as groundbreaking, but to many at the time they were not enough. In the streets the struggle to end discrimination was bloody and halting, as shown by massive resistance to school integration, high Black unemployment, stark residential segregation, poverty rates affecting a near majority of all African Americans and spectacular waves of police violence against peaceful civil rights marchers. Corrective action in the form of demonstrable, affirmative action toward material racial inclusion had to accompany the passage of federal nondiscrimination statutes. Equality finally had to impose real costs on the owners of racial privilege.

The first was President Kennedy's Executive Order 10925, which introduced the idea of "positive steps" toward racial equality in federal contracting. "It is the policy of the executive branch of the government to encourage by positive measures equal opportunity for all qualified persons within the Government."[21] Couched as procedural fairness, 10925 shifted the burden of nondiscrimination onto employers and contractors to eliminate discriminatory practices that had existed for decades. Furthermore, "the contractor will take affirmative action to ensure that all applicants are employed, and that employees are treated during employment, without regard to their race, creed, color or national origin."[22] Kennedy included incentives – merit certificates for businesses that complied – and disincentives – exclusion from future federal contracts for noncompliance – that would become a feature of subsequent affirmative action policies.[23] The Order established the President's Committee on Equal Employment Opportunity (PCEEO).[24] The PCEEO worked with contractors to develop "Plans for Progress," or employment action plans for companies to work toward compliance with Executive Order 10925.[25] All federal agencies were also required to include specific antidiscrimination provisions in all contracts moving forward.[26] Here are the seeds of a well-intentioned but poorly supported hope that presidential directives about a shared norm of antidiscrimination would be enough to alter racist behavior in the federal realm, resetting business norms beyond it.

That hope wouldn't hold, a fact begrudgingly accepted by many civil rights leaders and demonstrated by two summers of devastating urban riots. After Kennedy's assassination, President Johnson embarked on the road toward affirmative action we might still know today were it not for the invention of the diversity rationale in 1977. The first step was passage of the Civil Rights Act of 1964, the centerpiece of the Civil Rights Movement and a Kennedy aspiration before his death. The Act contains two critical provisions. First was Title VII, the basis for nondiscrimination in employment. Second was the creation of the Equal Employment Opportunity Commission (EEOC). While discrimination in the workplace was a violation of Title VII, so was "preferential treatment to any group who had suffered discrimination."[27] These components – a federal law of nondiscrimination in employment backed up by a federal agency (as well as the Department of Labor) and an explicit prohibition on preferential treatment – fueled the controversy we've yet to resolve. The central question then and now is how to achieve racial equality, not how to achieve antidiscrimination.

The problem was and is equity. President Johnson soon recognized that Title VII alone wasn't enough to overcome racial inequality and issued Executive Order 11246 the next year. In June, Johnson gave a commencement speech at Howard University, "To Fulfill These Rights," and he articulated as well as any US president the imperative of racial equity as a condition of racial equality. It was also the basis for affirmative action's primary justification: remediation of societal discrimination, or compensatory justice.

> This is the next and the more profound stage of the battle for civil rights. We seek not just freedom but opportunity. We seek not just legal equity but human ability, not just equality as a right and a theory but equality as a fact and equality as a result. For the task is to give 20 million [Black Americans] the same chance as every other American to learn and grow, to work and share in society, to develop their abilities – physical, mental and spiritual, and to pursue their individual happiness. To this end equal opportunity is essential, but not enough, not enough.[28]

The federal agencies that took this charge most seriously were the EEOC and the Labor Department's Office of Federal Contract Compliance. They created the architecture of affirmative action plans among unions, employers and contractors that actualized the idea that racial equality required compulsion and planning if it was to counteract several generations of racist recalcitrance. Over the next several decades, companies cooperating with federal agencies crafted detailed affirmative action plans, goals and timetables, hiring according to population proportionality and measuring compliance with concepts like "utilization" in business.

Affirmative action policies were advanced without complaint by Republican administrations and accepted as a business certainty by conservative businesspeople. In the 1970s, the idea that Black progress in employment or segregated schools was stymied by "societal discrimination" was not a radical notion. For example, it was a Republican president, Richard Nixon, who enforced and expanded the Philadelphia Plan. Trade unions there had discriminated against Black workers since the Industrial Revolution. Seniority rules and federally funded apprenticeship programs guaranteed that white workers passed jobs down to their sons.[29] Ironically, all-white construction trades were employed by President Johnson's Great Society Programs to build new structures in cities coping with the ravages of urban renewal, ghettoization and white flight. Blacks had been boycotting companies that didn't hire them. Of 1.3 million construction workers in the US, only 106,000 were Black.[30] When Nixon took office, $550 million in contracts were going to be dispersed in Philadelphia, a city that had a large Black population but still hypersegregated construction trade unions.[31] Then Secretary of Labor George Shultz and assistant secretary Arthur Fletcher devised the Philadelphia Plan – later codified for national use as Executive Order 11625 – which initially "required construction companies that had federal contracts to set numerical goals for hiring" Black workers.[32] The unions pushed back, as they would at multiple points. Shultz threatened to withhold government contracts. Minority employment increased from 4 percent to 26 percent between 1969 and 1973. The Plan expanded to nine other cities.[33]

The fact is routinely forgotten but affirmative action worked – and not just for white women. It produced measurable material access to the working and middle class for Black people during the period in the late 1970s leading up to the *Bakke* decision and the hostility of the Reagan Administration that arrived in 1981. Multiple studies show that in both employment and education – another push by the Johnson administration – Black mobility increased in terms of employment, educational access, income and reduced poverty.[34] Affirmative action was a success at marginally closing the inequality gap. More importantly, compensatory justice did not return equal and opposite material harms to whites. The contemporary idea that "hard" affirmative action – programs that either set aside admissions seats or contracts – creates "zero-sum" outcomes that do tangible racial harm to whites is not supported by much evidence. That is, white male overrepresentation in institutions that practiced some form of affirmative action in its 1970s heyday decreased, according to some estimates, by between 1.2 and 15 percent.[35] Educational enrollments increased more dramatically than employment gains during the same period, especially in graduate and professional programs, though studies are mixed regarding the extent to which racial preferences played a role (e.g., in admitting Blacks and other minorities versus whites).[36] Given overall rates of exclusion and overrepresentation, it's fair to assume that there will be some number of the dominant group who may lose dominance in some selective opportunities (there are *always* qualified people who will be excluded from truly selective opportunities). Yet it's that small faction on which the fight over the meaning of antidiscrimination turned rightward.

REMEDIATION KRYPTONITE

What should have been a starting point, however, became the end game. The issue was not necessarily "affirmative action," with its slate of mechanics (e.g., goals, timetables, preferences, quotas, set asides). It was remediation – and still is. Even though affirmative action tried to level the playing field, it was a forward-looking project that merely recognized past racial injustices, as if there were no serious generational consequences to those injustices. Remediation was not central to the discussion. Remediation is not strictly a Black and white issue either. If the compelling national interest is overcoming racial inequality, accountability reckoning must come up with substantive ways to remedy the cumulative effects of past and continuing racial disadvantage against Black people. As we discussed in Chapter 2, that means materially altering the resources available to succeed as an individual and a community. Though we made real progress, we didn't do enough accountability before white supremacy imposed a conceptual and legal barricade against remediation.

Imagine there are three basic ways to address the racial inequality that Black people in the US still face. First is reparations – that is, paying for race-based thefts, the many things *stolen*, such as labor, property, votes, wealth, clean air and water, or access, all as a result of slavery and its progeny of institutionalized racisms, like poll taxes, peonage, convict leasing, redlining, urban renewal etc. Reparations might be the most powerful form of accountability because it would come with acknowledgment of wrongfulness and an objective calculation of the price of the harm. It's what civil courts do every day. Reparations for stolen valuables doesn't depend on antidiscrimination to define either wrongfulness or injury, just theft against Black people because they were Black. Although reparations may be a policy fight we're currently having, suffice it to say it's never been done for African Americans. (It's been done for white former slaveholders reimbursed the value of their emancipated labor force after the Civil War and for Japanese Americans interned during World War II.)[37]

A second way to account for racial inequality is to pay for societal discrimination where it's been proven. In this case the injury comes from a denial of opportunity because of race discrimination. An example is the federal–local policy of racial segregation in Chapter 3 and the wealth harms it reproduces. It is the denial of benefits and opportunities, not the theft, that must be made whole. This form of accountability is what most of us mean when we talk about antidiscrimination rules. The issue is whether American constitutional law will allow claims based on societal discrimination (however defined) or whether it demands a narrower one-to-one intentional act-based idea of discrimination. As we saw in Chapter 2, the latter idea of antidiscrimination gave us colorblindness and strict scrutiny, with a vast ocean of societal discrimination arbitrarily immune to any means to account for it.

The third way is the most popular and indirect: make incremental policy gains against "the Struggle." This is so common we don't often think of it in terms of accountability. Rather we debate it in safety-net terms like "welfare" or redistribution. The goal for policymakers is to relieve people's burdens to a more tolerable point, to avoid being an unconscionable government, so that people can meet their basic needs for health care, shelter, economic assistance, child welfare, unemployment and energy discounts. We argue over who deserves this "aid" and what they owe in return. Because we know that these folks are disproportionately Black, but not even a majority so, these policies of struggle-mitigation can be thought of indirectly as accountability for racial inequality. No one would confuse government assistance for remediation.

The only one of these three forms of racial accountability that had an active chance at doing the remediation needed to overcome racial inequality was programs to pay for societal discrimination. It was consistent with the antidiscrimination principle and introduced the necessity of equity to modify the meaning of equality. Yet it ran afoul of denial and avoidance rules, so it failed in favor of diversity.

Left with little else, there's a contested and inconsistent fourth way to address racial inequality. That alternative is DEI.

THE MAKING AND UNMAKING OF DEI

Conservative thought gave us DEI.

While the executive and legislative branches of government embraced the notion of affirmative action and set-aside quotas, the courts took a much more conservative approach, while still endorsing the notion that moving forward, government needed to take some form of action to make sure that, at least prospectively, some form of racial equal opportunity was needed. Ironically, from a civil rights standpoint, diversity, equity and inclusion arose out of begrudging compromise from the diversity rationale in *Bakke*. The case overturned the University of California medical school's affirmative action admissions program on the grounds that its use of racial quotas to admit Black and Latino students violated the equal protection rights of white applicants like Alan Bakke, who claimed that he was denied admission solely on the basis of his race. The diversity rationale that conservative Justice Lewis Powell suggested could alone justify the limited use of race in admissions concerns the enhancement of the general educational experience. Powell opined that a diverse learning environment can justifiably promote awareness of, and appreciation for, racial and other kinds of differences for the benefit, not of a maligned group that has paid undue costs in racial injury, but for everybody in the environment on equal terms. The opinion praised the "Harvard model," that eschewed racial quotas in favor of a more holistic view of applicants that considered being a racial minority a plus to the entire school community. "DEI" was the expansion of these ideas into realms that used race as one factor among many in their community composition, such as hiring and retention. From an HR department standpoint, for instance, DEI represented necessity. Everyone in between was probably experimenting with how to operationalize institutional rules for an increasingly diverse world without getting sued for reverse discrimination.

Antidiscrimination talk made the institutionalization of the diversity idea possible. Since *Bakke*, conservative politicians and jurists have made great effectiveness of the elegant assertion that antidiscrimination is not open to exception; it is an absolute. But talk is cheap. "[I]t is to participate in an abstracted discourse,"[38] Kimberlé Crenshaw wrote, where the calculus of racial injury alternates meaninglessly between the material and the theoretical. It pendulates between Black people's (and some other minorities') injuries from limited mobility, wealth, health and voice versus white people's "constitutional" injuries from the very act of treating people differently by race. Yet as Randall Kennedy has said, "Nondiscrimination ... is better understood not as a 'principle' but as a tool. The pertinent principle should be racial justice."[39]

We have DEI because we lost that interest in remedial racial justice and replaced it with colorblindness. From the late 1970s to the Trump era, conservatives successfully exploited white resentment and doctrinal ambiguity to inflame white resentment and make the goal of substantive equality seem radical. It took three category-collapsing moves over the course of several Supreme Court affirmative action decisions to incapacitate the idea of remedial justice. First was to blur the important distinctions that had developed between different realms in which various affirmative action policies were deployed. Second was to eviscerate the distinction between "invidious" and benign discrimination. Third was to march all the category collapsing into the dead-end of a colorblind strict-scrutiny framework where racial justice would die. All three have absolutism in common. Let's take each briefly in turn.

It started with blurring the sector distinctions that mattered. The bureaucratic heft of affirmative action that conservatives deride arose from distinctions made among firms, sectors and practices, rather than a one-size-fits-all approach. Workplace discrimination is not the same as educational discrimination because they operate differently. The infrastructure of sticks, carrots and affirmative action plans was developed primarily in the employment realm by the EEOC. Under director counsel Al Blumrosen, the EEOC included onerous and detailed data collection, so that the agency could not only monitor employment patterns among companies and unions but sanction them where necessary.[40] Workplace exclusions weren't uniform; indeed, many sectors were willing voluntarily to use hiring and promotion goals and timetables to correct for past discrimination while others fought every inch of change. For many, clear numerical targets bred business certainty. Different patterns called for different approaches. According to Frank Dobbin in *Inventing Equal Opportunity*, the first cottage industry created by affirmative action consisted of the human relations (HR) departments of large corporations and their lawyers who "codified ... internal corporate legal codes."[41]

> Corporate equal opportunity experts speculated about how interpretation of the law might evolve, and how legislation might change. The speculations often followed some new social scientific ideas, such as the idea of institutional discrimination or the idea of cognitive bias. Experts then set up their own regulatory systems within firms consisting of practices ranging

> from bureaucratic promotion procedures to halt institutional discrimination to mandatory diversity awareness programs to end cognitive bias. Discrimination came to be defined as the absence of such measures.[42]

And what worked in manufacturing involved different interests and dynamics than in an entirely different realm like university admissions. The histories of exclusion were different; institutional needs, market pressures, relevant consumers and goals were all different, complex. Not without conflict, they were working them out in sector-specific ways that demanded a flexibility against one-size-fits-all rules of equality.

Yet the *Bakke* case created a template for collapsing those different approaches. Yes, Justice Powell's plurality opinion seemed to rest on education-specific considerations, such as the diversity of viewpoints in a freshman classroom. But it was the rejection of *remedial* rationales that would create a constraining colorblind uniformity beyond educational affirmative action that gave us diversity as the primary basis for using race in any kind of policy. Powell rejected the three other affirmative action rationales put forth by the University of California in defense of its admissions practices: countering societal discrimination, increasing the number of practicing physicians in underserved areas and correcting for the historic deficit of traditionally disfavored minorities in the medical profession.[43] These were akin to rationales that underlaid affirmative action efforts in the employment realm. Each of these rationales remedied a well-established discriminatory denial, such as racial misdiagnosis of disease, not enough doctors and stereotypes of who can be successful. *Bakke* heralded their elimination. The validity of voluntarily undertaken affirmative action plans once upheld in the *Weber* employment case,[44] the Title VII "presumptively necessary" idea of "sharing the burden of past discrimination" in *Franks v. Bowman*[45] or recognizing the aim of barring future discrimination in *Albemarle*[46] were closed door after door, case after case. When the Court decided *Wygant*[47] in 1986, a case that denied a school system the ability to bypass seniority in order to overcome embedded privilege and again rejected societal discrimination as a compelling interest to support affirmative action policies, only the diversity rationale remained available for most institutions. Racial diversity erased racial remediation as a means to end racial inequality.

The second move in the conservative logic of affirmative action was to create equivalency between what was always understood as "invidious" racism and "benign" race-conscious remediation. Invidious discrimination is the traditional kind of racial targeting while benign discrimination is the marginal cost to others who aren't due the remedy. We commit benign discrimination every time we distinguish the treatment appropriate for some group in order to accommodate them, either because they need it (e.g., disability) or are owed it (e.g., race), and we want to end their previous condition of exclusion. The rest of us pay a small price for wider doorways or more effective health care. The difference between invidious and benign discrimination is that one is the reason for remediation and the other provides it. What principle justifies the difference? Equity.

Yet suddenly, invidious and benign were joined by the Supreme Court, without distinction, by the mere fact that each took race into account. Again, this false equivalency was easiest to assert in the educational cases of *Bakke*, *Gratz*, *Grutter* and *Fisher*, because the Court had completely ignored evidence of past discrimination, assuming that the playing field was always equal. Without accounting for historically racist college admissions policies (through the 1970s) and segregated, underfunded schools overwhelmingly attended by Black children (still today), students could be presumed to come from level playing fields and should, in fairness, play by the same rules. If we presume a world without active discrimination, there is no longer a reason to distinguish between types of discrimination. There's only classification by race, which becomes per se discrimination, and no one's claim is any different or better than anyone else's. The bank that advertises no Blacks allowed is no more racist than the bank that remedied decades of redlining by promising more branches in Black neighborhoods because of its history. Equality without equity becomes merely a figure of speech, a slogan lacking substance.

The fantastical reasoning of radical equality swept into realms where the present effects of previous race discrimination had been more formally recognized, such as government contracting – the thing that started it all. Yet in an important reverse-discrimination contracting case, *City of Richmond v. J.A. Croson, Co.*,[48] the Supreme Court poked holes in the very premise that there was such a thing as historic discrimination impeding

Black and minority-owned companies from doing business with the government, even a local government considered the second capitol of the Confederacy. According to the conservative Court majority, setting aside some contracts for the victims of unproven invidious discrimination was a remedy without a wrong and constituted a *new* constitutional injury against white contractors. Did Black and other minority contractors suffer discrimination in the construction trades that prevented them from competing on lucrative government contracts? Undoubtedly. Could the city prove it? Perhaps, but the Court rejected every attempt. (Note how the same analysis presumes with less proof that white contractors are racially injured by the program.) *Croson* was later affirmed for all government contracts in *Adarand.*[49] Today, it is the heart of catch-all arguments against any use of race anywhere. Racial equivalency of injury triggers reciprocity of attack, as white plaintiffs sue to vindicate any perceived advantage given to nonwhites.

The third move was to invent an impregnable framework for review: strict scrutiny. Strict judicial scrutiny will strike down any use of a racial classification by the state or its grantees that does not further a compelling state interest. Conservative justices on the Court unsurprisingly have declared that the United States does not consider overcoming its persistent history of race discrimination a compelling state interest. Think about that for a moment. Antidiscrimination is a compelling state interest, but *remedying* racial discrimination is not. Some constitutional scholars argue that this distinction was the greatest coup of all, the triumph of Federalist Society jurisprudence (though the quest began shortly before the Federalists officially formed). Again, an absolutist approach was gratuitous. A compelling interest could have been phrased in more than one way to allow certain forms of affirmative action to survive equal-protection analysis. For instance, strict remediation could be a compelling interest, where a party would have a higher standard of proof to show the previous and lasting discrimination their policy seeks to reckon. Or it could have meant some demonstrated level of invidiousness as determined by proof and precedent, where a party had to defend its use of race based on the severity of race discrimination involved and the degree of harm it caused. It could also have remained diversity – specifically, racial diversity. Instead, it has effectively and absolutely meant none – no use of race survives strict scrutiny – whether remedial or not.[50]

THE DEI INDUSTRY

If diversity made racial remediation impossible, then the corporatized DEI industry that evolved out of *Bakke* should offer little hope for racial reckoning beyond enhanced awareness of identity dynamics. But racial accountability is more complicated than that, which is probably why DEI was vigorously revived as a target of Trumpism. It turns out that DEI was doing a lot more than annoying people in training sessions on unconscious bias. It was establishing a certainty of institutional and social norms amid changing demographic realities, which is a growth industry. It was also embodying, albeit sometimes clumsily, the notion of racial reckoning.

DEI had begun developing as a global field of academic and business inquiry since at least the start of the century. The international literature is vast and varied, underlying a cottage industry of jobs, departments, titles, consultants, programs and certificates known generally as DEI or some variant of its terms. The racial reckoning in 2020 briefly sent the sector into overdrive. According to McKinsey, the global market expenditures by companies on DEI-related activities, including Employee Resource Groups (ERGs), was $7.5 billion in 2020 and this was projected to double by 2026.[51] DEI officers of various labels have proliferated in nonprofit organizations, Fortune 500 companies and universities. Their work runs the gamut from very specific initiative-driven HR programming and strategic plans to more general rules of institutional operation. Despite the variety of program aims, the industry has professionalized and DEI professionals often communicate in a data-driven language (probably influenced by employment discrimination lawsuits) that emphasize such things as "significant, quantifiable, scalable, and sustainable impact."[52]

The expansive language of DEI across so many contexts reflects an almost circular intersectionality about the industry. You can, for example, enroll in Stanford Business School's DEI certificate program so that you can get a job at Stanford University's admissions office.[53] Leadership programs there include a range of subgroups, such as Asian, LGBTQ, Black, Women and Veterans.[54] Generally, DEI certificate programs range in price from a few hundred dollars for online courses offered by the Academy to Innovate HR to Harvard's multi-thousand-dollar program.

The survival of this corporate-leaning sector may depend on the goals of the DEI industry – and here's the complication for racial reckoning. The less DEI aims at actually altering the power dynamics that limit opportunities for underrepresented racial groups, the more likely it is to survive. The more its goals creep closer to remedying the persistent effects of racial hierarchies, the more vulnerable it will be to constitutional and political attack. The Trump justice department can investigate all it wants, but it is unlikely to score any major legal victories claiming that DEI is "illegal." Most institutions built their DEI programming with hawklike attention to existing civil rights law, as early court cases have shown.[55] (Many are private and therefore outside the reach of the state action requirement for equal protection or Title VI claims.) The question is whether companies and organizations possess the institutional value of racial equity *and* the operational imperative of creating productive, inclusive environments. Making workplaces more comfortable for everybody is noble, but hardly exceptional HR practice. Companies willing to publicly state the goals of their DEI efforts often resort to the language of business necessity – attracting talent, expanding market share, improving engagement and employee retention. These in turn produce the goal of better performance and competitive advantage. But rarely do they mention gaining "critical knowledge and skills to address bias and marginalization and to foster an inclusive corporate culture," as Harvard's program does.[56] Scholars have offered trenchant critiques of the DEI industry, from its high rhetoric and empty promises in their own fields[57] to its failure to do enough to remedy the continued effects of racial marginalization through more structural approaches,[58] especially for Blacks. They are, of course, pointing out the central role of racial avoidance again.

It's more than that. We've seen how DEI attracts a lot of legitimate criticism from the right and left sides of the affirmative action issue. Yet even within its own terms, corporatized DEI often manifests a hypocrisy that devalues continuing racial struggle and limits opportunities for reckoning. Specifically, DEI rarely centers the Blackness from which it comes. Decentering Blackness and the specific means by which Blacks have been systematically discriminated against across institutions, corporatized DEI can't credibly call for racially reparative remedies. DEI departments don't often speak truth to power. Instead, race is mediated mostly through euphemism, not confrontation. When DEI then becomes the only game in town, its proponents seem comfortable letting corrective action go as a reason to encourage diversification and inclusion. It was this very compromise on remediation that gave unnecessary support to the racial equivalency arguments that doomed diversity to become an all-things-to-all-people idea. When the racial reckoning occurred in 2020 and became ensconced in so many DEI fora, it wasn't surprising that affirmative steps at racial remediation were barely present. This was a lost opportunity for Black people that reeked of institutional opportunism for DEI programming. As Randall Kennedy argued, nothing prevented DEI from unapologetically valorizing Blackness even more.

> The diversity rationale moves the spotlight from the perceived deficiencies of blacks to their perceived strengths ... Indeed, the most striking and historically significant aspect of the diversity rationale is that it enables coloredness for the first time in American history to be seen as a valuable credential.[59]

The potential for these meritocratic arguments revaluing Blackness in DEI programming was sacrificed to the practices of a more careful industry that is strategically, if not ideologically, more comfortable abandoning racial remediation. Ironically, no amount of caution spared it from being the target of the anti-DEI saturation bombing campaign of Trump II.

HOW DEI CAN REMEDIATE

Amid this hostile environment, I've come around to the belief that some strains of diversity, equity and inclusion policies can do more, including remediation for embedded racial disadvantage. The problems of industrial capture, virtue signaling, racial avoidance and excessive rigidity aren't insoluble and have always coexisted alongside concerns for racial equality in some parts of DEI thinking. Here are three brief examples of how DEI-informed policy can have remedial impacts on the three areas of racial reckoning discussed in this book: the racial wealth gap, racial health disparities and policing.

First, to promote the goal of wealth accumulation in underrepresented – that is, Black – communities, the DEI priorities of efficiency, equity, transparency and inclusive growth can alter state corporate tax incentives criteria. Corporate tax incentives are extremely common transfers of public wealth to private companies for a "public purpose," such as filmmaking, job creation or other business development. Legislation forgoes billions in tax revenues to qualified businesses, thus reducing business costs and hopefully incentivizing investment, jobs or both. This transfers private-industry market costs onto taxpayers. The public's return on these subsidies, however, is rarely publicized; costly programs go on for years without proving themselves while the winning interests in an otherwise free market are being helped by government involvement. DEI-informed policies could make this common practice more efficient and transparent by adding equitable considerations to public purpose. Public dollars should be used to jumpstart labor markets, nourish markets in geographic areas of the state that need it, fill unmet consumer needs and build future capacity in key industries. They can be identified geographically and demographically through disparities studies. These are good governance considerations in spreading the benefits of economic growth to untapped areas of the state's population, but they also involve economic fairness and the avoidance of concentrations of market power. Many of the businesses that would be included in these benefits are Black owned, who disproportionately hire more Black labor and often provide goods and services to predominantly Black-identified regions of the state economy simply because of where they operate. That's a benefit. Pockets of underutilization are costly to all state taxpayers. There's a clear race-neutral public purpose in growing these businesses, jobs and markets through equitable regulation of corporate tax incentives, which converges with the remediation goal of closing the racial wealth gap. Without DEI, that kind of public-interested policymaking might be lost.

To promote the goal of reduced health disparities by race, DEI principles can provide the means to an end through research funding. The continuing interest in studying racial health disparities launched by *Unequal Treatment* and other texts discussed in Chapter 4 illustrates the remedial potential of DEI-informed research on Black health. Who gets studied, what the priority questions are and who participates in the work are all traditional DEI issues. For instance, medical students clearly sensitized to algorithmic bias in nephrology questioned the racial scoring of a common blood measure of kidney health, the eGFR. A few years of research later, it was debunked as racial fiction, adding 300,000 Black people to lists of patients eligible for enhanced kidney care, screening and transplants.[60] As Dr. Jennifer Tsai, an author of one of the studies, said, "When we teach that race is biological and that it's something that changes how your kidney works, what your blood vessels do, how your heart beats, how thick your skin is – these are all false ideas that contribute to research and practices that are disparate in terms of what you do when the patient in front of you is Black or white."[61] (Incidentally, it appears that most of the authors of the transformative study happened to be medical students of color.)

Finally, to promote the goal of reduced police violence, DEI policies can engender trust between law enforcement and communities at statistical risk of victimization. Again, there are good crime prevention strategies for engendering trust, just as there are non-DEI-related reasons to use corporate tax credits equitably or to conduct public health research on populations at most acute risk of harmful conditions. Truly remedial reckoning of unjustified police violence should be legal deterrence, as I argued in Chapter 5. Yet there is a role for both DEI-informed research and trainings in altering the conditions of trust that may reduce fatal incidents with police. Research by criminologists like those at the Newark Public Safety Collaborative recognizes that certain neighborhoods need better safety tools and are unjustly denied because of a policing history that led its department to enter into a civil rights consent decree.[62] Better data-driven research on how and where crimes occur and the propensity for police use of force applies DEI principles to remedial conduct. Beyond research, one city even used a DEI-informed approach to *atonement* for police racism in order to improve trust and lower crime. Stockton, California, experimented with a program of curated police–community conversations designed to acknowledge the underpinnings of racial distrust.[63] Modeled after truth-and-reconciliation methods, Stockton police officers actually apologized to community members for the history of racially motivated police misconduct that had bred so much more distrust and violence.

So, one defense of DEI is that it actually can advance racial remediation.

DEFENDING DEI AGAINST A RACIAL NDA

Another defense of DEI is that it constitutes speech and expression protected by the First Amendment. Just because there's a contest over what DEI means doesn't deny its meaningfulness.

In their overregulation of DEI, both right-wing politics and conservative legal reasoning would make a lot of Black identity disappear, one by command, the other by sleight of doctrinal hand. Conservative thinker Leonard Leo refers to DEI, reckoning and CRT as a "brand" that MAGA will turn "toxic, as we put all of the various cultural insanities under that brand category."[64] The earlier backlash against racial reckoning was aimed at symbols of "woke ideology" and tried to ban DEI in schools. The greater war of erasure was ferociously relaunched by Trump II: no DEI in public agencies or private entities receiving federal funds, no more funding schools participating in PhD pipeline programs for minorities,[65] no use of words that are even associated with DEI like "environmental justice," "equity," "trauma" or "disparity."[66] The MAGA attack on the arts and its best-known institutions – the Smithsonian's National Museum of African American History and Culture, the National Endowment for the Humanities, the Kennedy Center takeover and book bans of Black history – perceives Black culture as a danger.[67] The political supports the legal. As we've seen, conservative civil rights doctrine tries to ban group identity in strict favor of individual rights whenever it gets a chance. To use race is to see it, they might argue, and colorblindness strictly scrutinizes any attempt to do so. Regulation imposes a kind of racial nondisclosure agreement where it's understood that the race targeted most for silence is Black.

Erasure crosses the constitutional line, however, and shows why "DEI" should legally survive this bout with autocracy. First Amendment law is pretty clear about why government regulation of viewpoints is unconstitutional. DEI constitutes a set of views about how organizations should function according to certain values. DEI creates its own questions, some common, some specific to a field, and generates an endless amount of content. The DEI trainings that annoyed some people reflect studied frameworks with which you're free to disagree. We did and we still do. That's the point. Require diversity statements of job applicants? Introduce yourself with pronouns? There was no consensus. MAGA didn't start the debate, and it can't shut it down.

Whether we call it woke ideology, belonging or some other branding, a DEI policy framework has a message that's understood by those who hear it, especially if they don't like it. "[A] principal function of free speech under our system of government is to invite dispute," the Supreme Court has held. "It may indeed best serve its high purpose when it induces a condition of unrest, creates dissatisfaction with conditions as they are, or even stirs people to anger."[68] The more concerned with public affairs, the more robust, wide open and uninhibited the public discussions should be.[69] The more government believes the ideas are offensive or repugnant, the more they're entitled to constitutional protection from government regulation.[70] By singling out DEI for elimination from all federally funded public discourse, the federal and many state governments have selected the content they don't like and penalized those viewpoints on that basis, blatantly violating First Amendment rights upheld in a long line of Supreme Court cases.[71] The Court has even directly prohibited the punitive withholding of government funding,[72] a Trump administration strategy, and the banning of a philosophical perspective in the classroom,[73] as the administration has done to universities and K-12 schools. There is little question that silencing of DEI beliefs, teachings and policies by executive fiat is unconstitutional viewpoint discrimination and cannot stand, as several courts ruled early on.[74]

The harder question is whether Black people's expressed identification with reckoning, because of their association with DEI, can be defended against concerted attempts to erase them by insult, regulation and defunding. Even before Trump's reelection, you heard less explicit references to racial equality and few defenses of DEI. The Harris presidential campaign was almost devoid of them. After Trump's election, DEI all but vanished. Symbolically, Black people's interests in reckoning has been increasingly perceived through a powerful negative stereotype: "illegal, divisive, repugnant, unworthy DEI." Practically, Black people's already dwindling presence in many places could compel their silence, erasing the identification with racial reckoning. As it becomes more widely accepted, the stereotype justifies the gradual disappearance of the people it represents and the erasure of the reckoning with which they're associated. With no one to push back, it just sort of happens.

None of this was anticipated by the original reckoning. Yet just a few years later, as many Americans fret about the "existential threat" Trump's second administration poses for the country's democratic institutions, silencing the remaining Black voices of racial reckoning is part of the deal. Given Trump's successful attacks on DEI, the capacity to communicate Black people's interests may be sacrificed in another racial bargain. Just a few years later, we could be right back to the place we were at the start of the 2020 racial reckoning – reacting to years of suppressed racial marginalization – only this time, the structure would have changed to preempt any meaningful reckoning.

Let me elaborate on both points. Trump II has reshaped federal power in ways that resemble how it has reshaped racial justice. First, the administration asserted the power to ban things on the pretext of legality, such as dissolving agencies or declaring DEI illegal, based on a symbiotic relationship with the Supreme Court that created grey areas where clear distinctions once existed. Without the threat of Supreme Court sanction, the administration took extralegal action, knowing its targets will either see the transaction risks of fighting with no leverage as too much (e.g., elite universities who settle allegations without a formal investigation) or that litigating up to the Supreme Court will result in too costly a legal loss (e.g., immigration overreaches without due process). The "unitary executive" idea, from which this strategy comes, scored powerful wins under the Supreme Court's emergency or "shadow" docket, where cases are decided without justification, often on procedural grounds, that allow the administration's conduct to stand for an indefinite period of time. A researcher at Stanford reported that within the first six months of Trump II, district courts had found against the administration's practices 94.3 percent of the time; those cases that were appealed to the Supreme Court's shadow docket, however, were revered in Trump's favor 93.7 percent of the time.[75] The administration pushed ahead. The fundamental threat to democracy lies in becoming a system where the executive has unchecked authority to impose its will. Rather than political or legal constraints, most conflicts will boil down to whether a target can withstand the threat of federal penalties. Most can't.

As dangerous as this is to democracy in general, it is especially lethal for Black-identified interests like racial reckoning. The first chess move was to brand Black people with a discredited stereotype in DEI. The second was to suggest its illegality was supported by the Supreme Court's equal protection jurisprudence. Neither is completely true. Yet the associations combined with the threats to resisters will probably preempt a lot of initiatives aimed at remedying racial inequality. More and more people seem convinced that colorblindness is the right way to enshrine the constitutional norm of protecting *individual* rights, not group rights. Racial reckoning by its terms necessarily blurs that line.

The personal is inescapably political for many Black people, who risk punishment if they act on such thinking.

Consider this example. You're a Black reader of this book – a teacher, a law-firm lawyer, a receptionist at a manufacturer that does business with the government. You're persuaded that the arguments about wealth and health inequities reflect not only your beliefs but your experiences. You have personal stories about encounters with police you think are racist. These beliefs are twofold: they affect you as an individual and they threaten you and many people you love as a member of a race. You want your beliefs to have impact. You want to put them into action locally – say, to examine complaints about the fairness of student discipline patterns that seem to target Black boys while ignoring racist taunts by bullies, or to offer free representation to indigent, mostly Black tenants facing aggressive eviction campaigns, or to replace that expensive corporate caterer with the local Black restaurant people have been raving about. But as a teacher, you and your school face headwinds from parents angry about CRT. As a Black lawyer, the number of Black lawyers in big firms like yours have been shrinking for years and now your firm faces scrutiny for "DEI hiring practices" *and* for the kinds of pro bono it takes on. As a manufacturer, your company no longer believes it has equitable procurement obligations. Nevertheless, you believe all three can do better and that racial justice in some small way demands it. Your desires are instantly recognizable as "DEI," which in schools, law firms and government contractors means your ideas now put the whole enterprise at risk of an investigation, possibly fines, bad press, loss of business, whistle-blowers, lay-offs or private lawsuits. You'll be accused of equating your individual interests with a proscribed group interest in race, which the constitution now forbids. Maybe the thought of DEI will make some faction believe *you're* the racist. Therefore, you won't sue and you shouldn't talk about it and you're sure it can't make much of a difference anymore. Communication of your beliefs now comes with real risks to your livelihood. Any attempt to speak out could mean an HR rabbit hole of endless, expensive resistance – you're laid off suddenly, demoted, suspended, reassigned – with no guarantees that you'll get a fair chance to be heard. People like you are boxed in by their own sense of justice. In the ironic words of Kendrick Lamar, "Be humble. Sit down."

It's not clear if we will, but we shouldn't have to. The First Amendment should protect us.

More than a hundred years after writing *The Souls of Black Folks*, W.E.B. DuBois remains right about the "double consciousness" among Black Americans. To oversimplify, he meant that our social identities are constructed from within, where we are our individual selves, and also from without, where we see ourselves as we believe white society sees us. It is often a conflict, but whatever it means to any of us, it must be managed, even today. Managing a dual American identity is part of the foundation for self-awareness, which in turn enables self-determination. DEI didn't always deliver for Black people, but its tendencies toward awareness reckoning for all groups promised the institutionalized space for the expressive identity in one's Blackness.

Whether or not using DEI as a slur should be so closely associated with African Americans, DEI frameworks have had genuine significance for many Black people. The connections to its principles and values may have been different than for others. DEI jobs, trainings and initiatives offered opportunities to address the hardship of double consciousness by inviting Black voices to share honestly about their experiences with racism away from home. These disclosures were rare and meaningful, a breakthrough for many, however fleeting. Black professionals at the top of their fields, earning competitive corporate salaries, flocked to DEI positions. Contrary to MAGA taunts, the proliferation of DEI job titles was seen by many who took them as the rare convergence of personal values and organizational efficiencies. Putting aside DEI's annoying excesses, it was an exciting moment of positive potential. A vengeful Trump administration has worked actively to make those credentials a scarlet letter, forcing these same professionals to choose between writing away their experience or defending it somehow in a rapidly diminishing market for their skills and values. But the slurs do not redefine the choices.

Perhaps nowhere was the DEI identification more salient than with younger Black people who were my students' and children's ages, many of whom might not even use the DEI moniker. Nevertheless, they saw themselves in key elements of the initiatives. The language of DEI could often communicate their self-beliefs and their expectations socially, academically, professionally, politically. Inside this diffuse worldview was not only the foundation for resistance to a recharged white supremacy they've had to grow up with, but it also offered the confidence of hope. DEI affirms a sense of dignity. They owned it with a purpose.

Part of that purpose is survival. Young Black people are the only racial group (except Native Americans) for whom typical American notions of progress are contested, if not unlikely. They know that the anti-DEI movement's success will come at their material expense. While other groups' young people expect to do as well or better than their parents, not so Blacks – for example, in life expectancy, college admissions, employment, wealth creation, homeownership or death by police. Take Barack Obama, the nation's first Black president and the most salient symbol of racial progress. When he entered Harvard Law School in 1988, there were *significantly* more Black students beside him than today and for the foreseeable future. When he graduated in 1991, the NALP reported that 19.6 percent of Black male law grads and 18.2 percent of Black women went to work for large law firms like the ones targeted for their diversity efforts by the Trump administration. Yet in 2021, before Trump's return, the Black male percentage had been more than halved to 8.3 percent; Black women had declined to 12.4 percent.[76] The examples of such disappearance are only mounting, which diminishes the experience of competency, camaraderie and belonging for the next generation of Black people. Meanwhile, their non-Black peers are being taught again the lessons learned by many of their grandparents: these people are less than you.

Yet the final chess move – the threatened checkmate – is to shut down both the institutional DEI work *and* the personal identifications to it without legal, organizational or other recourse. The actual threat need never be carried out in order to constitute a prior restraint on Black expression. Long term, as Kimberlé Crenshaw noted years ago, the structures of suppression erected since the reckoning can "hamper efforts of African Americans to name their reality and to remain capable of engaging in collective action in the future."[77] Black people can't force a racial reckoning alone. Our interests prevail mostly when they're shared with others'. But self-censorship abounds. Silence portends erasure. In the racial bargain, others will also lose.

This makes reckoning an existential problem. How can you reckon with a racial identity you're not comfortable naming in public? How can Black people be secure in their identities as both individuals and members of a group if that very identity is chronically undermined because of the very efforts to uplift it?

African-American self-awareness is at the root of all racial reckoning, but it's only made manifest if it can be expressed. This too must be vigorously protected by the First Amendment. As Justice Thurgood Marshall wrote long ago:

> The First Amendment serves not only the needs of the polity but also those of the human spirit – a spirit that demands self-expression. Such expression is an integral part of the development of ideas and a sense of identity. To suppress expression is to reject the basic human desire for recognition and affront the individual's worth and dignity.[78]

In the most practical terms, DEI work must continue to uphold the right of Black people to be who we say we are. It must be fortified to stand against erasure.

RECKONING

Unlike other aspects of accountability reckoning that can be conducted through local institutional reforms and/or race-neutral policies, the DEI defense must be primarily conducted through litigation. This is especially true for counteracting the erasure of racial identity expression. The two-pronged attack of politically punitive anti-DEI policies backed up by the threat of legal action to enforce extreme colorblind norms puts fundamental rights at risk. The right to self-expression cannot be negotiated or politically waited out. These cases must be brought and won. A society that can pendulate between Black Lives Matter one year and silent acquiescence in renouncing it just a few years later can't be trusted to protect Black people's rights to seek what I argue is necessary redress for racial inequality – whether DEI policies, reparations or something else in which race must be named.

Successful litigation will change the power imbalance between governments on one side and institutions and their members on the other. This, in turn, will reopen a marketplace of ideas where people can again advocate for remedial diversity, equity and inclusion frameworks or whatever one chooses to call them. The goal is to reincorporate racial equity as a principle of institutional life so that stereotype, exclusion and silencing no longer subvert the good work of a diverse and deserving people.

CHAPTER 7

Looking for Vibranium

The social eruption for which there was no word became "the racial reckoning." Propelled by a vague sense of racial justice and directed by the strong antiracism rhetoric of Black Lives Matter and the friendly precepts of DEI organizational strategies, the reckoning achieved a brief pluralistic awareness of contemporary inequality, without meaningful accountability, before being overcome by the white backlash and subsequent reckoning of the MAGA movement. It could and should have been so much more. By 2020, new generations of Americans caught a glimpse of the racist vestiges of twentieth-century mistakes, schemes and policy atrocities. The story of African-American successes and failures had not yet been taken into twenty-first-century account, imprisoned in vague recollections of 1980s and 1990s reference points. The ways in which the structure of racial inequality had changed for African Americans – sometimes to isolate us, sometimes to align us with the experiences of diverse others – were being lived quietly by households, documented by academics and attacked mercilessly by conservative judges. But not reckoned with by the broader American public. A reckoning was overdue. By the spring of 2020, there was an undeniable sense that Black support for American democracy, 400 years in the giving, had not been sufficiently rewarded and that we continued to fall behind. George Floyd's horrific police lynching, complete with his plaintive pleas, and the casual indifference of the officers waiting for his life to leave him, all before a crowd of people standing outside in a pandemic that seemed to come specially for them, joined the unruly unimaginable of Trump's first term and set things off. The problem for this book, written just a few years later, is why couldn't the racial reckoning have meant as much as it warranted?

I have mostly tried to answer that question with an analysis of structural inequality that demonstrates how we should have focused on racial accountability for, rather than awareness of, the very real disparate impacts demonstrated in the racial wealth gap, racial health disparities and de facto immunity for racist policing. We have the evidence. The reckoning was a rare chance to make progress against the Struggle by informing a new generation's awareness of longstanding disparities for the purpose of accountability. Accountability demands a change in material outcomes, not sympathy, and therefore concrete policies of remediation. In police brutality, we had a brief window to direct public consciousness to unaddressed cruelties committed under color of state authority in order to enact reforms that would meaningfully deter excessive force. In health, this was a moment to surface the sources and causes of inflamed underlying health conditions so that structural changes would thereafter prevent the unimaginable losses of a pandemic from ever happening again. And in wealth inequality, 2020 was a time of intense housing insecurity that followed a decade of systemic wealth loss. During Covid this revealed to the nation a racial wealth gap whose cumulative waves of disinvestment, disproportionate taxation, gentrification, eviction, appraisal discrimination and all manner of predatory business behavior should have been enough to advance a public discourse about remedies.

It didn't.

The emphasis on accountability for Black life, like so many halfhearted efforts to address racial inequality, barely got started before fatigue, dilution and avoidance conditioned the resentment and faux victimization of white backlash. With Trump II, the original reckoning is as good as long gone.

In its place, however, are several things within Black agency. The big idea of national reckoning obscured the power of place to provide the resources for greater wealth, better health outcomes and more responsive public safety. Through more internal migrations than any other group since 2000, Blacks were trying to find their own reckoning.

It's time to conclude this examination of racial reckoning through a different lens. Some Black people led the racial reckoning and many participated, but no doubt the vast majority were preoccupied with a broader but related issue: well-being. What if the question of racial reckoning is better asked as, what do African Americans themselves seek in achieving a greater sense of well-being? After all, people all over the world demonstrate their desire for greater well-being through migration. The social upheavals in Europe and the United States today are contests between the demand to risk well-being elsewhere and the demand to preserve some idea of it by keeping others out. The Great Migration of African Americans from the South to Northern, Midwestern and Western cities between 1915 and 1970 amply showed the indomitable spirit of exit as a means of expressing dissatisfaction with one place-based reality in favor of another place-based reality somewhere else. Law and policy caught up with this idea of spatial determinacy. In the 1990s, the federal government experimented with the Moving to Opportunity demonstration project, which followed the housing segregation *Gautreaux* litigation, in which urban public housing residents sued to live in nonisolated, "high-opportunity" suburban neighborhoods.[1] The idea then and now is to facilitate racial and economic integration of high-opportunity areas by overcoming native resistance with regulatory sticks and carrots. Raj Chetty and other researchers' work on place and mobility has confirmed many of the basic assumptions about the benefits that would flow. However, years of HUD fair housing policies later, the good idea of encouraging antisegregation mobility strategies has had only mixed results.

But that's assuming we downplay the mobility choices and constraints of Black people themselves, which we won't.

AGAIN, MANY THOUSANDS GONE

Instead, as a final piece of research on racial reckoning, I went looking for "vibranium" – or rather, the evidence of what Black folk may believe is vibranium. The 2018 film "Black Panther" was a stunning box office success (almost $1.4 billion worldwide) and a cultural landmark for Black audiences, thrilled by the depiction of an all-Black paradise in Africa, called Wakanda. A study about the destinations that African Americans most often seek out and the places they leave the most would seem like a candidate for putting Wakanda in the title. But there might be many Wakandas or none. Migration suggests it's not the place itself that brings well-being, but the qualities of the place that help one achieve it. In *Black Panther*, that quality was a precious mineral found only in

Wakanda: vibranium. Vibranium's properties were so robust that it alone advanced educational and technological output, was an endless source of material resources and could be weaponized in order to keep Black people safe from all others. For that reason, it was sought after as a universal human asset (but, in the movie, by people who wanted to do really bad things like world war). My colleagues and I at the Rutgers Center on Law, Inequality and Metropolitan Equity (CLiME) wondered if the migrations and depopulations by and among African Americans in the twenty-first century suggested the ingredients of a kind of vibranium of Black well-being – and if, like the mineral in the movie, it was actually something that could benefit all people. The quantitative and qualitative "vibranium project" was on.

The findings are astonishing. It turns out that much of the movement for racial justice is just that: movement.

In the last quarter-century, Black population dynamics have quietly but dramatically changed their sense of spatial identity, defying twentieth-century characterizations of an "inner-city" people usually associated with ten major US cities across the North and West. Migration and population loss has been significant – more than for any other group during that period – and represents a self-reckoning tied consistently to complex notions of affordability. Sometimes we learn a lot from people's voting patterns, polling responses or consumer purchases. Yet as last century's Great Migration showed, nothing is as revealing as mobility. The amount of movement also reflects the disproportionate impacts of housing displacement brought about by the Great Recession (2008–11). Black households experienced high rates of eviction and foreclosure from which many took years to recover. Also, African Americans are mostly renters, and renters move more than homeowners for a variety of reasons. Indeed, African Americans' reasons for moving across the United States reflect several distinct trends, but underlying them all is a defining characteristic of contemporary capitalism: limited affordability, especially in housing, and a desire for a better place.

We looked for the top forty destinations in the country attracting African-American in-migration over the last twenty-five years ("pull places") and the top forty places Black folks exited during that period ("push places").[2] To do this, we looked at raw numbers for inbound, outbound and net migration of Black households, and then we examined

Black population change from 2000 to 2025. In order to make sense of these patterns, we looked at a range of qualitative sources to learn why people moved the way they did and what specific factors accounted for making a place a pull destination, a push jurisdiction or a place in flux. Ultimately, these factors were compiled into a weighted taxonomy that included multiple variables for housing, employment, health, education, public safety, wealth and segregation. Hundreds of places with over 10,000 Black people were scored. We tried to reconcile what we learned with a distinct sense of African-American well-being – the "vibranium" at the base of racial reckoning. Affordability runs through all the findings, though not always in ways one would suspect.

Four broad storylines emerged from the study.

First, Blacks are rapidly depopulating all of the Great Migration cities that became synonymous with Black identity during the twentieth century. In about twenty-five years, fourteen of the cities with the greatest number of Black residents have lost almost 1.5 million, compared to a total of 6 million Blacks who moved over sixty years in the Great Migration. The numbers in some cities are overwhelming. Chicago lost almost 300,000 Black people during the first quarter-century, New York City 200,000, Detroit 287,000, Los Angeles lost about 87,000 and Washington, DC, over 52,000. The gains were mainly in Southern cities, though New Orleans and Miami saw dramatic decreases in Black population.

Second, economic duress in the form of displacement, through gentrification, foreclosures and evictions, has caused a tremendous amount of movement within and around major cities. This aspect of general housing affordability has a distinctly disparate impact on Black households and reflects many of the cumulative disadvantages in housing wealth we saw in Chapter 3. There is no vibranium in housing insecurity.

Third, the largest category of moves are for better options within the same region, typically made by Black households who are dissatisfied with their current neighborhoods and want affordable quality-of-life improvements. This can mean different things in different parts of the country – suburbia or exurbia or small cities in the same metropolitan area. This category may represent the most resonant aspects of place-based well-being, affecting the most movers.

Fourth may be the closest thing to vibranium, in the form of larger, longer relocations to one of several mostly Southern destinations – what some call the "reverse migration" or "New Great Migration" – of more educated, affluent, younger Blacks. This is a mobility story where Blacks with resources take them to places in Georgia, Texas and North Carolina in order to convert those resources into more wealth, health and culture.

Let's look a little more closely at each.

EVACUATING CITIES

The large swaths of Black households that left major cities in the first quarter of this century were not pushed away without a fight. Urban identities are a lot to lose, especially as many cities recovered economically during this period. Coastal cities like Los Angeles, Boston, Seattle and New York were seen as the heart of US economic vibrancy beginning in the late 1980s. Yet Blacks were already starting to look elsewhere, without replenishing population with new births, or they were simply leaving them. It's been a quiet transformation in plain sight. Black folks *were* what cities are, a people often identified as "urban." New Orleans could not be New Orleans without the living history, culture and language of Black family life. Washington, DC, and Detroit were quintessential "chocolate cities" to be as much revered by Blacks as feared by others. Harlem, Bed-Stuy "Do or Die," "Oaktown," "South Central LA" – go on down the list: Blacks endured them when they were abandoned, helped build, lead and work them, suffered their poverty and near bankruptcies, created their cultures for others to copy and for a country, eventually, to adopt. Leaving them in large numbers would mean sacrificing political power and seniority, judgeships and organizational leadership, as well as the ability to influence the electoral votes of solidly Democratic states, missing out on the expanding tech sector that had revitalized urban regions from the Bay Area to Boston. By 2000, the most pressing question was, if cities were back, which ones, and would the millions of Black people identified with them share in their prosperity? Affordability is often negatively correlated with economic opportunity; leave economic growth for cheaper pastures at your peril. This has been the quandary for many Black households in traditional urban centers.

As we crossed the millennium, the narrative of what big cities mean, and for whom, fundamentally changed for many thousands of urban Blacks outside the South. An array of trends in economic urbanization dislodged both expectations and people: the housing whipsaw of predatory lending, subprime targeting and a devastating foreclosure crisis changing whole neighborhoods; gentrification and spiraling rents restarting after the Great Recession; the growth of a technology sector with a distinctly two-tiered employment and wage structure; housing competition with immigrant groups whose numbers, needs and preferences swelled during these decades yet whose settlement was often adjacent to Black-identified areas, if not in them (e.g., South LA); crime, racial profiling and what some simply called "nonsense"; affordability, affordability, affordability – and the corresponding desire for something better for the price. A given household's options were defined by their economic and cultural resources as well as their geographies, aspirations, age and opportunities. Many Americans faced these choices. However, the effect for many Black people was to launch three different kinds of searches for "vibranium."

DISPLACEMENT

The first group had little choice. Economic inequality widened dramatically during this period.[3] Save for the aughts before the 2008 crash, the twenty-first century has fine-tuned an affordability crisis into a weapon of displacement for many Americans, but disproportionately Black Americans. Displacement from New Orleans, for example, may have been started by the devastating racial cruelty of Hurricane Katrina in 2005 – the city lost more than 14,600 Black households from 2005 through 2009 and over 118,000 Black residents since 2000. However, those households shared a common acute economic vulnerability with those in other cities. During the aughts, predatory and subprime lenders concentrated their products in Black communities, offering homeownership at the price of unsustainable risk. Owners risked being underwater or facing increased costs, fees and taxes; renters faced spiraling rents and growing scarcity. The Great Recession wiped out a tremendous amount of Black wealth in just a few years, mostly in housing, where its ripple effects still linger.[4] Many Black homeowners became renters again, and the competition for affordable units became even harder.

The financialization of housing made it a more global business and less a local one. This changed the pace and rules of residential building and created scarcity[5] while creating new avenues to extract value from places through securitization on secondary markets. Tighter credit in turn created new opportunities for investors to become corporate landlords of foreclosed homes and – with the help and encouragement of the federal government – to buy up homes in predominantly Black neighborhoods and turn occupants who had been homeowners into renters.[6] Beginning around 2010, this buy-to-rent asset class of homes that were once the starter stuff of dreams has led to higher rents, fewer homes for sale and a new breed of more adversarial landlords who rely more on growing rents as passive income to investors than good relations with tenants. It's a wildly profitable business for investors in a market of scarcity, but the activity clearly drives up housing prices in myriad ways. The investor playbook used by both Wall Street firms and private equity spread rapidly across the South, Southwest and Midwest where investors bought thousands of foreclosed homes at government auctions. Since then, investors in single-family homes have learned strategies for serial purchases wherever they can buy low (often for cash or lower-cost financing) and rent high.

By the time of the pandemic in 2020, an eviction crisis was well underway, as scholars like Mathew Desmond have shown.[7] After Covid-era moratoria expired, eviction returned, uncured by state law interventions that failed to incorporate lessons about the numerous costs of displacement on families, especially children, and communities. These market-based ravages of unaffordability spurred a lot of Black households into less expensive inner-ring suburbs, substandard housing units they dare not complain about and a lot of rent burden – in Newark, for instance, a quarter of the population pays over half their incomes in rent.[8] Predictably, a growing percentage will leave for cheaper destinations, if they can find them.

Of all national moves CLiME studied, these represent the 16 percent of survey respondents who said they were "forced to move by a landlord, a bank, other financial institution, or government."[9]

Another way to be displaced is gentrification, something researchers on Harlem told us did not result in displacement as recently as 2004.[10] Yet just a few years later, the census revealed that Harlem lost 5,000 Black people between 2010 and 2020 while gaining 9,000 whites.[11] Bedford-Stuyvesant lost 28,000 Blacks while gaining 30,000 whites during the same period. Overall, the share of Black children in New York City schools declined from 35 percent in 2005 to 20 percent in 2023. We found similar patterns emerging in Jersey City and Newark, NJ.[12] According to a comprehensive report by the National Community Reinvestment Coalition, in the period between 1980 and 2020, gentrification's impact on 523 majority-Black neighborhoods yielded full racial turnover in a *third* of them (155), mostly in cities like Washington, DC, New York City, Philadelphia, New Orleans, Atlanta and the San Francisco Bay area.[13]

Gentrification has always eluded easy definition, but the term was coined in 1964 by Ruth Glass in order to describe a changing social landscape from working-class residents to middle- and upper-middle class people of any race. However, the class aspect has always been modified by race in the US, because gentrification is attached to development, a market business that responds quickly to changes in the profit potential of relatively less expensive land and the government incentives (e.g., tax breaks, subsidies; see Chapter 3) that often come with its redevelopment. Gentrification is not merely opportunistic real estate market strategy; it's government policy. It relies on lower-income urban people occupying the right spatial and economic circumstances to bring in more affluent newcomers at higher prices. Race has historically affected land values and neighborhood location. In Chapter 3, we saw how leveraging this grand racial bargain was behind the failed economic logic of urban renewal policy, beginning in downtown neighborhoods. Gentrification has always been the other side of local government redevelopment policies. Unlike the demolitions and forced removals of urban renewal, however, displacement by gentrification can include an accumulation of feelings associated with social fit as much as runaway costs. Sometimes people leave because the rent has increased 30 percent and there's no alternative to eviction. Other times, they decide it's time to leave when their Black child becomes one of only three in his once-diverse third grade, and the social isolations of economic status and race raise doubts about whether he'll become a target for excessive discipline.[14] Gentrification to the gentrified represents a loss not only of identification with a place but with the diversity and inclusion that made connection so valuable.

As a transplanted Harlemite, I remember watching it come over Fort Greene, Brooklyn, a neighborhood in the 1990s that was associated with the youthful energy of Black twenty- and thirty-somethings, Spike Lee's 40 Acres and a Mule production company and the distinct business sense of a cultural vanguard in literature, film, dance and the fine arts. This was organically grown vibranium, as we felt empowered by the productivity of each other's shared interests and presence, just as parents experienced that for their children playing on its brownstoned streets, or the comfort seniors felt growing old in a place near friends and church with the status of elders. Fort Greene was the place to be until all that artistic energy and lovely nineteenth-century architecture helped it become someone else's place to be. In 2000, Fort Greene was 41.8% Black, 31% white, 19.3% Hispanic and 4.2% Asian – and there were housing projects on both sides of the Brooklyn Queens Expressway. By 2023, Fort Greene had become 18.3% Black, 47.8% white, 14.4% Hispanic, and 10.7% Asian. The median income jumped several-fold to $156,870.[15] Some of the projects are gone, a result of more restrictive public housing authority policies, evictions and contractions. A few blocks away stand teeming residential skyscrapers that feature some of the highest rents in the city, indoor pools, rooftop decks, playrooms and minitheaters for residents only. (I left Brooklyn in 2011.)

Lost in these "neighborhood revitalizations" is not just affordability for Black people whose incomes and ownership rates didn't keep up with price inflation, but also the noneconomic aspects of vibranium's inherent well-being. The new vibranium catered to tastes that became more exclusive, condescending and less welcoming to long-time Black residents. The newcomers transformed the standards of place, attracting, if not demanding, the resources that Chetty described as beneficial to mobility. Displacement occurs when these benefits can't be shared and are no longer the product of broad community decision-making. In this sense, Fort Greene and neighborhoods like Capitol Hill in DC, Potrero Hill in San Francisco and Auburn-Gresham in Chicago represent the racial triumph of urban renewal's original plan. They reflect the distinctive displacement of social, cultural and economic marginalization. Undoubtedly, Blacks are not the only lower-income people gentrified out of their communities. But the losses are significant and harder to replace in tighter, more expensive urban housing markets. This is partly why many housing-insecure Black people moved to the exurbs of the

Pocono Mountains from New York City and Newark, or from Oakland, CA to Stockton or Antioch. Rolanda J.W. Spencer, whose family moved out to the Inland Empire, describes the experience of Black families like hers leaving their up-and-coming Los Angeles neighborhood of Inglewood as a "Blaxit":

> Time allowed us to play outside in Inglewood. We'd swim, skate, ride bikes, be fast, act out, be too grown and have a childhood all at the same time. We all knew each other, and it was all love. I loved Inglewood and thought Inglewood loved us enough to keep us forever. But it couldn't because everything we loved about Inglewood, everybody else began to love too.[16]

THE SEARCH NEARBY

The second group of movers is the largest – Black households whose sense of vibranium led them to more affordable places within the same region. Responses to the American Housing Survey show that quality-of-life indicators like better schools, better homes, lower poverty rates, more diversity, increased employment opportunities, cleaner air and a substantial Black presence represent the hope for vibranium within financial reach. Unlike the previous category of population losses, these are not characterized as displacement under duress but rather voluntary, sometimes with good results, sometimes with long commutes and acute regret. Most Black households' relocations were local (within the same county). Neighboring counties tend to be the top destinations of choice across the board, reflecting a movement of Black households from large cities to the fringes of metropolitan areas, trading the benefit of increased housing affordability for the burden of longer commutes to jobs in the urban core. Housing affordability is the critical determinant in this migration trend, though affordability does not necessarily translate to homeownership. These regional "pull" jurisdictions are represented by smaller cities, suburbs and exurbs of the Baltimore to Washington, DC, corridor; Lansing, Calumet City, Park Forest and South Holland near Chicago; Lancaster and Palmdale outside of Los Angeles; and suburban Detroit.

The sum of vibranium elements does not always add up to paradise. Look, for example, in Southern California where there has been a hollowing out of what was once the epicenter of Los Angeles from traditional settlements of Blacks in Compton, Carson, Hawthorne and other South LA communities to the deserts of the Inland Empire and Antelope Valley. These moves represented the mixed promise of cheaper land, less crime and sheer hope but yielded extremely long commutes and isolation. Since 2000, Lancaster and Palmdale – adjacent cities of about 170,000 people each – saw an influx of Black households of 17,000 and 6,000, respectively. The Antelope Valley is far north of LA jobs, with commutes into the city of sometimes two and three hours each way. Subdivisions proliferated on its desert flatlands, drawing Blacks from traditional South LA areas like Watts and Compton that are now over three-quarters Latino. But "anti-Black racism tends to follow Black people wherever they go," as one observer put it.[17] Losing political power and social support networks in South LA, some Blacks who moved north discovered a racial hostility in the desert, expressed in attitudes, policies and policing.[18] For instance, Lancaster was among many cities that reacted to changing demographics by adopting restrictive "crime-free housing" rules that train landlords to deny rental applicants with criminal histories and requires landlords to evict tenants even accused of breaking the law, a policy that disproportionately affected Blacks and Latinos. According to the *Los Angeles Times*, "Among the 20 California cities with the largest increases in Black residents since 1990, 85% have approved crime-free housing policies."[19] Racially charged incidents like the hanging death of young Robert Fuller in 2020 elicited fears of Palmdale's fraught racial history.[20]

A different version of the mobility search emerges from the DC–Baltimore corridor where geography and a more established Black presence have expanded the number of jurisdictions where Black people seeking more affordable options have moved since 2000. In that time, Washington, DC lost 52,540 Blacks and Baltimore lost 72,416. Most of the Black moves are to relatively nearby jurisdictions along the I-95 corridor. The largest increase in Black population was in Bowie, MD, which gained 17,188 Black residents from 2000 to 2023. Bowie has low poverty, low unemployment, affordable housing prices and a large Black population. Importantly, more than half of Black households have college degrees, and Bowie has a high wealth index score. Similarly, Waldorf, MD, is in Charles County, which lies just south of Prince George's County. Though Waldorf is further out, it has seen a Black population increase of 33,791 from 2000 through 2023. Again, our taxonomy showed that Waldorf, like Bowie, has good affordability, low poverty, low unemployment, and a decent wealth index score. The pull to a sense of vibranium is strong, especially for middle-class Blacks with resources. By 2019, 56 percent of new residents in Charles County had moved there from Prince George's County.[21] As K.R. Lacy argues, middle-class Black families often desire communities where their children can grow up surrounded by other successful Black individuals, fostering a normalized perception of Black success.[22] According to the American Community Survey, Charles County is now the highest-income majority-Black county in the United States, with a median household income of $104,000. Its population gains, like most of the others in this corridor, come from people already familiar with the region who are seeking the advantages of a perceived vibranium closer to a former home.

RELOCATING FOR VIBRANIUM

And then there are those intrepid, perhaps connected, often younger Blacks, with jobs and resources, who are willing to do as their grand and great-grandparents did and relocate to an entirely new state of opportunity, usually in the South. This is a true mobility story of reckoning by relocation. Our research confirmed much of the so-called "reverse migration" or "New Great Migration" research that scholars like William Frey at Brookings have written about.[23] This is the phenomenon of Black households leaving cities with large traditional Black populations in the North to return to cities and suburbs in Southern states like North Carolina, Georgia and Texas. Specifically, they're pulled to Raleigh, Greensboro and Charlotte, the Atlanta suburban metro, Dallas and Houston. (There are also a few places in Florida, Ohio and Minnesota.) Unlike the Great Migration, the travel routes do not always fit neatly along train and bus routes, though they tend to be somewhat regional. The economic "Blaxit" from California has either landed in Texas cities from which many Black Californians came originally, or into places where there was no significant Black presence at all until recently: Phoenix and Las Vegas. In Phoenix, 87 percent of Black households moving in are from out of state, and for Las Vegas it's 98 percent. These Southern cities are attracting in-migrants from local areas, too.

Nearly all these moves of spatial self-determination were anchored in economic opportunity. Our findings reaffirm how Black well-being draws sustenance from the availability of employment, business ecosystems that support Black entrepreneurship, and political systems that support Black economic success. In places where such economic scaffolding is present, we see conditions in which Black individuals and families can thrive, not merely survive. In contrast, we observed a systematic exodus of residents from places like Detroit that were not perceived to have the same supportive networks for Black entrepreneurship or career building. Metropolitan Atlanta, for instance, is often championed as the dynamic center of this economic, cultural and political universe. The writer Charles Blow has made a mission out of attracting African Americans to retake the political power that their ancestors were building there after Reconstruction.[24] Indeed, we found that the Atlanta in-migration has spread to other parts of Georgia, including much smaller towns and suburbs.

However, North Carolina has emerged as a key destination in the "New Great Migration," attracting a significant share of the Black American population relocating within the United States. Of the top twenty jurisdictions with the highest number of Black in-migrants over the past two decades, four are located in North Carolina: Charlotte, Raleigh, Greensboro and Kinston. According to Ben Sprung-Keyser, Nathaniel Hendren and Sonya Porter, Charlotte and Raleigh rank as the seventh and eighth most popular destinations for Black millennials (those born between 1984 and 1992) who have moved away from their childhood homes.[25] These migration flows reflect broader labor market dynamics and demographic shifts, as younger, college-educated Black professionals seek out regions that offer job opportunities as well as safety, and a sense of belonging. Consequently, these cities' rapid Black population growth is also drawn from relatively low unemployment rates, strong public education systems, and neighborhood-level racial diversity.[26] North Carolina is also a thriving center of Black-owned businesses. Charlotte alone is home to more than 13,000 Black-owned enterprises and is a regional hub for several Fortune 500 companies.[27] The physical landscape and urban design of North Carolina's major cities also serve as pull factors. Compared to many coastal metropolitan areas, cities like Charlotte and Raleigh are less congested, offer greater ease of transportation and provide more affordable homeownership opportunities. Home prices are comparatively affordable in Raleigh and Charlotte. Planned infrastructure projects, such as the GoTriangle commuter rail system, aim to improve mobility between suburban zones and urban employment centers in Raleigh.[28] This combination of affordability, access and investment in transit makes North Carolina's urban development increasingly appealing for upwardly mobile Black families and individuals.

Importantly, well-being is not only economic and not all Black migrants are motivated by material necessity. Many are already middle-class professionals relocating for lifestyle considerations. They are in search of *cultural ecosystems* – spaces that affirm their racial identity, creative pursuits and collective aspirations. They found spaces where the aesthetics of Black life (art, music, fashion, leisure) are not only visible, but dynamically reproduced and reimagined. And critically, these are often environments that offer psychological safety and modes of being unencumbered by hypersurveillance or social erasure. High-vibranium localities are frequently described as "Black-friendly," offering a strong sense of place rooted in cultural expression and civic participation while, as one respondent told a *Washington Post* reporter, allowing her to be "inconspicuously Black."[29] Charlotte's repeated inclusion in *Essence* magazine's list of top destinations for Black Americans further affirms its cultural significance. Importantly, the growing political power of the Black population in Charlotte has contributed to transforming North Carolina from a traditionally conservative stronghold into a more politically competitive, purple state.

The search for vibranium as seen in these distance moves modifies an old local government idea of exit power. The academic literature on localism has long exalted economist Charles Tiebout's idea of the "consumer-voter,"[30] who votes with their feet and thereby forces communities to accommodate their preferences or risk losing them to other jurisdictions. This 1950s-based idea always seemed to assume a white middle-class consumer-voter. Our research shows that the consumer-voter in the twenty-first century is quite often Black, and they won't stand for their preferences – and dollars – being overlooked, overcharged and undercounted either. More importantly, they have the economic resources to demand the purchase of noneconomic resources in return. Their mobility patterns strike a different bargain for basic goods and services tied to place, one no longer devalued by race. And this group – younger, more affluent and educated – will relocate across state lines to find it. Although the 1950s consumer-voter, like the rational white actor from Chapter 3, usually sought to preserve racial homogeneity, the twenty-first-century update suggests two things. First, Tiebout's thesis may have supported 1960s open housing advocacy by capturing the consumer-voter's rational racism. Those laws eventually opened up housing options once closed. However, Black consumer-voters seem distinctly less interested in integrating white neighborhoods in order to avail themselves of superior public goods. Second, today Black consumer-voters nevertheless prefer to live in less segregated neighborhoods, confirming the evidence that Black sociologists taught us decades ago about Black households preferences compared to whites, Hispanics or Asians.[31] What enriches vibranium for them, however, is the substantial presence of other African Americans, too.

CONCLUSION

So, what does the vibranium metaphor ultimately mean for reckoning? Is it a kind of well-being that belongs to African Americans, who are consigned, like the Black Panther story, to safeguard it from theft by others?

The 2020–22 racial reckoning and its continuing (as of this writing) backlash taught that an episodic moment of recognition of the African-American struggle against structural inequality is always fleeting because racial injury is automatically contested, diluted by similar claims against antidemocratic structures and organized into various awareness fora where the Rules of Avoidance, Denial and the heartbeat of cynical pendulation consistently defeat the accountability mechanisms that would actually remedy it. The structural backlash at the state and national levels is seemingly indefatigable. Racism works too well as a strategy to defeat the exigencies of equity – not just racial equity – in our politics and our judicial doctrines. These are hard truths for a generation of Americans committed to the demands of racial justice. The surgical attacks on DEI, health equity, environmental justice and affirmative action in the cynical name of antidiscrimination and white victimhood studied in these pages show it will be hard to extend Black lives as long as other lives, to remedy the cumulative disadvantages of so-called meritocracy and "race-neutral" denials of access, to upend the ravages of racial bargaining and market-justified displacement that undermine wealth opportunity and housing security and to perpetuate the immoral horror of undeterred police violence. Without a pervasive value of racial equity active in our primary institutions, the Struggle continues.

However, most of the lessons are local. National policies at the Congressional and executive level have no doubt consumed our attention because they are powerful, incendiary and no doubt consequential. Yet the struggle to remedy cumulative disparate racial impacts of so many aspects of wealth, health and policing inequality are fundamentally local. The ingredients of wealth creation are mostly local. Housing policies, economic development and employment patterns, sources of labor income, markets for businesses and entrepreneurship as well as taxes, fees and eviction-foreclosure policies are largely determined locally. Rules about development, landlord–tenant relationships, contracting and small-business opportunities, rent regulation and the fees and fines we levy on productive activity are mostly creatures of local government policy, informed by the states. That's federalism and localism at work. Similarly, racial heath disparities accrue in large part because of local social determinants of health, the availability of low-cost quality food distribution and state laws about medical care administered by local health-care providers. Policing and public safety, the third prong of the racial reckoning, is mostly carried out through state and local police power mandates, rules and institutional practices. The federal government is only a junior partner in the public safety you experience. These are all *local* public goods and services. They are the very thesis of self-government in our democratic system. The quality of all of them vary dramatically based on place, one of the only attributes we can individually and collectively control.

Hence the African-American search for well-being, like the promise of racial reckoning, relies on what we make of where we are.

My vibranium experiment demonstrates that Black people have been very attuned to the relative prospects for their own material, political and cultural reckoning in a nation still wedded to white supremacy and the manifest inequalities of "late-stage" capitalism. Like our twentieth-century forebears, this chapter has shown that we are not waiting to be saved.

African-American agency is resplendent and many-faceted, and one of its many strategies – shared by millions of others around the country and the world – is to move to our own opportunities. The mass deidentification with the cities in which our great-grandparents, grandparents and parents became associated is demonstrably possible. We will go where we can grow.

In this way, vibranium is us; we can be our own vibranium. It is what we make of our own hardworking resources, even if we must leave our historic places to make it in another. We find or remake different local structures. We understand affordability in complex ways. Vibranium is the democratic power we wield through struggle, clear purpose and enlightened self-interest. When allies drop off, it's still ours to make. When the federal government attacks our freedoms with slurs, executive orders and the inequitable permutations of ahistorical colorblindness, they are our freedoms to retake. To be unyoked from the constraints of structural inequality is freedom. Vibranium is freedom.

Yet we are not all so free. Many of us still struggle to harness its power. The relative promise of vibranium is still class-based. We cannot all leave even when we're displaced. Millions of Black people still want to be in the cities where they live (and the inner-ring suburbs and rural areas where they're rooted). Local agency, therefore, requires policies of equitable growth, significant investments in public health and a dedication to the trust that comes with true public safety. I'll recite but a few here from earlier chapters. We must ensure affordability of the resources necessary for success, and we must remedy the constraints on Black dignity and liberty. This means policies like living wages, guaranteed income and rental assistance, access to daycare and adequate transportation infrastructure. Predatory capitalism – often subsidized at the state and local levels – must be regulated by demonstrable enforcement against corporate landlording, equitable tax credit policies that don't fuel gentrification and rent controls that lower both housing costs and profits on displacement. The standards for health-care professionals and law enforcement must demonstrate increased trust, lower crime and effective interventions while deterring malfeasance through community-based partnership and accountable deterrence penalties. Overall, we need a governing ethos that values the dignity of working people and their families. This is only as radical as a suburban American dream created decades ago for generations of some Americans. If that's what makes America great, we can do it again for all.

So, is vibranium merely a Black notion of well-being, a self-reckoning whose chemical properties are at risk of being stolen by others? This has been a book about racial reckoning on behalf of African Americans that reflects my years of study as a scholar-advocate. It was a deliberate decision on my part not to attempt to show at every turn the parallels to Native Americans, Latinos or oppressed minorities of any kind. That was not only for the sake of concision. That focus reflected my deep belief that what is generally good for Black people – in wealth fairness, health outcomes and policing justice – is generally good for *all* people. The disparate impacts of a national affordability crisis, to take one example, shows not just disparity but broad impact. I hope many non-Black readers see their own experiences and struggles in these pages. What the contest against inequality shows, of course, is a contest for democracy, equity and inclusion against structural forces that have been well orchestrated to limit opportunity for far too many of us whatever our identity. If Black people's lives are lengthened and enriched by addressing the social determinants of health, so will the lives of their neighbors. If we enforce policies to prevent neighborhood predation and discriminatory housing practices, that will redound to all similarly vulnerable Americans. When racism ceases to infect policing, many more lives will be saved, and more trust will save others. Vibranium can't be stolen because others have it, too. It's already shared. But we must put it to greater use.

Epilogue: Principles and Strategies to Account for Well-Being

One of the most mistaken assumptions of the 2020 racial reckoning was that it would occur at a national level – large policy shifts, broadly implemented, based on an enhanced awareness of systemic racism. When that didn't happen and, worse, an anti-woke backlash ripened into a full-on federal counter-reckoning, many proponents of racial justice felt the dual sting of betrayal and hopelessness. Fortunately, that view overlooks the possibilities for change in the particular communities where we actually live. Federal tax policy and constitutional standards no doubt influence the chances for a racially just society. Yet racial inequality is mostly mediated by more mundane stuff like land use and housing policy, police and school district practices, state tax incentive programs, public health investments, regional banking regulation and the persistence and priorities of community-based organizations, nonprofits and foundations. These things affect us in more immediate and material respects. One way to imagine racial reckoning, as we saw in the last chapter on internal migration, is Black well-being.

For these reasons, racial reckoning in the immediate future will be conducted primarily at the state and local levels where the goals of racial justice and remediation can be addressed through the public and private race-neutral policies and strategies pursued by influential institutions. Place is nearly as determinative of justice as race, because it is the market for the exchange of public goods. This reflects the mostly local truth about racial inequality dynamics and also the current hostile state of federal policy. The foregoing chapters reckoned with strategy mishaps of the original reckoning, the backlash and structural counter-reckoning and the empirical case to be made for material reforms in closing the racial wealth gap, reducing racial health disparities and deterring racially disparate police misconduct. I bracketed these discussions with analyses of what we mean by the problem to be solved – racial inequality – and what can still be made of the most popular means to do it – DEI programming. Ultimately, I boiled reckoning down to a question: where can Black well-being be found in the US? Black well-being, it turns out, might resemble everybody else's well-being with the exception of institutional racism – perhaps the single most destructive flaw in American democracy. This epilogue summarizes the actions proposed along the way.

Although I've raised more questions than answers, I hope to contribute more than an artful redescription of miserable situations. My approach to reckoning gives rise to a template of solutions, no doubt incomplete, but a summary framework for future action by real people. Below, I organize the summary around the different chapter topics, but it moves from the abstract to the specific: principles and values first, followed by broad goals, then responsible institutions, strategies last.

The principles of accountability reckoning explored throughout this book come down to the following:

- Reckoning means accounting for the material demands of demonstrated racial inequality.
- Racial inequality must be shown, not merely asserted.
- Reducing the demonstrated effects of racial inequality is more consistent with the intent of equal protection than preserving some hypothetical equality.
- Equity demands accountability.
- Racial reckoning entails making racial equity a value that unavoidably takes race into account.
- Accountability for the harms of racial inequality entails actual racial remediation.
- The scope of remediation includes many kinds of direct and indirect racial harms, the traceable past as well as the continuing present.
- Racial harm may be caused cumulatively and by disparate impact.
- Any policy that advances the premise of white supremacy is harmful regardless of what it specifically produces.
- Democracy relies on trust.

As for goals, the first is fundamental: Black people must be able to expect generational progress in every material aspect of well-being like everyone else. This is a bedrock American assumption that applies to all groups except the two most overdue for accountability reckoning: African Americans and Native Americans. The idea that Black representation in university classrooms, boardrooms and positions of access not only stagnates but dramatically declines over time, while Black representation among drug overdoses, homelessness and deaths by police continues to grow demands structural remedies, whoever the nation's president happens to be.

The second goal is epistemic: we have to know what. That is, we need the institutional resources to generate reliable data and other modes of information about the issues we address in the name of reckoning. It seems as easy as saying we need to know what we're talking about, but reliable knowledge production is expensive, contested and offers a maze of delays and complications, especially in an age of separate digital universes. However, we can't address specific policy needs without a sophisticated understanding of the problems. Once we know, we can set realistic targets, reach them or hold each other accountable for failing to do so.

Third, place-based development strategies should rely on a theory of equitable growth, where growth is viewed not strictly in economic terms and equity modifies every notion of who benefits. Nearly every facet of American life sees progress through the necessity of growth, often at all costs. Equity shapes growth for the benefit of a larger public, and publicly assisted growth should be justified on that basis.

Fourth, housing security is paramount. Practically every variable in people's lives – job access, social determinants of health, mental stress levels, educational access, wealth capacity, relationship to law enforcement – tracks back to whether people have safe and stable homes.

Fifth, civil rights enforcement must be predictable in both civil and criminal matters, including policing. Many aspects of racial reckoning involve violations of existing antidiscrimination laws unenforced because of a lack of public infrastructure or by doctrinal design.

Sixth, collaborative, all-in efforts to produce structural change should replace more competitive models. Too often at the local level we address problems of racial inequality in piecemeal, fragmented ways where multiple individual entities decide unilaterally to devote scarce resources to solving, say, health and housing issues. While they may satisfy other individual or institutional goals, their diffusion of efforts wastes opportunities to concentrate resources on historically difficult problems and dilutes lessons learned.

Seventh, everything we call social services should be consciously humanized in order to deliver dignity to the recipients. The disadvantaged, differently abled and people otherwise in need of public assistance are too often punished for their status in what they get and how they get it. Affirming their dignity with the services we provide builds trust, and trust is a growth strategy.

Institutions and strategies fall under the subject areas below.

RACIAL INEQUALITY

Racial inequality is, as I've asserted, the race-based denial of resources necessary for the opportunity to flourish as an individual and a community. This entails mostly a material analysis of unequal inputs and outcomes, which means it can be measured and proven. These can include examples like access to K-12 trajectories with Advance Placement curricula, participation in capital-building business training, career internships or online counseling services. Some resources are provided publicly, some privately, many are both; most come with the place you're in. Consensus proof of race-based inequality would get us a long way toward determining the problems we're committing to remedy. It also helps disprove harms asserted in the name of abstract colorblindness. Facts shouldn't divide us. Claims of meritocracy shouldn't absolve us of quantifying unfair advantage. Valuing racial equity is a necessary feature of these efforts, not an afterthought. Once persistent racial inequality is demonstrated to a generation of people blind to it, simple fairness compels us to adopt equitable policies that share the burdens, remedy cumulative disadvantages and design for a greater good. Continuing a raw competition for scarce spoils fuels inequality. The underlying goal should be a deconcentration of social capital – that is, ensuring that people underrepresented among those with access to growth resources can consistently access them too.

Most institutions contribute to the persistence of racial inequality, but all should have an obligation to reduce racial inequality whether or not it arises from antidiscrimination law. Defining those obligations is the work of local institutions – school districts, public and private employers, universities, police departments, state and local public agencies – but it requires identifying the inequities of procedure that produce concrete inequalities. You can't solve what you don't know. It often requires research. The research can be produced by educational institutions such as universities, nonprofit research institutes and public research divisions in housing or health departments to prioritize regular monitoring of unequal outcomes and policy performance. Private philanthropies offer another important source of institutional leadership on racial inequality, because their mission, credibility and status allow them to act without government interference on the principle that racial equity requires resources. Public interest lawyers should counsel on what models of equitable procedure look like.

THE WEALTH GAP

Chapter 3 on the wealth gap and racial bargaining focused on race-conscious neighborhood displacement policies that codified segregation at mid-century and laid the groundwork for depressed wealth opportunities in Black-identified neighborhoods ever since. This was municipal and regional wealth planning for both its beneficiaries and its victims. Therefore, we can think of it under policies of equitable growth. These can be enacted at the state, county or municipal level. They are a way to harness growth on behalf of all, especially current residents, and prevent the displacement we saw in Chapters 3 and 7.

The primary institutions involved are government, private developers (including community and nonprofit developers), public housing authorities, state taxing and economic development authorities, community-based service and advocacy organizations and legislative bodies. The point is to modify the growth-at-all-cost perspective of many localities that see their fate within a finite competition for affluent new (young, childless) residents, and to reimagine growth trajectories that plan for the life cycles of residents of all socioeconomic classes. In fact, growth is equitable when it creates avenues for opportunity among people currently outside of it. As one mayor put it, it means policies that promote "gentrification from within."

Strategically, this premise accompanies findings on just who is systematically disadvantaged by past and present growth initiatives, which inevitably leads us back to the intersection of race and good governance. This can mean policies like affordability monitoring where crossing thresholds triggers regulatory action; local hiring mandates and contracting incentives to circulate investments and grow the capacity of small businesses and business clusters; tax-base sharing to reduce intermunicipal competition; equitable tax incentive programs, where the public's return on investment precludes wealth transfers of public dollars to affluent corporations with little demonstrated return; rental and down-payment housing assistance; baby bonds and similar cost-effective wealth-building entitlements; guaranteed income programs for eligible recipients; and social services audits, where providers are accountable both for *what* services they deliver to low-income people and *how* they do it.

REPARATIONS FOR URBAN RENEWAL

Because my original analysis described one specific federal–local policy and its implications at length, it's important to set out a few conceptual buckets of what accountability reckoning could look like. Since the Supreme Court has said that traceable racial harms arising from race-conscious government policies might be actionable, and since records exist that could theoretically result in direct damages to identifiable claimants, I consider this a form of reparations. It warrants an overview. (Readers can read more in my article on which Chapter 3 is based.[1])

We start with the character of the wrongs. Urban renewal consisted of both intentional and negligent harms; that is, as federal–local government policy, it constituted both intentional racism as well as disparate impact racial harm from facially neutral rules and practices.

There are many ways to value what was lost by these wrongs, each with their own causal complexity. A simplified analysis might create three buckets or categories – urban renewal's direct and indirect costs to Black displacees and urban renewal's more lasting segregative effects on Black wealth.

In the first bucket, direct contemporaneous harms, records identify owners and renters who received little to no compensation or relocation assistance; they or their heirs would receive that plus interest. They should also receive a portion of the improved value of the confiscated land resulting from their forcible removal and some of the future value that actual recipients accrued. Their involuntary sacrifice made these gains possible.

The second bucket consists of urban renewal's contemporaneous indirect costs on both Black displacees as well as eligible Blacks who were excluded because of race from a given region's homeownership opportunities. This might be comprised of lost opportunity costs – the price of exclusion from homeownership offers their white coworkers received. Another indirect cost is the monetary value of access to social capital that came with suburban homeownership.

The third bucket values the peculiar indirect costs that urban renewal's plan of segregation set in motion. These are the neighborhood-based costs arising from federal and local government policies that conditioned Black-identified markets beginning at mid-century. Restitution for this bucket of harms can come in many forms, such as discounted mortgage rates for eligible applicants, tax benefits for zone-based consumer transactions or hiring plans, and direct subsidies for underfunded public goods; most target the cumulative history of disinvestment, though neighborhoods change along with their resident beneficiaries.

Finally, there are the myriad costs of racial bargaining – another extension of the cumulative segregative effects bucket. While causation dynamics might be hard to overcome conceptually, we could certainly do a lot more to protect existing Black wealth from the waves of predatory economic activity to which it's been periodically vulnerable. Consumer fraud enforcement, real estate regulation and equitable local taxation rules could do a lot to lower costs and increase certainty. Racial bargaining is a set of economic norms that can be deterred through regulation.

RACIAL HEALTH DISPARITIES

Chapter 4 chronicled a large body of physical and mental health research in order to understand how Covid made black the color of viral risk and excess death. (Readers can find more detail about these findings in my article on which the chapter is based.[2]) We asked, if so much boils down to "underlying conditions," why do Black people suffer from so many that imperil their health? The answers came from two areas of research – environments and medical treatment. The social determinants of health and the disparate treatment by the medical profession structure the inequality of health outcomes, or "racial health disparities."

Three racial reckoning goals follow. First, the neighborhood must keep the score. Because Black-identified areas carry greater health risks for the people who live there, those risks should be standardized, regularly assessed, publicized and made part of a treatment plan that governs how public health dollars are spent. It's imperative that the numbers improve – on diabetes control, neonatal visits, blood pressure compliance, prostate monitoring etc. If they don't, there must be accountability imposed from state agencies, with funding implications and provider contracts put at risk until *neighborhoods* meet adequacy standards.

Second, make industry providers defend against the evidence. Professional accountability in the United States usually results from one of three sources – the oversight of professional licensing organizations like the American Medical Association, the market or malpractice lawsuits. The first two have not done enough to challenge the position of doctors and medical organizations to overcome patterns of substandard care, often as a result of implicit bias. This leaves lawsuits. Successful malpractice suits for implicit bias against doctors causing avoidable harm to Black patients would open up a new line of liability exposure that would lead to new institutional treatment norms and the greater caregiver–patient trust so critical to health maintenance. A state attorney general's office, however, could investigate it and either recommend legislative changes to ease the way for lawsuits or bring one itself. A few successful cases would establish a clear record of unlawful conduct, legally binding standards of care and an insurance industry incentivized to impose change on medical treatment norms. Malpractice by implicit bias should become rare.

Third, this era cannot stand. Because not all public health is state and local, the nation will need to rebuild the federal infrastructure supporting public health that Trump has dismantled. To do otherwise is to reinforce the structural racism that produces distinctly shorter and sicker lives by race. Federal tax dollars subsidize our health-care system. No functioning democracy ignores the disproportionate health outcomes of its population because of their race.

POLICE DETERRENCE

My argument in Chapter 5 is that the system of law enforcement oversight is not designed to deter police misconduct. As a result, racist and racially disparate conduct will largely go without consequence until we commit to deterrence in the rules and policies that govern the use of state-sponsored force. Although many potential constraints are found in federal law, police accountability is clearly within the purview of local control – the source of most funding. Adjacent police departments can have radically different use-of-force cultures, as we saw. (Readers can find more detail about these findings in my article on which the chapter is based.[3]) The George Floyd Justice in Policing Act, along with other federal incentive programs, would have significantly advanced the sort of consistent local reforms that accountability reckoning demands. Yet it contains many basic tenets of misconduct deterrence that can be adopted by state and local agencies and departments. These include vigilant use-of-force recordkeeping, including about individual police officers, and transparency in making records public. Access to police misconduct records is essential for victims of police brutality, lawmakers responsible for regulating and allocating funds to police departments, and criminal defendants claiming police abuse in their arrest or investigation.[4] The National Registry of Exonerations found in 2020 that "[i]n 54% of exonerations, official misconduct contributed to the false convictions; usually more than one type of misconduct."[5] As of 2021, police misconduct records were kept partially or entirely confidential in thirty-five states.[6]

States can seek a consistent set of conduct standards. There is currently no national definition for "reasonable," "necessary," or "excessive" use of force.[7] There is also no national, centralized database that tracks police use of force.[8] In "the most comprehensive analysis of police use of force ever conducted in the United States," the organization Mapping Police Violence was only able to obtain data from law enforcement agencies covering 60 percent of the US population.[9]

Doctrinal legal reforms like the proposed modification of qualified immunity remain possible under state law. Given the stagnancy in Congress and slow, if any, shift in the doctrine in the federal courts,[10] states and municipalities are considering a cause of action equivalent to §1983 that bars the defense of qualified immunity.[11] Colorado, New Mexico, and New York City have all created causes of action against the conduct of peace officers, government actors or police officers who deprive citizens of their state constitutional rights, to which officers may not assert qualified immunity as a defense.[12]

In general, a host of reforms have proven effective in deescalating interactions and saving lives. States and localities could increase the investigatory powers of independent bodies, ban no-knock warrants in drug cases, incentivize a ban on chokeholds, require body cameras, prohibit racial profiling, improve training and hiring of diverse law enforcement departments and study ways to change the warrior culture of law enforcement. States and localities should limit the collective bargaining power of police unions to receive a range of exculpatory exclusions described in the chapter that impede investigations and undermine deterrence. Local police departments can also determine, based on substantial evidence, that certain conduct is needlessly risky. For instance, the benefits of certain kinds of traffic stops are simply not worth the cost in lives and the heightened risk of lawsuits during those encounters. Police brutality is too often a cost business. State policies can change who internalizes the costs of bad behavior. Police brutality may not yet be expensive enough for the departments whose officers are most responsible for it. The public should not subsidize violations of civil rights. Finally, beyond deterrence is trust, which can be rebuilt with many models of the community-based criminal justice programs at work around the country.

DIVERSITY, EQUITY AND INCLUSION

Unlike other aspects of accountability reckoning that can be conducted through local institutional reforms and/or race-neutral policies, the defense of DEI must be conducted primarily through litigation. This is especially true for counteracting the erasure of racial identity expression. The two-pronged attack of politically punitive anti-DEI policies backed up by the threat of legal action to enforce extreme colorblind norms has put fundamental rights at risk. The right to self-expression can't be negotiated or politically waited out. These cases must be brought and won. A society that can pendulate between Black Lives Matter one year and silent acquiescence in renouncing it just a few years later can't be trusted to protect Black people's rights to seek what I argue is necessary redress for racial inequality – whether DEI policies, reparations or something else in which race must be named. Successful litigation will change the power imbalance between governments on one side and institutions and their members on the other. This, in turn, will reopen a marketplace of ideas where people can again advocate for remedial diversity, equity and inclusion frameworks or whatever one chooses to call them.

Restoring efforts to remedy the concentration of social capital among a privileged few groups in our institutions will take more than litigation. It will demand much greater energy for inclusion and belonging than we've seen amid the backlash to racial reckoning. Generations of Black and other young people rely on a broad dedication to racial equity as a core national value that resides in classrooms with them, is unquestioned among their peers, informs their prospective employers and constitutes a background of decency in all their interactions. The goal is to reincorporate racial equity as a principle of institutional life so that stereotype, exclusion and silencing no longer dictate the good work of a diverse and deserving people. The legacy of this era cannot be performance and then surrender to retributive supremacy, but rather reconciliation and rededication to democratic justice.

LOCAL RESOURCES – VIBRANIUM

In Chapter 7, I discussed original research that showed how for at least twenty-five years many thousands of Black households have been seeking their own reckoning in different places, quietly migrating away from traditional urban settings and looking elsewhere for a kind of "vibranium" of resources. I suggested we might think of reckoning instead as improved well-being. We may not yet know exactly what constitutes well-being, but we have some idea based upon the most voluntary moves. Affordability connects all categories of movers. In fact, affordability itself seems to be a consideration in valuing the resources people believe they need to thrive and not merely survive. If I cannot afford to flourish here, where should I go where I can?

We can't all leave unaffordable, inequitable places, but we can seek greater racial equity and affordability where we are. The mix of resources may come from public or private sources – the schools, health-care providers, employment. The housing infrastructure should accommodate a substantial middle class, with a range of affordability safeguards. These places should offer myriad answers to questions like, what activities can children of *all* ages do here? What transportation options allow people of all ages and abilities to be mobile? Is there enough access to healthy food? What makes people feel safe? How do we celebrate our excellence and lift each other up? We're seeking well-resourced localities. A few strategies illustrate the point.

In housing, jurisdictions often fail to adequately embed fair housing policies into their master plans, housing codes and other residential regulations. If they did, we'd have a market freer of many arbitrary exclusions. While not always discriminatory in the traditional sense, lease provisions that ban people with criminal records or women who seek police intervention for domestic violence are just as discriminatory as failing to accommodate people with disabilities. Aggressive patterns of evictions exceed normal levels of market exclusion and burden all taxpayers with the costs of displacement and homelessness. A lack of code enforcement is a direct contributor to the social determinants of health. A fair housing policy incorporated into housing policy would add a layer of protections that tame market excesses and allow more people to live with security. Strategies like a right to counsel for indigent tenants prevents many unwarranted eviction actions. Rent control and rent stabilization come in many forms and can be tailored to local housing conditions and lead to more stable tenure and profits for tenant and landlord. During Covid, countless rental assistance programs proved themselves effective and cost effective; they should expand. Predatory real estate practices – often subsidized at the state and local levels – must be regulated at the state and local levels before they completely subvert homeownership and rental markets in entire neighborhoods. The growing interest group of corporate landlords (1–4 unit homes) is becoming a powerful lobbying presence that threatens local democracy. Tax credit policies offer important incentives but must contain guardrails against gentrification – for instance, no subsidies for luxury new development.

Behind the wealth gap is, among other things, a concentration of the resources necessary for developing social capital. Three strategies illustrate how to address both wealth gaps and resource hoarding: community schools, promoting unions and investing in child care.

As a subject, education is too big for this book, but one model conceives of schools as social determinants of well-being. In the community schools approach, a community school or district is responsive to the "needs, assets, and priorities" of the surrounding community, incorporating supports such as health clinics, dental care, housing support, year-round programming, family skills development courses, vocational training, and neighborhood improvement initiatives.[13]

Employment is also a subject that deserves robust analysis, but I single out unionization for its positive effects on closing the wealth gap. Studies show that the "union advantage" or "union premium" is "even stronger for Black and Hispanic households, meaning that the racial wealth gap among union members is substantially lower than for nonunion households."[14] Similarly, "[u]nion membership also makes it less likely that a family has no or negative wealth, which could occur if they have no savings, few valuable assets, and/or a large amount of debt"; the share of Black households with no wealth is 20.2 percent in nonunion households versus 12.5 percent in union households.[15] Black union members have higher rates of wealth across all "key assets," including homeownership.[16]

Finally, access to affordable child care serves as a barrier to wealth building for many Black families.[17] A 2021 study found that Black and low-income families were more likely to report a lack of access to child care, and about 20 percent of these families report that an adult or parent had to leave a job because of this.[18] In 2022, New Mexico became the "first state to offer free child care" to virtually all New Mexico families.[19] Others should follow.

*

Many writers shy from trying to solve the problems they raise because critics inevitably point out how they are wrong. Mine will no doubt do the same. Some will argue my views are too progressive, others that they're too liberal. Sometimes the critique is that you failed to emphasize the one factor the critic believes in, like family structure and personal responsibility or class over race. Inevitably, empirically minded critics will fault a lack of studies, as if everything that should be quantified has been accurately answered in an academic paper. Others will find I exaggerated the findings of some research (probably a fair objection and a common mistake). The legal conclusions may seem too dire or shortsighted and require a deeper dive in order to see the silver linings behind some recent cases. I further expect that some find the entire premise of a book about Black racial reckoning divisively Afrocentric, as if the systemic marginalization faced by other people of color is secondary, unrelated or merely a subset of anti-Black racism. Alternatively, it all amounts to camouflage for reparations. Why not just say it? And the most anticipated criticism of all: Everything here has been tried before. Nothing I've proposed is new.

If you've come this far with me, you'll probably agree with some of the above. We've covered a lot of ground. My response to the criticism is twofold. First, everything *has* been tried before. Using the tools we have, however, we could have done a lot more to achieve racial accountability by now were we not blind to the lived consequences of structural racism. American political and legal culture has been colorblind too long in defiance of a societal reality that is clearly not colorblind. Avoidance, denial and now racial revenge truncate every gain, forcing the racial pendulum back again. Colorblindness works like an attention deficit disorder deliberately imposed against justice, so we are constantly starting over from fresh losses. The fault is not in the solutions but in ourselves, preventing the accountings needed for a just democracy. Race will matter until we commit to work all the way through it. This book testifies to the distance yet to travel.

The second thought is that no, nothing I've proposed is new. It's the quality of our efforts that must change. Most of what we know to do requires the addition of racial equity, a chronically missing ingredient. The negligence on which structural or institutional racism rests can be counteracted by more conscious efforts to act equitably with respect to race. Think of the tremendous strides we've made with accessibility, for example. Generations of structures have been built that completely ignored the needs of people with disabilities. With greater awareness of what to them has always been obvious, we've learned to stop avoiding our shared obligations by imposing regulations that changed norms and behavior. Recognizing the need for accountability, we penalize actors who continue to deny accommodations. As a result, the structure of embedded inequality for disabled people is being undone, and what we understand as discrimination against them becomes less commonplace. Racial equity is similar, though it requires the more difficult step of acknowledging that racism and the institutions it's informed has not always acted negligently, but purposefully, to advance white supremacy. So, when we design for school district funding, or multifamily zoning, or impose property tax burdens or grant abatements, our well-known protocols have to also take racial equity into account. We have to measure whether or not they promote racial inequality. Of course, this also means that we'll have to unyoke from the stranglehold of colorblindness, at least in limited ways, to reckon with yawning racial disparities traced directly and indirectly to racist practices. The key, however, is to understand that the distribution of place-based resources necessary for well-being are racially conditioned, a fact only unearthed with scrutiny and a focus on fairness. In this way, the mundane work of all we already know can one day become the routine stuff of a democracy enriched by racial justice. And move on.

Acknowledgments

One of the gifts of being a writer is to count all the blessings among the people whose support, scrutiny, intellect and love underwrite my daily work. It begins at home. I'm grateful for the people with whom I share my life – my wife Shawn and my daughters Naima and Jasmine, who do more than they can know to push me to the end of each thought, sentence and hope for the future. They are the reason to do the best that I can. I also thank my sisters, Margot Troutt Keys and Eve Troutt Powell for the example of their perseverance, our family's tradition of advocacy and scholarship and the kindness of their love.

I am particularly grateful to rely on a team of extraordinary researchers at the Rutgers Law School Center on Law, Inequality and Metropolitan Equity (CLiME). Dr. Katherine Nelson has been the ultimate colleague at so many incalculable points along the way. Our papers together are woven within these pages. Her quantitative and policy chops give depth, accuracy and meaning to so many discoveries here in housing, public health and creative analysis. Anna Griffith, CLiME's Senior Research Fellow, has unlimited energy for excellent legal research and analysis; brilliant beyond her years, she is also an indispensable partner in this work. I am deeply indebted to the prodigious expertise of two of my faculty colleagues, Penny Venetis and Carlos Gonzalez, who tirelessly weighed in when I went astray and taught me so much I could never know about civil rights and constitutional law. Penny's relentless intellect was indispensable at several points along the way. Professors David Lopez, Bernard Bell and Rachel Godsil helped fashion arguments and perspective in critical ways for which I'm also thankful. I am deeply indebted to the endless time and profound learning I gained from years of discussions and drafts discussed with Dr. Denise Rodgers and Dr. Alicia Lukatchko, without whom public health would have remained a foreign subject. Jean-Marc Coicaud was always an ear I needed. A great many student researchers' fingerprints run throughout this work, including Gatien Loral, Ryan Houser, Tiani Bhopeah and Ayo Bowman. Erica Coleman's work on urban renewal was simply extraordinary. Joshua Miller contributed excellent research on the traditions of US policing. The vibranium project would not have been possible without the tireless research of Dr. Tashanna Walker and Dr. Michela Zonta, who worked with grace and rigor. I appreciate comments on three law review articles whose details are included here and for my faculty's contributions at colloquia, including talks I gave to the Local Government Scholarship Conference and the American Bar Foundation. My friends on the Newark Equitable Advisory Commission have kept me honest for several years, especially Joe Dellafave and Richard Camerieri.

At Rutgers University where I have spent most of my academic career, I simply would not have had the extraordinary resources to cover so much intellectual ground. Universities are more than centers of knowledge production, but nurturing homes for rigorous empathy and the inquiring mind. My former chancellor Dr. Nancy Cantor's support and intellectual inspiration over many years made CLiME what it is and me who I am. Her successor, Dr. Jeffrey Robinson, was tireless in keeping me on track. Dr. Kevin Lyons is a ride-or-die colleague, laser-focused on economic equity in so many exemplary ways. Vice Chancellor Shante Palmer worked her magic many times in support of the mission of this work. I am deeply honored to receive the support of the State of New Jersey. At Rutgers Law School, Jeff Balog and Rosie Correia rescued me from countless jams. I would also like to thank my dean, Johanna Bond, for her unquestioned support. Katie Sferra helped the center run.

I am grateful for the support and insights of my editor at Cambridge University Press, Cecelia Cancellaro, who was quick, kind and wise throughout the process. Jem Langworthy dotted every *i* with charm. Lisa Carter carried us over the line.

Key perspectives and motivations often come from the love of family. I am grateful to my cousins Nina Lewis and George "Alex" Vary. Barry Nelson shared invaluable observations that helped ground analyses of places life has taken him. Many friends hold me up but none as well or as long as my best one, Keith Coleman, who always believes what I seek to accomplish is possible. Mentors like the late Derrick Bell, Charles Ogletree and June Jordan will always remain in my head, pushing me onward.

And there is no one for whom I am more grateful than my mother, Dr. Bobbye Vary Troutt, who made the way I am fortunate to take, with each example of hard work and relentless curiosity.

Notes

Chapter 1

1 See a discussion of this phenomenon in Tracie McMillan, The White Bonus: Five Families and the Cash Value of Racism in America, 20 (2024).

2 Katherine Schaeffer, *Black Workers' Views and Experiences in the U.S. Labor Force Stand Out in Key Ways*, Pew Rsch. Ctr. (Aug. 31, 2023), www.pewresearch.org/short-reads/2023/08/31/black-workers-views-and-experiences-in-the-us-labor-force-stand-out-in-key-ways/.

3 Serena Summer, *The Untold Struggles of Black Families in the Sandwich Generation*, Rolling Out (Dec. 21, 2024), https://rollingout.com/2024/12/21/black-sandwich-generation-challenges/.

4 *E.g.*, John Rawls, A Theory of Justice (1971); Will Kymlicka, Liberalism, Community, and Culture (1989); Joseph Raz, The Morality of Freedom (1988).

5 Kim Parker, Juliana Menasce Horowitz & Monica Anderson, *Amid Protests, Majorities Across Racial and Ethnic Groups Express Support for the Black Lives Matter Movement*, Pew Rsch. Ctr. (June 12, 2020), www.pewresearch.org/social-trends/2020/06/12/amid-protests-majorities-across-racial-and-ethnic-groups-express-support-for-the-black-lives-matter-movement/.

6 Obama Foundation, *A Conversation with President Obama: Reimagining Policing in the Wake of Continued Police Violence*, YouTube, 7:33 (June 7, 2020), www.youtube.com/watch?v=q_qB6SsErpA&t=1s&ab_channel=ObamaFoundation.

7 *See, e.g.*, Emma Goldberg, *How Companies Are Navigating the D.E.I. Backlash*, N.Y. Times (Feb. 10, 2025), www.nytimes.com/2025/02/10/us/politics/dei-corporate-america.html.

8 *See* Ryan Grim, *Elephant in the Zoom: Meltdowns Have Brought Progressive Advocacy Groups to a Standstill at a Critical Moment in World History*, Intercept (June 13, 2022), https://theintercept.com/2022/06/13/progressive-organizing-infighting-callout-culture/.

9 Brandi Buchman, *Right Wingers Want Trump to Issue More Pardons – and They're Incredibly Controversial,* HUFFPOST (May 5, 2025), www.huffpost.com/entry/republicans-want-trump-pardon-derek-chauvin_n_67c88df8e4b0931288b66fe4.

10 Chronicle Staff, *DEI Legislation Tracker,* CHRON. HIGHER EDUC., www.chronicle.com/article/here-are-the-states-where-lawmakers-are-seeking-to-ban-colleges-dei-efforts.

11 *See, e.g., Report of a Special Committee: Political Interference and Academic Freedom in Florida's Public Higher Education System,* AM. ASS'N UNIV. PROFESSORS (Dec. 2023), www.aaup.org/sites/default/files/AAUP_Florida_final.pdf; Greg Allen, *Fla. Gov. DeSantis Is Now Looking to Overhaul the State's Colleges and Universities,* NPR (Feb. 1, 2023), www.npr.org/2023/02/01/1153150917/fla-gov-desantis-is-now-looking-to-overhaul-the-state-s-colleges-and-universitie.

12 Oana Dumitru, *What Do Americans Think About the U.S. Prison System?,* YOUGOV (Aug. 10, 2023), https://today.yougov.com/politics/articles/45975-what-americans-think-about-prison-system-poll. ("Americans 65 and older and white Americans are more likely to say the U.S. imprisons too few people than are younger adults and Black and Hispanic Americans.")

13 Muzaffar Chishti & Julia Gelatt, *Busing and Flights of Migrants by GOP Governors Mark a New Twist in State Intervention on Immigration,* MIGRATION POL'Y INST. (Sept. 28, 2022), www.migrationpolicy.org/article/migrant-asylum-seeker-busing.

14 *See* RICHARD HANANIA, THE ORIGINS OF WOKE: CIVIL RIGHTS LAW, CORPORATE AMERICA, AND THE TRIUMPH OF IDENTITY POLITICS, Chs. 2, 6–7 (2023).

15 Ross Douthat, *The Anti-D.E.I. Crusader Who Wants to Dismantle the Department of Education,* N.Y. TIMES (Mar. 7, 2025), www.nytimes.com/2025/03/07/opinion/chris-rufo-trump-anti-dei-education.html (transcript of Douthat's interview with Christopher Rufo).

16 Exec. Order No. 14151, 90 Fed. Reg. 8339 (Jan. 20, 2025).

17 Exec. Order No. 14173, 90 Fed. Reg. 8633 (Jan. 21, 2025).

18 Exec. Order No. 14188, 90 Fed. Reg. 8847 (Jan. 29, 2025).

19 U.S. Dep't of Educ., Off. for Civ. Rts., Dear Colleague Letter: *SFFA* v. *Harvard,* Feb. 14, 2025, www.ed.gov/media/document/dear-colleague-letter-sffa-v-harvard-109506.pdf.

20 Emma Green, *What Comes After D.E.I.?,* NEW YORKER (Apr. 14, 2025), www.newyorker.com/magazine/2025/04/21/what-comes-after-dei (published in the print edition of the Apr. 21, 2025 issue, with the headline "The Pluralism Pivot").

21 Derrick A. Bell, *The Racism Is Permanent Thesis: Courageous Revelation or Unconscious Denial of Racial Genocide,* 22 CAP. UNIV. L. REV. 571 (1993).

Chapter 2

1 Congress as an institution overrepresents whites in almost every category, including staffer internships. *See* James Jones, *Congress Has Decided to Stay Far Too White*, IN THESE TIMES (Apr. 10, 2024), https://inthesetimes.com/article/house-office-diversity-inclusion-dei-congress-government-shutdown. One pipeline issue in STEM is the underrepresentation of Black faculty in STEM fields. *Study Finds Widening Racial Diversity Gap in STEM and Non-STEM Fields*, J. BLACKS HIGHER EDUC. (Sept. 16, 2024), https://jbhe.com/2024/09/study-finds-widening-racial-diversity-gaps-between-stem-and-non-stem-fields/, *discussing* Sofia P. Baker & Cory Koedel, *Diversity Trends Among Faculty in STEM and Non-STEM Fields at Selective Public Universities in the U.S. from 2016 to 2023*, 11 HUMANS. & SOC. SCI. COMMC'NS 1149 (Sept. 6, 2024), https://doi.org/10.1057/s41599-024-03687-x.

2 *Chief Diversity Officer Demographics and Statistics in the US*, ZIPPIA, www.zippia.com/chief-diversity-officer-jobs/demographics/.

3 *Prison Warden Salary New Jersey*, SALARYEXPERT, www.salaryexpert.com/salary/job/prison-warden/united-states/new-jersey.

4 *See Economics of Incarceration: Research on the Economic Drivers and Consequences of Mass Incarceration*, PRISON POL'Y INITIATIVE, www.prisonpolicy.org/research/economics_of_incarceration/.

5 For prisoner race, see *BOP Statistics: Inmate Race*, FED. BUREAU PRISONS, www.bop.gov/about/statistics/statistics_inmate_race.jsp. For warden race, see *Warden Demographics and Statistics in the US*, ZIPPIA, www.zippia.com/warden-jobs/demographics/. Yet 76.5% of wardens are white.

6 ALLIANCE FOR BOARD DIVERSITY, MISSING PIECES REPORT: A BOARD DIVERSITY CENSUS OF WOMEN AND UNDERREPRESENTED RACIAL AND ETHNIC GROUPS ON FORTUNE 500 BOARDS, 7th ed. (2023), https://iasplus.com/content/e85fd5e1-85e1–4bf0-a94f-87b6fb56e200.

7 *See* Commissioner's Corner, *More than a Century of Occupational Changes Among African American Workers*, U.S. BUREAU LAB. STAT. (Feb. 27, 2024), www.bls.gov/blog/2024/more-than-a-century-of-occupational-changes-among-african-american-workers.htm.

8 Erica E. Meade, *Research Brief: Overview of Community Characteristics in Areas with Concentrated Poverty*, ASPE OFF. HUM. SERV. POL'Y (Apr. 2014), https://aspe.hhs.gov/sites/default/files/migrated_legacy_files/130426/rb_concentratedpoverty.pdf.

9 *See Neighborhood Poverty: All Neighborhoods Should Be Communities of Opportunity*, NAT'L EQUITY ATLAS, https://nationalequityatlas.org/indicators/Neighborhood_poverty.

10 George Galster & Patrick Sharkey, *Spatial Foundations of Inequality: A Conceptual Model and Empirical Overview*, 3 RSF: RUSSELL SAGE FOUND. J. SOC. SCI. 1 (Feb. 2017), https://doi.org/10.7758/rsf.2017.3.2.01.

11 *Id.*

12 Raj Chetty et al., *The Opportunity Atlas: Mapping the Childhood Roots of Social Mobility*, OPPORTUNITY INSIGHTS & U.S. CENSUS BUREAU (Jan. 2025), https://opportunityinsights.org/wp-content/uploads/2018/10/atlas_paper.pdf.

13 Raj Chetty & Nathaniel Hendren, *The Impacts of Neighborhoods on Intergenerational Mobility: Childhood Exposure Effects and County-Level Estimates*, OPPORTUNITY INSIGHTS (April 2015), https://opportunityinsights.org/wp-content/uploads/2018/03/nbhds_exec_summary.pdf.

14 *See* Raj Chetty et al., *Executive Summary: The Opportunity Atlas: Mapping the Childhood Roots of Social Mobility*, OPPORTUNITY INSIGHTS & U.S. CENSUS BUREAU (Jan. 2020), https://opportunityinsights.org/wp-content/uploads/2018/10/atlas_summary.pdf.

15 Raj Chetty et al., *Race and Economic Opportunity in the United States: An Intergenerational Perspective*, OPPORTUNITY INSIGHTS & U.S. CENSUS BUREAU (Dec. 2019), https://opportunityinsights.org/wp-content/uploads/2018/04/race_paper.pdf.

16 William H. Frey, *Neighborhood Segregation Persists for Black, Latino or Hispanic and Asian Americans*, BROOKINGS INST. (Apr. 6, 2021), www.brookings.edu/articles/neighborhood-segregation-persists-for-black-latino-or-hispanic-and-asian-americans/.

17 Stephen Menendian et al., *The Roots of Structural Racism Project: Twenty-First Century Racial Residential Segregation in the United States*, OTHERING & BELONGING INST. (June 21, 2021), https://belonging.berkeley.edu/roots-structural-racism.

18 *See, e.g.*, KENNETH T. JACKSON, CRABGRASS FRONTIER: THE SUBURBANIZATION OF THE UNITED STATES (1985).

19 *See* DAVID RUSK, CITIES WITHOUT SUBURBS (1993).

20 Village of Belle Terre v. Boraas, 416 U.S. 1, 100 (1980).

21 TRACIE MCMILLAN, THE WHITE BONUS: FIVE FAMILIES AND THE CASH VALUE OF RACISM IN AMERICA (2024).

22 *Id.* at 309.

23 Marianne Bertrand & Sendhil Mullainathan, *Are Emily and Greg More Employable than Lakisha and Jamal? A Field Experiment on Labor Market Discrimination*, 94 AM. ECON. REV. 991 (Sept. 2004), www.aeaweb.org/articles?id=10.1257/0002828042002561.

24 Martin Abel & Rulof Burger, Unpacking Name-Based Race Discrimination (IZA Inst. Lab. Econ., Discussion Paper No. 16254, June 2023), https://ssrn.com/abstract=4490163.

25 Devah Pager, Bruce Western & Naomi Sugie, *Sequencing Disadvantage: Barriers to Employment Facing Young Black and White Men with Criminal Records*, 623

Annals of Am. Acad. Pol. Sci. 195 (May 2009), https://doi.org/10.1177/0002716208330793. *See also* Devah Pager, *The Mark of a Criminal Record*, 108 Am. J. Socio. 937 (Mar. 2003), https://doi.org/10.1086/374403.

26 Susan Adams, *White High School Drop-Outs Are As Likely to Land Jobs as Black College Students*, Forbes (July 27, 2014), www.forbes.com/sites/susanadams/2014/06/27/white-high-school-drop-outs-are-as-likely-to-land-jobs-as-black-college-students/.

27 Jonathan Lanning, *Evidence of Discrimination in the $1.4 Trillion Auto Loan Market*, Fed. Rsrv. Bank Chi., ProfitWise News & Views (Jan. 2023), www.chicagofed.org/publications/profitwise-news-and-views/2023/discrimination-auto-loan-market. ("My analysis specifically shows that Black borrowers disproportionately pay what is generally the highest allowable interest rate markup – 2.0 percentage points – which results in nearly $1,400 in additional interest over the lifetime of a typical auto loan from the 2008–13 data set I used for my paper.")

28 Consumer Fin. Prot. Bureau, Matched-Pair Testing in Small Business Lending Markets (Nov. 2024), https://files.consumerfinance.gov/f/documents/cfpb_matched-pair-testing-report_2024-11.pdf.

29 U.S. Census Bureau, Income in the United States: 2022, Report No. P60–279 (Sept. 12, 2023), www.census.gov/library/publications/2023/demo/p60-279.html.

30 U.S. Census Bureau, Households with a White, Non-Hispanic Householder Were Ten Times Wealthier than Those with a Black Householder in 2021 (Apr. 23, 2024), www.census.gov/library/stories/2024/04/wealth-by-race.html.

31 These rates are for 2022. *See Rate of Homeownership in the United States in 2023, by Race*, Statista (2024), www.statista.com/statistics/639685/us-home-ownership-rate-by-race/.

32 U.S. Dep't Treasury, Racial Differences in Economic Security: Housing (Nov. 22, 2022), https://home.treasury.gov/news/featured-stories/racial-differences-in-economic-security-housing.

33 *Educational Attainment: Educational Equity Is Key to Building a Strong, Resilient Workforce*, Nat'l Equity Atlas, https://nationalequityatlas.org/indicators/Educational-attainment.

34 U.S. Bureau Lab. Stat., Rep. 1100, Labor Force Statistics by Race and Ethnicity, 2021 (Jan. 2023), www.bls.gov/opub/reports/race-and-ethnicity/2021/home.htm.

35 *Id.*

36 CDC, Infant Mortality in the United States, 2021: Data from the Period Linked Birth/Infant Death File, Nat'l Vital Stat.

REP. VOL. 72, NO. 11 (Sept. 12, 2023), www.cdc.gov/nchs/data/nvsr/nvsr72/nvsr72-11.pdf.

37 Latoya Hill & Samantha Artiga, *What Is Driving Widening Racial Disparities in Life Expectancy?*, KFF (May 23, 2023), www.kff.org/racial-equity-and-health-policy/issue-brief/what-is-driving-widening-racial-disparities-in-life-expectancy/.

38 Leah Wang, *Updated Data and Charts: Incarceration Stats by Race, Ethnicity, and Gender for All 50 States*, PRISON POL'Y INITIATIVE (Sept. 27, 2023), www.prisonpolicy.org/blog/2023/09/27/updated_race_data/.

39 *See, e.g.*, Staff Writer, *The Health Benefits of Trees*, HARV. T.H. CHAN SCH. PUB. HEALTH (Sept. 15, 2021), https://hsph.harvard.edu/news/the-health-benefits-of-trees/.

40 Richmond v. J.A. Croson Co., 488 U.S. 469 (1989).

41 Adarand Constructors v. Peña, 515 U.S. 200 (1995).

42 Milliken v. Bradley, 418 U.S. 717 (1974).

43 Griggs v. Duke Power Co., 401 U.S. 424 (1971). *Griggs* was subsequently modified by Wards Cove v. San Antonio, 490 U.S. 642 (1989), the Civil Rights Act of 1991, Pub. L. 102–66, Sec. 2., 42 U.S.C. § 2000e-2, and then Ricci v. DeStefano, 557 U.S. 557 (2009).

44 U.S. DEP'T JUST., CIV. RTS. DIV., TITLE VI LEGAL MANUAL, SECTION VII: PROVING DISCRIMINATION – DISPARATE IMPACT (www.prrac.org/title_vi_repository/doj/2017_title_vi_manual/title_vi_legal_manual_sec_7_impact_final1.pdf).

45 Olatunde C. Johnson, *The Agency Roots of Disparate Impact*, 49 HARV. C.R.-C.L. L. REV. 125, 136 (2014), https://scholarship.law.columbia.edu/faculty_scholarship/1099; Susan D. Carle, *A Social Movement History of Title VII Disparate Impact Analysis*, 63 FLA. L. REV. 251, 294–96 (2011), http://scholarship.law.ufl.edu/flr/vol63/iss1/7; Melissa Hart, *Disparate Impact Discrimination: The Limits of Litigation, the Possibilities for Internal Compliance*, 33 J.C. & U.L. 547, 548–49 (2007), https://scholar.law.colorado.edu/faculty-articles/328; George Rutherglen, *Disparate Impact, Discrimination, and the Essentially Contested Concept of Equality*, 74 FORDHAM L. REV. 2313 (2006), https://ir.lawnet.fordham.edu/flr/vol74/iss4/27.

46 Michael Selmi, *Was the Disparate Impact Theory a Mistake?*, 53 UCLA L. REV. 701 (2006).

47 *Id.*

48 I borrow the term from Randall Kennedy, *Colorblind Constitutionalism*, 82 FORDHAM L. REV. 1 (2013).

49 Raj Chetty, David J. Deming & John N. Friedman, Diversifying Society's Leaders? The Determinants and Causal Effects of Admission to Highly Selective Private Colleges, Opportunity Insights, IRS & NBER (Oct. 2023),

https://opportunityinsights.org/wp-content/uploads/2023/07/CollegeAdmissions_Paper.pdf.

50 *Id.* (the top 1% are more than twice as likely to attend).

51 White House, *Remarks by the President at a Campaign Event in Roanoke, Virginia,* NAT'L ARCHIVES (July 13, 2012), https://obamawhitehouse.archives.gov/the-press-office/2012/07/13/remarks-president-campaign-event-roanoke-Virginia:

> There are a lot of wealthy, successful Americans who agree with me – because they want to give something back. They know they didn't – look, if you've been successful, you didn't get there on your own. You didn't get there on your own. I'm always struck by people who think, well, it must be because I was just so smart. There are a lot of smart people out there. It must be because I worked harder than everybody else. Let me tell you something – there are a whole bunch of hardworking people out there. (Applause.)
>
> If you were successful, somebody along the line gave you some help. There was a great teacher somewhere in your life. Somebody helped to create this unbelievable American system that we have that allowed you to thrive. Somebody invested in roads and bridges. If you've got a business – you didn't build that. Somebody else made that happen. The Internet didn't get invented on its own. Government research created the Internet so that all the companies could make money off the Internet.

52 Vinay Harpalani, *Roberts Rules of (Dis)Order: Doctrinal Doublespeak on Affirmative Action and Stare Decisis,* 77 SMU L. REV. 61, 63–64 (2024); Larry J. Pittman, *The Supreme Court's Erroneous Equal Protection Clause Analysis: Societal Discrimination, the Harvard College Decision as the New* Plessy v. Ferguson-Lite, *and the Thirteenth Amendment,* 57 CREIGHTON L. REV. 189, 191 (2024); Angela Onwuachi-Willig, *Roberts's Revisions: A Narratological Reading of the Affirmative Action Cases,* 137 HARV. L. REV. 192, 200–201 (2023); Jonathan P. Feingold, *Affirmative Action After SFFA,* 48 J. COLL. & UNIV. L. 239, 244 (2023).

53 Students for Fair Admissions, Inc. v. President & Fellows of Harv. Coll., 600 U.S. 181, 318-319 (SOTOMAYOR, J., dissenting).

54 *Id.* at 385 (JACKSON, J., dissenting).

55 *Id.* at 299–300 (GORSUCH, J., concurring).

56 A federal district judge, ruling against the Trump administration's targeting of Blacks and other minorities with the research funding cuts contained in executive orders, said he had "never seen government racial discrimination like this." Zach Montague, *Trump's Cuts to NIH Grants Focused on Minority Groups Are Illegal,* N.Y. TIMES (June 16, 2025), www.nytimes.com/2025/06/16/us/

politics/trump-nih-grants-cut.html?smid=nytcore-ios-share&referringSource=articleShare.

Chapter 3

1 *Nearly Half of Renter Households Are Cost-Burdened, Proportions Differ by Race*, U.S. CENSUS BUREAU (Sept. 12, 2024), www.census.gov/newsroom/press-releases/2024/renter-households-cost-burdened-race.html.

2 *See* DAVID D. TROUTT & KATHARINE NELSON, WHO OWNS NEWARK? TRANSFERRING HOMEOWNER WEALTH TO CORPORATE BUYERS, Rutgers Center on Law, Inequality and Metropolitan Equity (May 2022), https://static1.squarespace.com/static/5b996f553917ee5e584ba742/t/626fd98bb8357d201cb8dcb5/1651497359130/Who+Owns+Newark+Final+1.pdf.

3 *What Causes Homelessness? Systemic Racism and Discrimination of Marginalized Groups*, NATIONAL ALLIANCE TO END HOMELESSNESS, https://endhomelessness.org/systemic-racism-and-marginalization/.

4 This was an extension of the racial bargain over New Deal legislation generally, like the Social Security Act, in which President Franklin Delano Roosevelt believed he had to accede to Southern Democrat demands in Congress that agricultural and domestic workers – both overwhelmingly Black – should be exempted from coverage under the Act in order to assure its passage. *See* HARVARD SITKOFF, A NEW DEAL FOR BLACKS: THE EMERGENCE OF CIVIL RIGHTS AS A NATIONAL ISSUE: THE DEPRESSION DECADE 34 (30th anniversary ed. 2009).

5 MARTIN ANDERSON, THE FEDERAL BULLDOZER: A CRITICAL ANALYSIS OF URBAN RENEWAL, 1949–1962 (1964); *and see* discussion on the estimates of Black displacees in this chapter, under the subheading "The Legacy of Displacement and Racial Bargaining."

6 These numbers represent the author's original calculations based on Urban Renewal Administration reports for specific cities and aggregate projects. *See* discussion in this chapter, under the subheading "Recognizing Mass Taking."

7 ANDERSON, *supra* note 5 at 69.

8 *See Inflation Calculator*, FEDERAL RESERVE BANK OF MINNEAPOLIS, www.minneapolisfed.org/about-us/monetary-policy/inflation-calculator.

9 ISABEL WILKERSON, THE WARMTH OF OTHER SUNS: THE EPIC STORY OF AMERICA'S GREAT MIGRATION 14–15 (2010).

10 KARL E. TAEUBER & ALMA F. TAEUBER, NEGROES IN CITIES: RESIDENTIAL SEGREGATION AND NEIGHBORHOOD CHANGE 12 (1965).

11 *Id.* at 24–25.

12 Sometimes called either dissimilarity or evenness, "dissimilarity measures the percentage of a group's population that would have to change residence for

each neighborhood to have the same percentage of that group as the metropolitan area overall. The index ranges from 0.0 (complete integration) to 1.0 (complete segregation)." *Housing Patterns: Appendix B: Measures of Segregation*, U.S. CENSUS BUREAU (Nov. 21, 2021), www.census.gov/topics/housing/housing-patterns/guidance/appendix-b.html.

13 TAEUBER & TAEUBER, *supra* note 10 at 54. For example, the segregation index for Cincinnati, OH was 47.3 in 1910, 57.2 in 1920, 72.8 in 1930 and 80.6 in 1950. The same numbers for Syracuse, NY were 64, 65.2. 86.7 and 85.8. *Id.* "The most consistent finding in these historical investigations for various cities is a sharp increase in residential segregation between 1910 and 1930 in every city, both Northern and Southern, for which we have data." *Id.*

14 ST. CLAIR DRAKE & HORACE R. CAYTON, BLACK METROPOLIS: A STUDY OF NEGRO LIFE IN A NORTHERN CITY 60 (2015).

15 At least one study debunks the widely held notion that most Black migrants of the Great Migration were poor farmhands with limited education whose passage to the North was paid for by labor bosses, companies or "carpetbaggers." *See* Carole Marks, *Black Workers and the Great Migration North*, 46 PHYLON 148 (1985). According to Marks, 1 million Black people – about 10% of the South's total Black population – left between 1910 and 1930, about 600,000 of them between 1916 and 1918. *Id.* Although originally farm laborers, many had already become mobile throughout the South in search of better pay; some went to Southern cities in search of industrial employment. *Id.* at 149. Typically, migrants had moved from the farm to Southern cities, acquired some educational literacy and worked long enough to afford the trip North. *Id.* at 157. "[T]here was a significant out-migration of literate Blacks." *Id.* at 158.

16 As Drake and Cayton explained in 1945,

> Negroes are not finally absorbed in the general population. Black Metropolis remains athwart the least desirable residential zones. Its population grows larger and larger, unable to expand freely or to scatter ... Black Metropolis as a community is the end result of one hundred and fifty years of intense competition among native-whites, Negroes, and foreign-born for living space, economic goods and prestige.

DRAKE & CAYTON, *supra* note 14 at 17.

17 MARKS, *supra* note 15 at 159.

18 RICHARD WRIGHT, 12 MILLION BLACK VOICES: A FOLK HISTORY OF THE NEGRO IN THE UNITED STATES 101–11 (1941).

19 *See, e.g.*, Prottoy A. Akbar et al., *Racial Segregation in Housing Markets and the Erosion of Black Wealth* (Nat'l Bureau of Econ. Rsch., Working Paper No. 25805, May 2019), www.nber.org/system/files/working_papers/w25805/w25805.pdf:

> We find that over a single decade rental prices soared by roughly 50 percent on city blocks that transitioned from all white to majority black. Meanwhile,

pioneering black families paid a 28 percent premium to buy a home on a majority white block. These homes then lost 10 percent of their original value as the block became majority black. These findings strongly suggest that segregated housing markets cost black families much of the gains associated with migrating to the North.

20 Arnold R. Hirsch, Making the Second Ghetto: Race and Housing in Chicago, 1940–1960, 29 (1983).

21 *Id.* at 18.

22 *Id.* at 23–24.

23 *Id.* at 31. *See also* Wendell Pritchett, *The "Public Menace" of Blight: Urban Renewal and the Private Uses of Eminent Domain*, 21 Yale L. & Pol'y Rev. 1, 21 (2003).

24 Brandi Blesset, *Urban Renewal and "Ghetto" Development in Baltimore: Two Sides of the Same Coin*, 50 Am. Rev. Pub. Admin. 838 (June 2020).

25 The pattern of designating "white" spaces and "Black" begins during the early twentieth century with racial zoning ordinances. These ordinances prohibited residential race mixing after a given block or street was deemed to have a majority Black or white population. Though struck down as unconstitutional in Buchanan v. Warley, 245 U.S. 60 (1917), these lines of demarcation remained along with the practice. Richard Rothstein describes the practice of the Public Works Administration to divide early public housing projects by race according to a "neighborhood composition rule" based on perceived or once-official racial zones. Richard Rothstein, The Color of Law: A Forgotten History of How Our Government Segregated America 21 (2017). For a more contemporary exegesis on the cumulative reproduction of Black- and white-identified spaces and their consequences, *see* Elise C. Boddie, *Racial Territoriality*, 58 UCLA L. Rev. 401 (2010).

26 These calculations are based on an original case study analysis of seven representative US cities by my research team at the Rutgers Law School Center on Law, Inequality and Metropolitan Equity (CLiME). The findings are available online at www.clime.rutgers.edu as the Urban Renewal Archives. The population counts are based on US Census Bureau data.

27 Detroit also experienced a dramatic change in its demographics just as redevelopment projects became a priority. In 1930, Blacks comprised only 7.6% of the city (120,066), a proportion that more than doubled to 16.2% (300,506) by 1950. Ten years later, the Black population was almost 29% of the total, or 482,223 people. Newark also saw a doubling of its Black population from 1930 to 1950, about 39,000 or 8% to about 75,000 or 17%. Ten years later, it would double again. Cleveland's demographic transformation as a result of Black migration is similar – a doubling of Black population between 1930 to 1950 from 71,899 (8%) to 147,847 (16.2%). During the first decade of urban renewal the Black population nearly doubled again to 250,818 (28.6%) in 1960. *See id.*

28 ROTHSTEIN, *supra* note 25 at 18–19.

29 Emergency Relief and Construction Act of 1932, Pub. L. No. 72-302, 89 Stat. 709 (codified as amended in scattered sections of 12 U.S.C.).

30 *See* CQ Researcher, *Slum Clearance: 1932–1952*, CQ PRESS (Nov. 22, 1952), https://library.cqpress.com/cqresearcher/document.php?id=cqresrre1952112200. The Act authorized the Reconstruction Finance Corporation to make loans for slum clearance and housing construction.

31 Katharine L. Shester, *The Local Economic Effects of Public Housing in the United States, 1940–1970*, 73 J. ECON. HIST. 978, 981 (Dec. 2013).

32 Wilton S. Sogg & Warren Wertheimer, *Legal and Governmental Issues in Urban Renewal*, *in* URBAN RENEWAL: THE RECORD AND THE CONTROVERSY, 126, 126–27 (James Q. Wilson ed., 1966); LAWRENCE V. VALE, PURGING THE POOREST: PUBLIC HOUSING AND THE DESIGN POLITICS OF TWICE-CLEARED COMMUNITIES 8 (2013).

33 Jay Rumney, *The Social Cost of Slums*, 7 J. SOC. ISSUES 69, 73 (Spring 1951), *cited in* CQ Researcher, *supra* note 30:

> One authority has listed the following symptoms of blight: scrambling of land uses for residential and non-residential purposes detrimental to both; invasion of an area by low-income minorities with no access to educational or recreational facilities; failure to keep buildings in repair. Other symptoms are disregard of zoning, housing, sanitation and safety codes; continued demolition of buildings with vacant land held for speculation; excessive building with insufficient public open space; increasing mortgage foreclosures and tax delinquencies; continuing flight of population to suburbs; physical and financial deterioration of central business districts.

34 *See* BRENT CEBUL, ILLUSIONS OF PROGRESS: BUSINESS, POVERTY, AND LIBERALISM IN THE AMERICAN CENTURY (2023).

35 42 U.S.C. § 1437(a)(1)(A)–(C).

36 ROTHSTEIN, *supra* note 25 at 17–18. World War II production efforts brought population increases that worsened existing housing shortages, especially as veterans returned from abroad. VALE, *supra* note 32 at 15.

37 VALE, *supra* note 32 at 14.

38 *Id.* at 12–13.

39 ROTHSTEIN, *supra* note 25 at 23 (citing US Housing Authority Manual directing the preservation of racially homogeneous communities in determining site selection). HIRSCH, *supra* note 20 at 10. Before that, the state's involvement was primarily through judicial enforcement of private restrictive covenants.

40 VALE, *supra* note 32 at 17.

41 Pub. L. No. 84–627, 70 Stat. 374 (1956) (current version at 23 U.S.C. § 101 et seq.).

42 Kenneth T. Jackson, Crabgrass Frontier: The Suburbanization of the United States 206 (1985).

43 *Id.* at 207. Jackson suggested that the FHA was more racist than the Home Owners Loan Corporation (which invented redlining) in its use of appraisal techniques that for decades favored all-white neighborhoods. *Id.* at 215.

44 Hirsch, *supra* note 20 at 28.

45 Jackson, *supra* note 42 at 206.

46 Pub. L. 81-171, 63 Stat. 413 (current version at 42 U.S.C. § 1441 et seq.).

47 *Id.* The declared purpose of the Housing Act is "the realization as soon as feasible of the goal of a decent home and a suitable living environment for every American family." 42 U.S.C. § 1441.

48 These were generally understood as consisting of project expenditures (planning, land acquisition and demolition) plus the local noncash grant-in-aid share less whatever proceeds came from sales to developers. Sogg & Wertheimer, *supra* note 32 at 135. Anderson, *supra* note 5 at 21, 34. *See also* Housing Act of 1949, *supra* note 46 at Title I § 110.

49 Just as the 1937 Act required the creation of Local Housing Authorities for participating municipalities.

50 Housing Act of 1954, Pub. L. No. 83-560, sec. 303, 68 Stat. 590, 623–24 (1954) (codified as amended at 42 U.S.C. § 1451). Ashley A. Foard & Hilbert Fefferman, *Federal Urban Renewal Legislation, in* Urban Renewal: The Record and the Controversy, 71, 97 (James Q. Wilson ed., 1966) (*reprinted from* 25 L. & Contemp. Probs. 635 (Fall 1960), https://scholarship.law.duke.edu/cgi/viewcontent.cgi?article=2856&context=lcp).

51 *See* Powelton Civic Home Owners Asso. v. Department of Housing & Urban Development, 284 F. Supp. 809, 818 (E.D. 1968):

> [A]lthough [HHFA] does not actually acquire or redevelop the properties, the agency is required to perform a planning control function; the availability of the advances, loans, and grants is conditioned upon whether the project plans satisfy certain specified federal criteria. For example, 42 U.S.C. § 1451 provides that the Secretary (or his delegate) must find that the local agency has met certain local responsibilities before authorizing a contract for a loan or capital grant. The Secretary's determination is to be based upon his review of a "workable plan for community improvement" submitted by the local public agency. 42 U.S.C. § 1451(c). That "workable plan" must be "of sufficient scope and content to furnish a basis for evaluation of the need for the urban renewal project". 42 U.S.C. § 1451(e). [citations omitted]

See also Anderson, *supra* note 5 at 17–18. Notice and hearing requirements were minimally observed, had little influence when they were and produced little accommodation. Sogg & Wertheimer, *supra* note 32.

52 As several authors note, public use became conflated with a public purpose consistent with police power objectives. *See, e.g.*, Sogg & Wertheimer, *supra* note 32 at 146.

53 This was in keeping with the political swings to Republican President Dwight Eisenhower's strict beliefs in federalism and disinterest in cities. ROGER BILES, THE FATE OF CITIES: URBAN AMERICA AND THE FEDERAL GOVERNMENT, 1945–2000, at 60–61 (2011).

54 Housing Act of 1956, Pub. L. No. 84-1020, sec. 303(d), 70 Stat. 1097, 1099 (1956) (codified at 42 U.S.C. § 1452(d)).

55 Housing Act of 1959, Pub. L. No. 86–372, 73 Stat. 654, 672 (1959) (codified at 42 U.S.C. § 1453).

56 Foard & Fefferman, *supra* note 50 at 121.

57 These guaranteed lower land costs for investors, who paid only for parcels discounted by the land clearance costs paid by the federal government. Foard & Fefferman, *supra* note 50 at n. 17.

58 William L. Slayton, *The Operation and Achievements of the Urban Renewal Program, in* URBAN RENEWAL: THE RECORD AND THE CONTROVERSY, 189, 223 (James Q. Wilson ed., 1966).

59 *Id.* at 222.

60 Foard & Fefferman, *supra* note 50 at 106.

61 *See* Pritchett, *supra* note 23 at 14–15.

62 Marc A. Weiss, *The Origins and Legacy of Urban Renewal, in* FEDERAL HOUSING POLICY & PROGRAMS: PAST AND PRESENT, 253, 255 (J. Paul Mitchell ed., 1986). By then it had already received an urgent push by Commerce Secretary Herbert Hoover, whose efforts in the 1920s to assemble experts to draft the first Standard State Zoning Enabling Acts were designed to adopt measures already in use in European cities in the service of a nascent American Dream. Pritchett, *supra* note 23 at 16–18.

63 Weiss, *supra* note 62 at 258.

64 According to HHFA Commissioner William Slayton's testimony, "[I]t appears that after redevelopment assessed values are averaging between four to five times the values prior to slum clearance." Slayton, *supra* note 58 at 222.

65 Foard & Fefferman, *supra* note 50 at 106. Historians had perhaps a different view. *See, e.g.*, Erica Avila and Mark H. Rose, *Race, Culture, Politics, and Urban Renewal: An Introduction*, 35 J. URB. HIST. 335, 339 (2009). ("When historians refer to 'urban renewal,' they are not describing one singular policy. Rather, they are describing a host of programs and policies that wrought a series of radical interventions on the urban built environment.")

66 348 U.S. 26 (1954). For more on the case, *see* Amy Lavine, *Urban Renewal and the Story of Berman v. Parker*, 42 URB. L. 423 (2010); Pritchett, *supra* note 23.

67 37 U.S. 483 (1954).

68 According to Berchmans Fitzpatrick, general counsel of the HHFA, *Brown*'s overturning of the "separate but equal" doctrine was inapplicable to housing. ROTHSTEIN, *supra* note 25 at 33.

69 Francesca Russello Ammon, *Commemoration Amid Criticism: The Mixed Legacy of Urban Renewal in Southwest Washington, D.C.*, 8 J. PLAN. HIST. 175, 202 (Aug. 2009), https://doi.org/10.1177/1538513209340630.

70 BERNARD J. FRIEDEN & LYNNE B. SAGALYN, DOWNTOWN, INC.: HOW AMERICA REBUILDS CITIES 31 (1989).

71 Ammon, *supra* note 69, at 202, *citing* 1960 ANNUAL REPORT, D.C. REDEV. LAND AGENCY, 16 (Sept. 28, 1960).

72 *Id.*, *citing* 1960 ANNUAL REPORT, *supra* note 71 at 21.

73 ELEANOR PAPERNO WOLF ET AL., CHANGE AND RENEWAL IN AN URBAN COMMUNITY: FIVE CASE STUDIES OF DETROIT 473 (1969).

74 *Id.* at 466.

75 According to an early study of forty-one cities' relocation practices, assistance varied by time and city size, with at least one-third of all eligible displacees receiving nothing. *See* Harold Reynolds, *Population Displacement in Urban Renewal*, 22 AM. J. ECON. & SOCIO. 113, 117 (1963).

76 ANDERSON, *supra* note 5 at 55–57. These results are consistent with David E. Pinsky, *Relocation Payments in Urban Renewal: More Just Compensation*, 11 N.Y.L.F. 80, 96 (1965) (who found in 1965 that 104,000 families received a total of $7,500,000 or an average of $72 each and 39,000 individuals who received $1.8 million or an average of $45 each.)

77 ANDERSON, *supra* note 5 at 59.

78 *Id.* at 61–62. He estimated that average rents for displaced families at $50-60 per month, with new private high-rise apartments (the goal of redevelopment) renting for an average of $124–158 per month. Between 1950 and 1960, 25,000 private units were built and only 3,000 public housing units. *Id.* at 59.

79 *Id.* at 67.

80 121 N.Y.S.2d 841 at 845.

81 Comment, *Standing to Challenge Administrative Agency Conduct: Recent Developments in the Federal Common Law*, 44 TUL. L. REV. 95, 110 (1969).

82 *See, e.g.*, Terry J. Tondro, *Urban Renewal Relocation: Problems in Enforcement of Conditions on Federal Grants to Local Agencies*, 117 U. PA. L. REV., 183, 184 (Dec. 1986); William Grigsby, *Housing Markets and Public Policy*, *in* URBAN RENEWAL: THE RECORD AND THE CONTROVERSY, 24, 30 (James Q. Wilson ed., 1966).

83 Note, *Family Relocation in Urban Renewal*, 82 HARV. L. REV. 864, 866 (Feb. 1969).

84 Pinsky, *supra* note 76 at 82.

85 *Id.*

86 *Family Relocation, supra* note 83 at 866; Note, *Judicial Review of Displacee Relocation in Urban Renewal.* 77 YALE L.J. 966 (1968); Reynolds, *supra* note 75 at 117 (finding that only approximately one-third of participating cities offered competent advice).

87 Chester Hartman, *The Housing of Relocated Families, in* URBAN RENEWAL: THE RECORD AND THE CONTROVERSY, 293, 321 (James Q. Wilson ed., 1966).

88 It might also have violated the Federal False Claims Act, 31 U.S.C. §§ 3729–33. That the federal government often looked the other way and provided certification complicates the analysis. FRIEDEN & SAGALYN, *supra* note 70 at 31.

89 Uniform Relocation Assistance and Real Properties Acquisition Policies Act of 1970 ("Uniform Relocation Act" or "URA"), 42 U.S.C. §§ 4601–55.

90 *See, e.g.*, James J. Kelly, *"We Shall Not Be Moved": Urban Communities, Eminent Domain and the Socioeconomics of Just Compensation,* 80 ST. JOHN'S L. REV. 923, 975 (2006). Kelly argues that "The Uniform Relocation Act only required that the condemning agency produce a plan that the funding agency found satisfactory; and failed to give condemnees, either directly or indirectly through meaningful judicial review, any means to control relocation. Yet, it gave condemning agencies a public relations kit for dealing with anxious residents of redevelopment districts."

91 DAVID DANTE TROUTT, THE PRICE OF PARADISE: THE COSTS OF INEQUALITY AND A VISION FOR A MORE EQUITABLE AMERICA (2013); SHERYLL CASHIN, THE FAILURES OF INTEGRATION: HOW RACE AND CLASS ARE UNDERMINING THE AMERICAN DREAM (2005); Sheryll Cashin, *Localism, Self-Interest, and the Tyranny of the Favored Quarter,* 88 GEO. L.J. 1985 (2000); Richard Briffault, *Smart Growth and American Land Use Law,* 21 ST. LOUIS PUBLIC L. REV. 253 (2002).

92 FEDERAL HOME LOAN MORTGAGE CORPORATION, THE SECONDARY MARKET IN RESIDENTIAL MORTGAGES, U.S. DEP'T HOUS. & URB. DEV. 12 (1982), www.huduser.gov/Publications/pdf/HUD-11648.pdf. *See also* LEO GREBLER, HOUSING ISSUES IN ECONOMIC STABILIZATION POLICY 11 (1960).

93 GREBLER, *id.* at 6.

94 Administrative exclusion at the local level was not limited to the South. Lending programs that privileged veteran status, for instance, continued to discriminate against Black borrowers. IRA KATZNELSON, WHEN AFFIRMATIVE ACTION WAS WHITE: AN UNTOLD HISTORY OF RACIAL INEQUALITY IN TWENTIETH-CENTURY AMERICA 139 (2005). Where discrimination was not express, few Blacks could ever qualify for loans. "In New York and the Northern New Jersey suburbs, fewer than 100 of the 67,000 mortgages insured by the GI Bill supported home purchases by non-whites." *Id.* at 140.

95 *Id.* at 111.

96 These immigrants were also in the cities, also redlined – or more often just a line or grade above. The FHA guidelines demanded a rigid racial hierarchy that punished racially mixed neighborhoods as "inharmonious," "antipathetic," "incompatible racial groupings" to be avoided at all cost. DAVID R. ROEDIGER, WORKING TOWARD WHITENESS: HOW AMERICA'S IMMIGRANTS BECAME WHITE 231 (2005). "New Deal housing policies empowered and advantaged new immigrants, but as whites, not as immigrants." *Id.* at 230.

97 *Id.* at 232.

98 For example, according to one analysis, the median price of a home in Michigan in 1950 was $7,496; its 2019 value was $169,600. Aine Givens, *How Much the Typical Home Cost in Your State in 1950*, CHI. TRIB. (Nov. 2, 2021), www.chicagotribune.com/real-estate/luxury-real-estate/sns-stacker-home-cost-state-midcentury-20211102-e5j7nzctlbdudhzmxafsbbecsu-photogallery.html. In 1950 New York, the median price was $10,152, which increased to $338,700 in 2019. *Id.* In Washington, DC, the gains were greatest: from $14,498 in 1950 to $646,500 in 2019. *Id. See also* Patrick Sisson, *Why Buying a House Today Is So Much Harder than in 1950*, CURBED (Apr. 10, 2018), https://archive.curbed.com/2018/4/10/17219786/buying-a-house-mortgage-government-gi-bill.

99 *See* Jay A. Fernandez, *Divided Highways*, ACLU MAGAZINE (Spring 2022), www.aclu.org/aclu-magazine/aclu-magazine-spring-2022.

100 16 U.S.C. § 503.

101 Andrew M. Giguere, "... and never the twain shall meet:" Baltimore's East–West Expressway and the Construction of the "Highway to Nowhere," 22 (June 2009) (Master's thesis, Ohio University), https://etd.ohiolink.edu/acprod/odb_etd/etd/r/1501/10?clear=10&p10_accession_num=ohiou1243 879048. *See generally* DEBORAH N. ARCHER, DIVIDING LINES: HOW TRANSPORTATION INFRASTRUCTURE REINFORCES RACIAL INEQUALITY (2025).

102 FRIEDEN & SAGALYN, *supra* note 70 at 28.

103 *Id.* at 29.

104 *Id.*

105 The Supreme Court invalidated these in Buchanan v. Warley, 245 U.S. 60 (1917). Carol Rose, *Property Law and Inequality: Lessons from Racially Restrictive Covenants*, 117 NW. U. L. REV. 225, 231 (2022).

106 RICHARD BROOKS & CAROL ROSE, SAVING THE NEIGHBORHOOD: RACIALLY RESTRICTIVE COVENANTS, LAW, AND SOCIAL NORMS (2013).

107 *Id.*

108 COLIN GORDON, MAPPING DECLINE: ST. LOUIS AND THE FATE OF THE AMERICAN CITY 73 (2008). Restrictive covenants were so effective in suburbia that many suburban municipalities used them instead of zoning until the 1940s. *Id.* at 75.

109 Alan Mallach, *Shifting the Redlining Paradigm: The Home Owners' Loan Corporation Maps and the Construction of Urban Racial Inequality*, 34 Hous. Pol'y Debate 891 (Mar. 11, 2024), https://doi.org/10.1080/10511482.2024.2321226.

110 Drake and Cayton, *supra* note 1, at 8-9.

111 *Id.*

112 *E.g.*, Daniel Aronson, Daniel Hartley & Bashkar Mazumder, *The Effects of the 1930s HOLC "Redlining" Maps*, 13 Am. Econ. J.: Econ. Pol'y 355 (Nov. 2021) (housing); Amber L. Pearson et al., *The Effects of Contemporary Redlining on the Mental Health of Black Residents*, 23 SSM Popul. Health 101462 (Sept. 2023) (mental health of residents); John Anders, *The Long Run Effects of De Jure Discrimination in the Credit Market: How Redlining Increased Crime*, 222 J. Pub. Econ. 104857 (June 2023) (crime rates).

113 Surprisingly few direct analyses exist that compare the relationship between redlining and the urban renewal program, though both relied heavily on demarcating neighborhood boundaries. The University of Richmond has provided some of the most authoritative, indispensable and accessible research on both through two groundbreaking interactive research portals, *Renewing Inequality*, https://dsl.richmond.edu/panorama/renewal/#view=0/0/1&viz=cartogram (urban renewal) and *Mapping Inequality*, https://dsl.richmond.edu/panorama/redlining/#loc=5/39.1/-94.58 (redlining).

114 Pub. L. No. 94-200, 89 Stat. 1124 (1975) (codified at 12 U.S.C. § 2801 et seq.)

115 Pub. L. No. 95–128, § 801, 91 Stat. 1111, 1147-48 (1977) (codified in 12 U.S.C. § 2901 et seq.)

116 Mary Patillo-McCoy, Black Picket Fences: Privilege and Peril Among the Black Middle Class (1999).

117 Biles, *supra* note 53, at 354 (discussing how the Department of Housing and Urban Development's shortcomings at its inception in 1965 reflected and continued to show the federal ambivalence toward stable, comprehensive urban policymaking).

118 Frieden & Sagalyn, *supra* note 70 at 31–32.

119 395 F.2d 920, 930–31 (2d Cir. 1968).

120 *E.g.*, William Julius Wilson, The Truly Disadvantaged: The Inner City, the Underclass, and Public Policy (1987); Oscar Lewis, La Vida: A Puerto Rican Family in the Culture of Poverty – San Juan and New York (1966).

121 *E.g.*, Douglas S. Massey & Nancy A. Denton, American Apartheid: Segregation and the Making of the Underclass (1993); Patrick Sharkey, Stuck in Place: Urban Neighborhoods and the End of Progress toward Racial Equality (2013); Paul A. Jargowsky, Poverty and Place: Ghettos, Barrios, and the American City (1997); Thomas Sugrue, The Origins of the Urban Crisis: Race

AND INEQUALITY IN A POSTWAR DETROIT (1996); DAVID SIBLEY, GEOGRAPHIES OF EXCLUSION: SOCIETY AND DIFFERENCE IN THE WEST (1995); Raj Chetty et al., *Is the United States Still a Land of Opportunity? Recent Trends in Intergenerational Mobility* (Nat'l Bureau of Econ. Rsch., Working Paper No. 19844, May 2014), www.nber.org/papers/w19844.

122 Jesse Coburn, *How the Trump Administration Is Weakening the Enforcement of Fair Housing Laws*, PROPUBLICA (Mar. 15, 2025), www.propublica.org/article/trump-hud-weakening-enforcement-fair-housing-laws.

Chapter 4

1 E.A. Rusoja & B.A. Thomas, *The COVID-19 Pandemic, Black Mistrust, and a Path Forward*, 35 ECLINICALMEDICINE 100868 (May 6, 2021), www.thelancet.com/journals/eclinm/article/PIIS2589-5370(21)00148-6/fulltext. Just 42% of Black Americans said in November they'd be willing to take a Covid vaccine. Martha Hostetter & Sarah Klein, *Understanding and Ameliorating Medical Mistrust Among Black Americans*, COMMONWEALTH FUND (Jan. 14, 2021), www.commonwealthfund.org/publications/newsletter-article/2021/jan/medical-mistrust-among-black-americans, *citing* Cary Funk & Alec Tyson, *Intent to Get a COVID-19 Vaccine Rises to 60% as Confidence in Research and Development Process Increases*, PEW RSCH. CTR. (Dec. 3, 2020), www.pewresearch.org/science/2020/12/03/intent-to-get-a-covid-19-vaccine-rises-to-60-as-confidence-in-research-and-development-process-increases/.

2 Emily A. Largent, *Public Health, Racism, and the Lasting Impact of Hospital Segregation*, 133 PUB. HEALTH REP. 715 (Nov. 2018), https://doi.org/10.1177/0033354918795891.

3 Cynthia Delgado et al., *A Unifying Approach for GFR Estimation: Recommendations of the NKF-ASN Task Force on Reassessing the Inclusion of Race in Diagnosing Kidney Disease*, 79 AM. J. KIDNEY DIS. 268 (Sept. 23, 2021), www.ajkd.org/action/showPdf?pii=S0272-6386%2821%2900828-3 ("[T]he National Kidney Foundation and the American Society of Nephrology established a Task Force to reassess inclusion of race in the estimation of glomerular filtration rate (GFR) in the United States" and recommended eliminating the race variable). *See also*, Prabhdeep Uppal, Benjamin L. Golden, Ashley Panicker, Omar A. Khan & Matthew J. Burday, *The Case Against Race-Based GFR*, 8 DEL. J. PUB. HEALTH 86 (Aug. 2022), https://pmc.ncbi.nlm.nih.gov/articles/PMC9495470/ ("Adjusting for Black race … accounts for an approximately 18% and 16% increase in eGFR, respectively. It was assumed that Black people have a higher average muscle mass … which has never been proven by any reputable research." Because of this artificial inflation, "[p]hysicians are failing to diagnose early stages of [chronic kidney disease] in the Black population, which leads to a delay in secondary prevention"); *and see* Dorothy Roberts, *The Problem with*

Race-Based Medicine, TEDMED 2015 (TED Nov. 2015), www.ted.com/talks/dorothy_roberts_the_problem_with_race_based_medicine.

4 The Dose Podcast, *Diagnosing Racism: How One Med Student Sparked a Big Change*, Commonwealth Fund (April 7, 2023), www.commonwealthfund.org/publications/podcast/2023/apr/diagnosing-racism-how-one-med-student-sparked-big-change.

5 *E.g.*, Kelsey Butler & Fiona Rutherford, *A US Medical Association is the Latest Battleground in Fight Over Diversity Programs*, Bloomberg (Feb. 29, 2024), www.bloomberg.com/news/articles/2024-02-29/skin-doctors-push-to-scrap-dei-programs-citing-antisemitism. Members of the American Academy of Dermatology (AAD) introduced a resolution at AAD's annual conference titled "Sunsetting All DEI Programs," charging the "DEI movement" as being antisemitic and divisive. The AAD ultimately rejected the proposal and upheld existing DEI initiatives. Lauren Buchanan, *American Academy of Dermatology Upholds Diversity Policies in Face of Anti-DEI Proposal*, Dermatology Times (Mar. 11, 2024), www.dermatologytimes.com/view/american-academy-of-dermatology-upholds-diversity-policies-in-face-of-anti-dei-proposal; Meena Singh (@drmeenasingh), Instagram (Mar. 10, 2024), www.instagram.com/p/C4WeK2esOpE/?hl=en.

6 CDC, Nat'l Vital Stat. Sys., Vol. 74 No. 7, Infant Mortality in the United States, 2023: Data From the Period Linked Birth/Infant Death File (June 12, 2025), www.cdc.gov/nchs/data/nvsr/nvsr74/nvsr74-07.pdf (infant mortality); CDC, Nat'l Ctr. Health Stat., No. 521, Mortality in the United States, 2023 (Dec. 2024), www.cdc.gov/nchs/data/databriefs/db521.pdf (death rates and life expectancy).

7 Inst. of Med., Unequal Treatment: Confronting Racial and Ethnic Disparities in Health Care (Brian D. Smedley, Adrienne Y. Stith & Alan R. Nelson eds., 2003), https://nap.nationalacademies.org/read/12875/chapter/1.

8 Nat'l Acad. Sci., Eng'g & Med., Ending Unequal Treatment: Strategies to Achieve Equitable Health Care and Optimal Health for All (Georges C. Benjamin, Jennifer E. DeVoe, Francis K. Amankwah & Sharyl J. Nass, eds., 2024), https://nap.nationalacademies.org/read/27820/chapter/1.

9 Dielle J. Lundberg, Elizabeth Wrigley-Field, Ahyoung Cho et al., *COVID-19 Mortality by Race and Ethnicity in US Metropolitan and Nonmetropolitan Areas, March 2020 to February 2022*, 6 JAMA Network Open e2311098 (May 2, 2023), https://doi.org/10.1001/jamanetworkopen.2023.11098.

10 Kendra Jason, Miguel Wilson, Jamel Catoe, Courtney Brown & Mayleen Gonzalez, *The Impact of the COVID-19 Pandemic on Black and Hispanic*

Americans' Work Outcomes: A Scoping Review, 11 J. RACIAL ETHN. HEALTH DISPARITIES 1157 (June 2024), https://doi.org/10.1007/s40615-023-01594-6.

11 Joanna Gaitens, Marian Condon, Eseosa Fernandes & Melissa McDiarmid, *COVID-19 and Essential Workers: A Narrative Review of Health Outcomes and Moral Injury,* 18 INT'L J. ENV'T RSCH. PUB. HEALTH 1446 (Feb. 4, 2021), https://doi.org/10.3390/ijerph18041446.

12 Radu Silaghi-Dumitrescu, Iulia Patrascu, Maria Lehene & Iulia Bercea, *Comorbidities of COVID-19 Patients,* 59 MEDICINA 1393 (July 29, 2023), https://doi.org/10.3390/medicina59081393; Paddy Ssentongo, Anna E. Ssentongo, Emily S. Heilbrunn, Djibril M. Ba & Vernon M Chinchilli, *Association of Cardiovascular Disease and 10 Other Pre-existing Comorbidities with COVID-19 Mortality: A Systematic Review and Meta-analysis,* 15 PLoS ONE e0238215 (Aug. 26, 2020), https://doi.org/10.1371/journal.pone.0238215.

13 Sharon Begley, *It's Not Just the Lungs: The Covid-19 Virus Attacks Like No Other "Respiratory" Infection,* STAT (June 26, 2020), www.statnews.com/2020/06/26/from-nose-to-toe-covid19-virus-attacks-like-no-other-respiratory-infection/; Ariel Bleicher & Katherine Conrad, *We Thought It Was Just a Respiratory Virus,* UCSF MAGAZINE (Summer 2020), www.ucsf.edu/magazine/covid-body.

14 Prashanth Vas, David Hopkins, Michael Feher, Francesco Rubino & Martin B. Whyte, *Diabetes, Obesity and COVID-19: A Complex Interplay,* 22 DIABETES, OBESITY & METABOLISM 1892 (Oct. 2020), https://doi.org/10.1111/dom.14134.

15 CDC, COVID-19 ASSOCIATED HOSPITALIZATION RELATED TO UNDERLYING MEDICAL CONDITIONS, https://web.archive.org/web/20200930193832/https://www.cdc.gov/coronavirus/2019-ncov/downloads/covid-data/hospitalization-underlying-medical-conditions.pdf (INTERNET ARCHIVE access from Sept. 30, 2020).

16 Matthew T. Oetjens, Jonathan Z. Luo, Alexander Chang et al., *Electronic Health Record Analysis Identifies Kidney Disease as the Leading Risk Factor for Hospitalization in Confirmed COVID-19 Patients,* 15 PLoS ONE, e0242182 (Nov. 12, 2020), https://doi.org/10.1371/journal.pone.0242182.

17 Justin M. Gregory, James C. Slaughter, Sara H. Duffus et al., *COVID-19 Severity Is Tripled in the Diabetes Community: A Prospective Analysis of the Pandemic's Impact in Type 1 and Type 2 Diabetes,* 44 DIABETES CARE 526 (Feb. 2021), https://doi.org/10.2337/dc20–2260.

18 *Obesity, Race/Ethnicity, and COVID-19,* CDC (last reviewed Feb. 5, 2024), www.cdc.gov/obesity/data/obesity-and-covid-19.html.

19 Nikhil Chatrath, Nandita Kaza, Punam A. Pabari et al., *The Effect of Concomitant COVID-19 Infection on Outcomes in Patients Hospitalized with Heart Failure,* 7 ESC HEART FAIL. 4443 (Oct. 11, 2020), https://doi.org/10.1002/ehf2.13059.

20 Heidi Ledford, *Millions of Black People Affected by Racial Bias in Health-Care Algorithms,* NATURE (Oct. 24, 2019), www.nature.com/articles/d41586-019-03228-6.

21 Zawn Villines, *What You Need to Know about Hypertension in African Americans,* MedicalNewsToday (Mar. 30, 2021), www.medicalnewstoday.com/articles/hypertension-in-african-americans (citing CDC data no longer publicly available).

22 CDC, National Diabetes Statistics Report 2020: Estimates of Diabetes and Its Burden in the United States, 2 (2020), https://diabetesresearch.org/wp-content/uploads/2022/05/national-diabetes-statistics-report-2020.pdf.

23 Ruth Petersen, Liping Pan & Heidi M Blanck, *Racial and Ethnic Disparities in Adult Obesity in the United States: CDC's Tracking to Inform State and Local Action,* 15 Prev. Chronic Dis. E46 (Apr. 11, 2019), https://doi.org/10.5888/pcd16.180579.

24 Rishi K. Wadhera, Jose F. Figueroa, Fatima Rodriguez et al., *Racial and Ethnic Disparities in Heart and Cerebrovascular Disease Deaths During the COVID-19 Pandemic in the United States,* 143 Circulation 2346 (June 15, 2021), https://doi.org/10.1161/CIRCULATIONAHA.121.054378.

25 Lauren Michele Jackson, *The Case that Being Black and Poor Is Bad for Your Health,* The New Yorker (May 31, 2023), www.newyorker.com/books/page-turner/the-case-that-being-poor-and-black-is-bad-for-your-health.

26 Allison L. Skinner-Dorkenoo, Apoorva Sarmal, Kasheena G. Rogbeer, Chloe J. André, Bhumi Patel & Leah Cha, *Highlighting COVID-19 Racial Disparities Can Reduce Support for Safety Precautions Among White U.S. Residents,* 301 Soc. Sci. Med. 114951 (May 2022), https://doi.org/10.1016/j.socscimed.2022.114951.

27 There's a class element to Black Covid deaths, too, *see* R.B. Hawkins, E.J. Charles & J.H. Mehaffey, *Socio-Economic Status and COVID-19–Related Cases and Fatalities,* 189 Pub. Health 129 (Dec. 2020), https://pubmed.ncbi.nlm.nih.gov/33227595/, including the collection of social determinants of health. Sarah B. Maness, Laura Merrell, Erika L. Thompson, Stacey B. Griner, Nolan Kline & Christopher Wheldon, *Social Determinants of Health and Health Disparities: COVID-19 Exposures and Mortality Among African American People in the United States,* 136 Pub. Health Rep. 18 (Jan.–Feb. 2021), https://pubmed.ncbi.nlm.nih.gov/33176112/.

28 Jonathan Daw, *Contribution of Four Comorbid Conditions to Racial/Ethnic Disparities in Mortality Risk,* 52 Am. J. Preventive Med. S95 (Jan. 2017), https://doi.org/10.1016/j.amepre.2016.07.036.

29 *E.g.,* Patrick Sisson, *The Other Housing Crisis: Too Many Sick, Aging Homes,* Bloomberg (Nov. 23, 2023), www.bloomberg.com/news/features/2023-11-27/america-s-aging-housing-stock-takes-toll-on-public-health; *Social Determinants of Health: Quality of Housing,* Healthy People 2030, https://odphp.health.gov/healthypeople/priority-areas/social-determinants-health/literature-summaries/quality-housing.

30 *E.g.*, James C. McCutcheon & Amanda D. Johnson, *Arson in Chicago: Patterns and Correlates*, 14 JUST. POL'Y J. (Fall 2017), www.cjcj.org/media/import/documents/arson_in_chicago_patterns_and_correlates_jpj.pdf.

31 *E.g.*, Robert D. Bullard, *Neighborhoods Zoned for Garbage*, *in* THE QUEST FOR ENVIRONMENTAL JUSTICE: HUMAN RIGHTS AND THE POLITICS OF POLLUTION (Robert D. Bullard ed., 2005) (discussing the siting of waste disposal in Black communities in Houston); Darryl Fears, *A Black Community in Northeast D.C. Is Surrounded by Industrial Pollution. The City Plans to Add More*, WASH. POST (Aug. 4, 2021), www.washingtonpost.com/climate-environment/2021/08/04/brentwood-pollution-racism-dc/ (discussing DC's plan "to build a sprawling school-bus terminal in the historically Black enclave of Brentwood, where residents have long lived amid industrial sites that discharge pollution into their community").

32 *E.g.*, Douglas S. Massey, *Getting Away with Murder: Segregation and Violent Crime in Urban America*, 143 U. PA. L. REV. 1203 (1995); Angela J. Haddad, Aupal Mondal, Chandra R. Bhat et al., *Pedestrian Crash Frequency: Unpacking the Effects of Contributing Factors and Racial Disparities*, 182 ACCIDENT ANALYSIS & PREVENTION 106954 (2023) https://doi.org/10.1016/j.aap.2023.106954.

33 *See, e.g.*, David R. Williams & Selina A. Mohammed, *Discrimination and Racial Disparities in Health: Evidence and Needed Research*, 32 J. BEHAV. MED. 20 (Feb. 2009), https://doi.org/10.1007/s10865-008-9185-0; April D. Thames, Michael R. Irwin, Elizabeth C. Breen & Steve W. Cole, *Experienced Discrimination and Racial Differences in Leukocyte Gene Expression*, 106 PSYCHONEUROENDOCRINOL OGY 277 (Aug. 2019), https://doi.org/10.1016/j.psyneuen.2019.04.016.

34 Arline T. Geronimus, Margaret Hicken, Danya Keene & John Bound, *"Weathering" and Age Patterns of Allostatic Load Scores Among Blacks and Whites in the United States*, 96 AM. J. PUB. HEALTH 826 (May 2006), https://doi.org/10.2105/AJPH.2004.060749.

35 Cynthia G. Colen, David M. Ramey, Elizabeth C. Cooksey & David R. Williams, *Racial Disparities in Health Among Nonpoor African Americans and Hispanics: The Role of Acute and Chronic Discrimination*, 199 SOC. SCI. MED. 167 (Feb. 2018), https://doi.org/10.1016/j.socscimed.2017.04.051.

36 Caryn N. Bell, Roland J. Thorpe, Jr., Janice V. Bowie & Thomas A. LaVeist, *Race Disparities in Cardiovascular Disease Risk Factors Within Socioeconomic Status Strata*, 28 ANNALS OF EPIDEMIOL. 147 (Mar. 2018), https://doi.org/10.1016/j.annepidem.2017.12.007.

37 John Gramlich, *What We Know About the Increase in U.S. Murders in 2020*, PEW RSCH. CTR. (Oct. 27, 2021), www.pewresearch.org/short-reads/2021/10/27/what-we-know-about-the-increase-in-u-s-murders-in-2020/.

38 *See Trauma*, AM. PSYCHOL. ASS'N, www.apa.org/topics/trauma/index.aspx.

39 Judith Herman, M.D., Trauma and Recovery: The Aftermath of Violence – From Domestic Abuse to Political Terror (1992).

40 *E.g.*, Andres J. Pumariega, Youngsuhk Jo, Brent Beck & Mariam Rahmani, *Trauma and US Minority Children and Youth*, 24 Curr. Psych. Rep. 285 (Mar. 14, 2022), https://doi.org/10.1007/s11920-022-01336-1.

41 *See* Laura J. Hickman et al., *How Much Does "How Much" Matter? Assessing the Relationship Between Children's Lifetime Exposure to Violence and Trauma Symptoms, Behavior Problems and Parenting Stress*, 28 J. Interpersonal Violence 1338 (2012) (only poly-victimization predicted child behavior problems, PTSD and parenting stress); Heather A. Turner et al., *Poly-Victimization in a National Sample of Children and Youth*, 38 Am. J. Preventive Med. 89 (2010); David Finkelhor et al., *Polyvictimization and Trauma in a National Longitudinal Cohort*, 19 Dev. & Psychopathology 149 (2007); David Finkelhor et al., *Poly-Victimization: A Neglected Component in Child Victimization*, 31 Child Abuse & Neglect 7 (2007).

42 E. Jane Costello et al., *The Prevalence of Potentially Traumatic Events in Childhood and Adolescence*, 15 J. Traumatic Stress 99, 110 (2002).

43 Vincent J. Felitti et al., *Relationship of Childhood Abuse and Household Dysfunction to Many of the Leading Causes of Death in Adults: The Adverse Childhood Experiences (ACE) Study*, 14 Am. J. Preventative Med. 245 (1998).

44 Finkelhor et al., *Poly-Victimization and Trauma in a National Longitudinal Cohort*, *supra* note 41.

45 Judith A. Cohen et al., *Childhood Traumatic Grief: Concepts and Controversies*, 3 Trauma, Violence, & Abuse 307 (2002); Eva Alisic et al., *Rates of Post-Traumatic Stress Disorder in Trauma-Exposed Children and Adolescents: Meta-Analysis*, 204 British J. Psychiatry 335 (2014).

46 Shelley E. Taylor et al., *Early Adversity and Adult Health Outcomes*, 23 Dev. & Psychopathology 939 (2011).

47 Costello et al., *supra* note 42, at 109–10.

48 Eugene Aisenberg & Ferol E. Mennen, *Children Exposed to Community Violence: Issues for Assessment and Treatment*, 17 Child & Adolescent Soc. Work J. 341 (2000); Linda C. Gallo et al., *Socioeconomic Status and Health: What Is the Role of Reserve Capacity?*, 18 Curr. Dir. Psych. Sci. 269 (2009).

49 For example, Lin, Neylan, Epel, and O'Donovan investigated the relation between childhood adversity (repeating a year of school, household dysfunction related to parent alcohol or drug abuse, physical abuse by parent), adult adversity (death of child; fire, flood, earthquake or natural disaster; combat exposure; family member addicted to drugs/alcohol; victim of a serious physical attack or assault; self, spouse or child experienced life-threatening illness or accident) and levels of an inflammatory biomarker, high sensitive C-reactive protein (hsCRP) in 11,198 adults aged fifty or older. The authors found that

the presence of any childhood or adult adversity and their greater frequency (continuous) each predicted significantly higher blood levels of hsCRP. This finding and another study comparing participants with no adult or childhood adversity, childhood but no adult adversity, adult but no childhood adversity, and childhood and adult adversity, points to the relation between childhood adversity, even more so than adult adversity, and inflammation, which is a pathway through which chronic stress is believed to increase risk of disease. Joy E. Lin et al., *Associations of Childhood Adversity and Adulthood Trauma with C-reactive Protein; A Cross-Sectional Population-Based Study*, 53 BRAIN, BEHAV. & IMMUNITY 105 (2016).

50 Aoife O'Donovan et al., *Childhood Trauma Associated with Short Leukocyte Telomere Length in Posttraumatic Stress Disorder*, 70 BIOLOGICAL PSYCHIATRY 465 (2011).

51 Bruce D. Perry, *The Neurodevelopmental Impact of Violence in Childhood*, *in* TEXTBOOK OF CHILD AND ADOLESCENT FORENSIC PSYCHIATRY, 221 (D. Schetky & E.P. Benedek eds., 2001) (available at www.healing-arts.org/healing_trauma_therapy/Perry_The_Neurodevelopmental_Impact_of_Violence_in_Childhood.pdf, 3–4).

52 *Id.* at 5.

53 Robert F. Anda et al., *Adverse Childhood Experiences, Alcoholic Parents, and Later Risk of Alcoholism and Depression*, 53 PSYCHIATRIC SERV. 1001 (2001); Daniel P. Chapman et al., *Adverse Childhood Experiences and the Risk of Depressive Disorders in Adulthood*, 82 J. AFFECTIVE DISORDERS 217 (2004); Ronald C. Kessler et al., *Childhood Adversity and Adult Psychiatric Disorder in the US National Comorbidity Survey*, 27 PSYCHOL. MED. 1101 (1997).

54 *See* Theodore Thompson, Jr. & Carol Rippey Massat, *Experiences of Violence, Post-Traumatic Stress, Academic Achievement and Behavior Problems of Urban African-American Children*, 22 CHILD & ADOLESCENT SOC. WORK J. 367 (2005).

55 Covid isolation alone increased PTSD symptomatology for adults during the pandemic. Katja I. Seitz, Katja Bertsch & Sabine C. Herpertz, *A Prospective Study of Mental Health During the COVID-19 Pandemic in Childhood Trauma-Exposed Individuals: Social Support Matters*, 34 J. TRAUMA STRESS. 477 (June 2021), https://doi.org/10.1002/jts.22660. *See* PATRICK SHARKEY, STUCK IN PLACE: URBAN NEIGHBORHOODS AND THE END OF PROGRESS TOWARD RACIAL EQUALITY (1st ed. 2013).

56 Rachel Young & Solomon Hsiang, *Mortality Caused by Tropical Cyclones in the United States*, 635 NATURE 121 (2024), https://doi.org/10.1038/s41586-024-07945-5.

57 Lisa A. Cooper, Debra L. Roter, Kathryn A. Carson et al., *The Associations of Clinicians' Implicit Attitudes About Race with Medical Visit Communication and Patient Ratings of Interpersonal Care*, 102 AM. J. PUB. HEALTH 979 (MAY 2012), https://doi.org/10.2105/AJPH.2011.300558.

58 INST. OF MED., *supra* note 6 at 396.

59 Rachel G. Logan, Ellen M. Daley, Cheryl A. Vamos, Adetola Louis-Jacques & Stephanie L. Marhefka, *"When Is Health Care Actually Going to Be Care?" The Lived Experience of Family Planning Care Among Young Black Women*, 31 QUALITATIVE HEALTH RSCH. 1169 (May 2021), https://doi.org/10.1177/1049732321993094.

60 INST. OF MED., *supra* note 6 at 396.

61 LIZ HAMEL, LUNNA LOPES, CAILEY MUÑANA, SAMANTHA ARTIGA & MOLLYANN BRODIE, RACE, HEALTH, AND COVID-19: THE VIEWS AND EXPERIENCES OF BLACK AMERICANS, KFF, 4 (Oct. 2020), https://files.kff.org/attachment/Report-Race-Health-and-COVID-19-The-Views-and-Experiences-of-Black-Americans.pdf.

62 Paige Nong, Minakshi Raj, Melissa Creary, Sharn L.R. Kardia & Jodyn E. Platt, *Patient-Reported Experiences of Discrimination in the US Health Care System*, 3 JAMA NETWORK OPEN e2029650 (Dec. 15, 2020), https://doi.org/10.1001/jamanetwork open.2020.29650.

63 Medicaid managed care enrollees who are members of racial and ethnic minority groups have historically reported worse care experiences than white enrollees. Compared with white enrollees, minority enrollees reported significantly worse care experiences. Overall adjusted disparities for Black enrollees ranged between 1.5 and 4.5 percentage points; 1.6–3.9 percentage points for Hispanic or Latino enrollees; and 9.0–17.4 percentage points for Asian American, Native Hawaiian, or other Pacific Islander enrollees. Disparities were largely attributable to worse experiences by race or ethnicity within the same plan. Kevin H. Nguyen, Ira B. Wilson, Anya R. Wallack & Amal N. Trivedi, *Racial and Ethnic Disparities in Patient Experience of Care Among Nonelderly Medicaid Managed Care Enrollees*, 41 HEALTH AFF. (MILLWOOD) 256 (Feb. 2022), https://doi.org/10.1377/hlthaff.2021.01331.

64 A 1994 study published in the Journal of the American Medical Association found that Medicare patients who are African American, poor and seriously ill receive worse care than other gravely ill Medicare patients in every type of hospital in America. K.L. Kahn, M.L. Pearson, E.R. Harrison et al., *Health Care for Black and Poor Hospitalized Medicare Patients*, 271 JAMA 1169 (Apr. 20, 1994), www.ncbi.nlm.nih.gov/pubmed/8151874. In a 1999 New England Journal of Medicine study, actors pretending to have heart problems described their symptoms to 720 physicians. Black female actors received the fewest referrals for specialized treatment – even though they related symptoms identical to those of white men, white women and Black men. K.A. Schulman, J.A. Berlin, W. Harless et al., *The Effect of Race and Sex on Physicians' Recommendations for Cardiac Catheterization*, 340 N. ENGL. J. MED. 618 (Feb. 25, 1999), https://doi.org/10.1056/nejm199902253400806.

65 Carolyn Johnson & Phil Drechsler, *After His Wife Died, Man Pushing to Change Laws to Protect More Women From Pregnancy-Related Deaths*, NBC L.A. (July 15,

2020), www.nbclosangeles.com/investigations/wife-died-giving-birth-change-laws-to-protect-more-women-pregnancy-related-deaths/2395401/.

66 Rachel L. Johnson et al., *Patient Race/Ethnicity and Quality of Patient–Physician Communication During Medical Visits*, 94 AM. J. PUB. HEALTH 2084 (Dec. 2004), https://doi.org/10.2105/AJPH.94.12.2084.

67 T.E. Finucane & J.A. Carrese, *Racial Bias in Presentation of Cases*, 5 J. GEN. INTERNAL MED. 120 (Mar. 1990), https://doi.org/10.1007/bf02600511; M. van Ryn & J. Burke, *The Effect of patient Race and Socio-economic Status on Physicians' Perceptions of Patients*, 50 SOC. SCI. & MED. 813 (Mar. 2000), https://doi.org/10.1016/s0277-9536(99)00338-x.

68 NAT'L RSCH. COUNCIL, UNDERSTANDING RACIAL AND ETHNIC DIFFERENCES IN HEALTH IN LATE LIFE: A RESEARCH AGENDA, 100 (Rodolfo A. Bulatao & Norman B. Anderson eds., 2004).

69 *See, e.g.*, Chloë FitzGerald & Samia Hurst, *Implicit Bias in Healthcare Professionals: A Systematic Review*, 18 BMC MED. ETHICS, 19 (Mar. 1, 2017), https://doi.org/10.1186/s12910-017-0179-8 (documenting thirty-five out of forty-two articles showing evidence of implicit bias lowering quality of care); Aiden Byrne & Alessandra Tanesini, *Instilling New Habits: Addressing Implicit Bias in Healthcare Professionals*, 20 ADV. HEALTH SCI. ED. 1255 (2015), https://doi.org/10.1007/s10459-015-9600-6 (Implicit Association Test evidence links disparities in health outcomes with unconscious social biases of physicians); Janice A. Sabin & Anthony G. Greenwald, *The Influence of Implicit Bias on Treatment Recommendations for 4 Common Pediatric Conditions: Pain, Urinary Tract Infection, Attention Deficit Hyperactivity Disorder, and Asthma*, 102 AM. J. PUB. HEALTH 988 (May 2012), https://doi.org/10.2105/AJPH.2011.300621 (suggesting health-care providers implicitly hold associations that Black patients are less compliant and less cooperative than white patients despite lack of evidence).

70 Rose Clark-Hitt, Jennifer Malat, Diana Burgess & Greta Friedemann-Sanchez, *Doctors' and Nurses' Explanations for Racial Disparities in Medical Treatment*, 21 J. HEALTH CARE POOR & UNDERSERVED 386 (Feb. 2010), https://doi.org/10.1353/hpu.0.0275.

71 INST. OF MED., *supra* note 6.

72 Marcella Alsan & Marianne Wanamaker, *Tuskegee and the Health of Black Men*, 133 Q.J. ECON. 407 (Feb. 2018), https://doi.org/10.1093/qje/qjx029; Sophia Chase, *The Bloody Truth: Examining America's Blood Industry and Its Tort Liability through the Arkansas Prison Plasma Scandal*, 3 WM. & MARY BUS. L. REV. 597 (2012).

73 Jesse Washington, *New Poll Shows Black Americans Put Far Less Trust in Doctors and Hospitals than White People*, ANDSCAPE: RACE & HEALTH CARE, https://theundefeated.com/features/new-poll-shows-black-americans-

put-far-less-trust-in-doctors-and-hospitals-than-white-people/ (Andscape formerly known as The Undefeated), *discussing* Hamel et al., *supra* note 61.

74 K.L. Kahn, M.L. Pearson, E.R. Harrison et al., *Health Care for Black and Poor Hospitalized Medicare Patients*, 271 JAMA 1169 (Apr. 20, 1994), https://pubmed.ncbi.nlm.nih.gov/8151874/. *See also* Juanita J. Chin, Iman K. Martin & Nicole Redmond, *Health Equity Among Black Women in the United States*, 30 J. WOMEN'S HEALTH 212 (2021), https://doi.org/10.1089/jwh.2020.8868.

75 Schulman et al., *supra* note 64. *See also* Molly Ginty, *Black Women at Higher Risk for Major Diseases*, WOMEN'S ENEWS (Feb. 25, 2005), https://womensenews.org/2005/02/black-women-at-higher-risk-major-diseases/.

76 In a study examining an algorithm used to refer patients for additional healthcare services, researchers found that the data input into the algorithm underestimated the average Black person's health risk because it based risk on the annual cost of care provided. While the cost of the average Black patient's care was significantly lower per year than the average white patient's, the average Black patient was substantially sicker. Because of this bias, only 17.7% of the patients referred for extra care were Black, but properly calculated based on the health of individual, 46.5% of referred patients would have been Black. Ledford, *supra* note 20.

77 *See, e.g.*, Liggon-Redding v. Voorhees, 2014 U.S. Dist. LEXIS 77815 (plaintiff minority patient's claim of a pattern of implicit bias malpractice dismissed for failure to establish professional standard of care).

78 Charles F. Parker & Eric K. Stern, *The Trump Administration and the COVID-19 Crisis: Exploring the Warning-Response Problems and Missed Opportunities of a Public Health Emergency*, 100 PUB. ADMIN. 616 (Sept. 2022), https://doi.org/10.1111/padm.12843.

79 Ryan Zamarripa, *Five Ways the Trump Administration's Policy Failures Compounded the Coronavirus-Induced Economic Crisis*, CTR. AM. PROGRESS (June 3, 2020), www.americanprogress.org/article/5-ways-trump-administrations-policy-failures-compounded-coronavirus-induced-economic-crisis/.

80 Steffie Woolhandler, David U. Himmelstein, Sameer Ahmed et al., *Public Policy and Health in the Trump Era*, 397 LANCET 705 (Feb. 20, 2021), www.thelancet.com/journals/lancet/article/PIIS0140-6736(20)32545-9/abstract.

81 Jenna Russell, *Federal Cuts Become "All Consuming" at Harvard's Public Health School*, N.Y. TIMES (May 21, 2025), www.nytimes.com/2025/05/21/us/harvard-chan-school-public-health-federal-funding-cuts.html. ("Then last week, the trickle became a flood, swamping a school where 59 percent of operating revenue comes from the federal government and other outside sponsors. By comparison, Harvard Medical School receives 35 percent of its revenue from such sponsors, the Graduate School of Education 22 percent, the Kennedy School of Government 16 percent, and Harvard Law School 3 percent.")

Chapter 5

1 Jesus Jiménez & Sara Ruberg, *Louisiana Trooper Avoids Jail Time in Death of Ronald Greene*, N.Y. TIMES (Oct. 28, 2024), www.nytimes.com/2024/10/28/us/louisiana-trooper-plea-ronald-greene-death.html.

2 Maanvi Singh, *How America's Broken Autopsy System Can Mask Police Violence*, THE GUARDIAN (July 2, 2020), https://amp.theguardian.com/us-news/2020/jul/02/autopsies-police-killings-medical-misleading; Anne Crawford Roberts et al., *George Floyd's Autopsy and the Structural Gaslighting of America*, SCI. AM. (June 6, 2020), https://nam02.safelinks.protection.outlook.com/GetUrlReputation.

3 The murder of Daniel Prude will not yield criminal action. Greg Hanlon, *Cops Won't Face Charges in Case of Daniel Prude, Black Man Who Died After Being Put in "Spit-Hood"*, PEOPLE (Feb. 23, 2021), https://people.com/crime/daniel-prude-police-no-charges-death-rochester-black-man/. The murder of Elijah McClain produced indictments of the three police officers who subdued and asphyxiated him, as well as two paramedics who are alleged to have failed to render timely assistance,. and a judge will decide if there is probable cause for the case to proceed. Carina Julig & Max Levy, *Trial Against Aurora Cops, Medics in Death of Elijah McClain Moved to August*, SENTINEL (Apr. 18, 2022), https://sentinelcolorado.com/news/metro/trial-against-aurora-cops-medics-in-death-of-elijah-mcclain-moved-to-august/. In Breonna Taylor's case, none of the officers were charged with state crimes for shooting her (though one was indicted for recklessly firing into Taylor's building and putting neighbors at risk). However, the U.S. Department of Justice has filed criminal civil rights charges against four police officers, including one at the scene, for conspiracy to deprive Taylor of her civil rights based on their fraudulent procurement of a no-knock warrant. *See* Dylan Lovan, *Breonna Taylor Supporters Relieved by Charges Against Officers Involved in Her Killing*, PBS (Aug. 5, 2022), www.pbs.org/news hour/nation/breonna-taylor-supporters-relieved-by-charges-against-police.
In an unprecedented result, Derek Chauvin, the former Minneapolis police officer primarily responsible for the murder of Derek Floyd, was convicted of state murder charges as well as federal criminal civil rights charges and sentenced to decades in prison. *See* note 35, *infra*.

4 *Fatal Force: Police Shootings Database*, WASH. POST, www.washingtonpost.com/graphics/investigations/police-shootings-database/. *See also* Elie Mystal, *The Cops Killed More People in 2023 than They Had in Years*, NATION (Jan. 11, 2023), www.thenation.com/article/archive/cops-killed-more-people-in-2023-than-in-years/; Curtis Bunn, *Report: Black People Are Still Killed at a Higher Rate than Other Groups*, NBC NEWS (Mar. 3, 2022), www.nbcnews.com/news/nbcblk/report-black-people-are-still-killed-police-higher-rate-groups-rcna17169.

5 *See, e.g.*, Anna North, *How Racist Policing Took Over American Cities, Explained by a Historian*, Vox (June 6, 2020), www.vox.com/2020/6/6/21280643/police-brutality-violence-protests-racism-khalil-muhammad, quoting Khalil Muhammad:

> But it wasn't really until the beginning of the 20th century, when streams of black migrants began to move to northern cities, and particularly during World War I and what became known as the Great Migration, that we began to see the increased ascription of black people as prone to criminality, as a dangerous race, as a way of essentially limiting their access to the full fruits of their freedom in the North.

6 *See, e.g.*, Off. of Surgeon Gen., U.S. Surgeon General's Advisory on Firearm Violence: A Public Health Crisis in America (2024), www.ncbi.nlm.nih.gov/books/NBK605169/pdf/Bookshelf_NBK605169.pdf (no longer accessible on the Office of the Surgeon General's HHS website); Daniel Kim, *Social Determinants of Health in Relation to Firearm-Related Homicides in the United States: A Nationwide Multilevel Cross-Sectional Study*, 16 PLoS Med. 1002978 (Dec. 17, 2019), https://pubmed.ncbi.nlm.nih.gov/31846474/.

7 *See generally* Kristin Hennings, The Rage of Innocence: How America Criminalizes Black Youth (2021).

8 Jill Lepore, *The Invention of the Police*, New Yorker (July 13, 2020), www.newyorker.com/magazine/2020/07/20/the-invention-of-the-police.

9 *Id.*

10 *See* Simone Weichselbaum, *Police with Military Experience More Likely to Shoot*, Marshall Project (Oct. 15, 2018), www.themarshallproject.org/2018/10/15/police-with-military-experience-more-likely-to-shoot (describing studies from multiple cities showing correlation between military service and officer shootings).

11 Lepore, *supra* note 8.

12 Howard Zinn, A People's History of the United States (1980).

13 *See generally* Khalil Gibran Muhammad, The Condemnation of Blackness: Race, Crime, and the Making of Modern Urban America 4 (2010). ("For white Americans of every ideological stripe – from radical southern racists to northern progressives – African American criminality became one of the most widely accepted bases for justifying prejudicial thinking, discriminatory treatment, and/or acceptance of racial violence as an instrument of public safety.")

14 The full text of Section 2, ratified December 6, 1865, reads: "Neither slavery nor involuntary servitude, except as a punishment for crime whereof the party shall have been duly convicted, shall exist within the United States, or any place subject to their jurisdiction." U.S. Const. amend. XIII § 2.

15 This is historically true, even though the Court in *The Civil Rights Cases* gave Congress the power to use the Thirteenth Amendment to eliminate "all badges and incidents of slavery." 109 U.S. 3, 20 (1883).

16 Monroe v. Pape, 365 U.S. 167, 174 (1961). ("This Act of April 20, 1871, sometimes called 'the third "force bill",' was passed by a Congress that had the Klan 'particularly in mind.' The debates are replete with references to the lawless conditions existing in the South in 1871.")

17 *Id.*

18 DERRICK A. BELL, RACE, RACISM AND AMERICAN LAW 374–77 (2nd ed. 1980).

19 *Monroe* represented a novel (at that time) question of Section 1983's reach to include local police abuses. Bell argues that its criminal parallel, Section 242, was not revived again until the 1960s. *Id.* at 379–80. *See also* United States v. Price, 383 U.S. 787 (1966).

20 *See* L. Song Richardson, *Police Racial Violence: Lessons from Social Psychology*, 83 FORDHAM L. REV. 2961, 2962 (2015).

21 *See* Amelia Thomson-DeVeaux, Nathaniel Rakich & Likhitha Butchireddygari, *Why It's So Rare for Police Officers to Face Legal Consequences*, FIVETHIRTYEIGHT (June 4, 2020), https://fivethirtyeight.com/features/why-its-still-so-rare-for-police-officers-to-face-legal-consequences-for-misconduct/, *citing Fatal Force, supra* note 4.

22 However, most are armed during the encounter. Charles Menifield, Geigunn Shin & Logan Strother, *Do White Law Enforcement Officers Target Minority Suspects?*, 79 PUB. ADMIN. REV. 56 (Jan. 2019).

23 *Id.* The same study found that white cops are *not* more likely to kill Blacks than nonwhite officers.

24 *See* Cheryl Thompson, *Fatal Police Shootings of Unarmed Black People Reveal Troubling Patterns*, NPR (Jan. 25, 2021), www.npr.org/2021/01/25/956177021/fatal-police-shootings-of-unarmed-black-people-reveal-troubling-patterns.

25 *Id.*

26 *See Official Misconduct*, INNOCENCE PROJECT, https://innocenceproject.org/official-misconduct/.

27 Rachel Harmon, *Why Do We (Still) Lack Data on Policing?*, 96 MARQ. L. REV. 4 (2014). Harmon argues that public policy and legal decisions about policing depend heavily on empirical judgments, but police chiefs and local government officials do not generate sufficient data about the police absent external regulation. The Bureau of Justice Statistics and the Federal Bureau of Investigation, the primary federal agencies charged with collecting information on policing, have focused on serving the law enforcement community rather than facilitating governance of the police. The consequence is that we do not have the information we need to secure effective and rights-protecting policing.

28 Thomson-DeVeaux et al., *supra* note 21; Ryan Gabrielson, Eric Sagara & Ryan Grochowski Jones, *Deadly Force in Black and White*, PROPUBLICA (Oct. 10, 2014), www.propublica.org/article/deadly-force-in-black-and-white (showing

that young Black men were twenty-one times more likely to be shot dead by police than their white counterparts).

29 *See Fatal Force*, *supra* note 4.

30 *Id.* For "an impartial, comprehensive and searchable national database of people killed during interactions with police," *see* FATAL ENCOUNTERS, https://FatalEncounters.org/.

31 *Id.* A database created by Bowling Green State University Professor Phillip M. Stinson documents instances of misconduct for over 10,000 criminal arrest cases, between 2005 and 2014, involving over 8,000 nonfederal sworn law enforcement officers. *See* Thomson-DeVeaux et al., *supra* note 21.

32 Craig McCarthy & S.P. Sullivan, *For 17 Years, N.J. Had the Chance to Stop Potentially Dangerous Cops. The State Failed to Do It*, NJ.COM (Nov. 29, 2018), www.nj.com/news/2018/11/nj_broken_system_for_stopping_potentially_abusive_police_officers.html.

33 *E.g.*, *Force Report: Millville Cumberland County*, NJ.COM, http://force.nj.com/database/pd-dept/millville-cumberland. For instance, in Millville in South Jersey, Black people faced police force at more than six times the rate of whites. In South Orange, it was nearly ten times. In Lakewood, it was twenty-two times. *See generally The Force Report*, NJ.COM: PROJECTS & INVESTIGATIONS, http://force.nj.com/.

34 McCarthy & Sullivan, *supra* note 32. New Jersey fails to monitor trends to flag officers who use disproportionately high amounts of force. The state recently implemented a new early warning system to identify potential problem officers but did not mandate tracking use-of-force trends as a criteria, which experts called a gaping hole in oversight.

35 Laurel Wesley, *Derek Chauvin Found Guilty of George Floyd's Murder*, NPR (Apr. 20, 2021), www.npr.org/sections/trial-over-killing-of-george-floyd/2021/04/20/987777911/court-says-jury-has-reached-verdict-in-derek-chauvins-murder-trial. Press Release, Former Minneapolis Police Officer Derek Chauvin Sentenced to More than 20 Years in Prison for Depriving George Floyd and a Minor Victim of their Constitutional Rights, U.S. Dep't Just. Off. Pub. Affs. (July 7, 2022), www.justice.gov/opa/pr/former-minneapolis-police-officer-derek-chauvin-sentenced-more-20-years-prison-depriving.

36 Shaila Dewan, *Few Police Officers Who Cause Deaths Are Charged or Convicted*, N.Y. TIMES (Sept. 24, 2020), www.nytimes.com/2020/09/24/us/police-killings-prosecution-charges.html?referringSource=articleShare.

37 Kimberly Kindy & Kimbriell Kelly, *Thousands Dead, Few Prosecuted: Fatal Shootings by On-Duty Officers: An Analysis*, WASH. POST (Apr. 11, 2015), www.washingtonpost.com/sf/investigative/2015/04/11/thousands-dead-few-prosecuted/?wpisrc=al_alerthttp://.

38 Dewan, *supra* note 36. *See also* Tom Jackman & Devlin Barrett, *Charging Officers with Crimes Is Still Difficult for Prosecutors*, WASH. POST (May 29, 2020), www.washingtonpost.com/crime-law/2020/05/29/charging-cops-with-crimes-is-still-difficult-prosecutors/. Jackman and Barrett note that prosecutors typically consider themselves part of the law enforcement "team" with police, and they may even know the potential defendant. And when a case finally goes to trial, juries tend to be sympathetic to the daily challenges faced by officers on the street and are more likely to find them not guilty.

39 ALEX S. VITALE, THE END OF POLICING 18 (2017). *See also* Kindy & Kelly, *supra* note 37.

40 *See* Dewan, *supra* note 36.

41 Associated Press, *Police in Misconduct Cases Stay on Force Through Arbitration*, VOA (June 24, 2020), www.voanews.com/a/usa_police-misconduct-cases-stay-force-through-arbitration/6191657.html.

42 Joanna Schwartz, *Myths and Mechanics of Deterrence: The Role of Lawsuits in Law Enforcement Decisionmaking*, 57 UCLA L. REV. 1023, 1040 (2010). Schwartz argues that it should not be presumed that civil rights lawsuits necessarily have a deterrent effect, because not all cities track, process, or respond to lawsuits filed against officers.

43 Kate Levine, *How We Prosecute the Police*, 104 GEO. L.J. 745, 749 (2016). Levine argues that, as criminal justice insiders, police have dealt themselves special protections from police questioning based on their knowledge of what protections a suspect need most when facing interrogation. Meanwhile, the police continue to argue that, without using these selfsame tactics on other suspects, their ability to catch and convict dangerous criminals will be hampered.

44 CARL B. KLOCKARS, SANJA KUTNJAK IVKOVICH, WILLIAM E. HARVER & MARIA R. HABERFIELD, RESEARCH IN BRIEF: THE MEASUREMENT OF POLICE INTEGRITY (May 2000), www.ncjrs.gov/pdffiles1/nij/181465.pdf.

45 Neal Trautman, Nat'l Inst. Ethics, *Police Code of Silence Facts Revealed*, INT'L ASSN. CHIEFS OF POLICE (2000), www.aele.org/loscode2000.html.

46 *Id.*

47 *See* Cleveland Bd. of Education v. Loudermill, 470 U.S. 532, 546 (1985) ("The tenured public employee is entitled to oral or written notice of the charges against him, an explanation of the employer's evidence, and an opportunity to present his side of the story"), *citing* Arnett v. Kennedy, 416 U.S. 134, 170–71 (1974) (POWELL, J., concurring).

48 Editorial Board, *To Hold Police Accountable, Ax the Arbitrators*, N.Y. TIMES (Oct. 3, 2020), www.nytimes.com/2020/10/03/opinion/sunday/police-arbitration-reform-unions.html?referringSource=articleShare.

49 *Id.*

50 *See* U.S. COMM'N ON CIV. RTS., No. 005-901-00074-0, REVISITING *WHO IS GUARDING THE GUARDIANS?*: A REPORT ON POLICE PRACTICES AND CIVIL RIGHTS IN AMERICA 64 (2000) ("The most common avenue of redress available to victims of police abuse is initiating a civil action for damages under state law"). *See, e.g.*, Wilson v. Isaacs, 929 N.E.2d 200, 203 (2010) ("a law enforcement officer's use of force is reasonable only 'if the officer reasonably believes that the force is necessary to effect a lawful arrest.' Ind. Code § 35-41-3-3(b). If an officer uses unnecessary or excessive force, the officer may commit the torts of assault and battery.") (citations omitted).

51 42 U.S.C. §1983.

52 Gomez v. Toledo, 446 U.S. 635, 640 (1980) (*citing* Monroe v. Pape, 365 U.S. at 171).

53 Calif. v. Hodari D., 499 U.S. 621, 628 (1991). No seizure occurs unless cops intentionally use physical force in effecting a stop, or a suspect submits to a show of authority.

54 471 U.S. 1, 7 (1985). ("While it is not always clear just when minimal police interference becomes a seizure . . . there can be no question that apprehension by the use of deadly force is a seizure subject to the reasonableness requirement of the Fourth Amendment.")

55 Brower v. County of Inyo, 489 U.S. 593, 597 (1989).

56 Kingsley v Hendrickson, 135 S. Ct. 2466, 2472 (2015).

57 490 U.S. 386, 387 (1989).

58 Plumhoff v. Rickard, 134 S.Ct. 2012, 2020 (2014).

59 Graham, 490 U.S. at 396.

60 MICHAEL AVERY, DAVID RUDOVSKY, KAREN BLUM & JENNIFER LAURIN, POLICE MISCONDUCT: LAW AND LITIGATION 132, sec. 2:19 (3rd ed. 2015–16). Commentators have called into question how often police actually face split-second decision-making, and whether they should receive deference in situations where, through unnecessary escalation, the officer himself creates the need for fast action. *See, e.g.*, Michael Avery, *Unreasonable Seizures of Unreasonable People: Defining the Totality of Circumstances Relevant to Assessing the Police Use of Force Against Emotionally Disturbed People*, 34 COL. HUMAN RTS. L. REV. 261, 320–23 (Spring, 2003) ("The Myth of Split-Second Decision-Making").

61 *See* Roger G. Dunham, Geoffrey P. Alpert, Dennis J. Kenny & Paul Cromwell, *High-Speed Pursuit: The Offenders' Perspective*, 25 CRIM. JUST. & BEHAV. 30 (Mar. 1998).

62 *See* Thompson, *supra* note 24. Regarding jury deference, Professor Stinson says, "The courts are very reluctant to second-guess the split-second decisions of police officers in potentially violent street encounters that might be life-or-death situations . . . They somehow seem to take everything that's been presented in the case, in the trial, and just disregard the legal standard." *Id.*

63 The relative danger to police from traffic stops, for example, is far less than police lead the public to believe. *See* Jordan Blair Woods, *Policing, Danger Narratives, and Routine Traffic Stops*, 117 MICH. L. REV. 635 (2019), https://repository.law.umich.edu/cgi/viewcontent.cgi?article=2484&context=mlr. ("Under a conservative estimate, the rate for a felonious killing of an officer during a routine traffic stop was only 1 in every 6.5 million stops, the rate for an assault resulting in serious injury to an officer was only 1 in every 361,111 stops, and the rate for an assault against officers (whether it results in injury or not) was only 1 in every 6,959 stops.")

64 Joseph Goldstein, *"Testilying" by Police: A Stubborn Problem*, N.Y. TIMES (Mar. 18, 2018), www.nytimes.com/2018/03/18/nyregion/testilying-police-perjury-new-york.html. *See also* Stephanie Agnew, *Police Perjury –"Testilying" – Perpetuates Institutional Racism, Violence, and Corruption*, CHI. APPLESEED (Nov. 9, 2020), www.chicagoappleseed.org/2020/11/09/testilying/.

65 AVERY, POLICE MISCONDUCT, *supra* note 60 at 132, sec. 2:19.

66 *See* Chiraag Bains, *After Creating Danger, Can Cops Use Force with Impunity?*, MARSHALL PROJECT (June 15, 2017), www.themarshallproject.org/2017/06/15/after-creating-danger-can-cops-use-force-with-impunity (discussing County of Los Angeles v. Mendez, 581 U.S. 420 (2017)).

67 For a comprehensive investigation of three illustrative police shootings, *see* Robin Stein, Haley Willis, Brenna Smith, Natalie Reneau, Rumsey Taylor, David Kirkpatrick et al., *Before the Final Frame: When Police Steps Create Danger*, N.Y. TIMES (Oct. 30, 2021), www.nytimes.com/interactive/2021/10/30/video/police-traffic-stops-danger-video.html?referringSource=articleShare.

68 *See, e.g.*, Blazovic v. Andrich, 124 N.J. 90, 112 (1991) (holding that verbal provocation by victim of violent assault constitutes contributory negligence comparable to intentional conduct).

69 *See generally* Joanna C. Schwartz, *How Qualified Immunity Fails*, 127 YALE L.J. 1 (2017), https://digitalcommons.law.yale.edu/ylj/vol127/iss1/1 (reviewing the findings of the largest and most comprehensive study to date of the role qualified immunity plays in constitutional litigation).

70 Pierson v. Ray, 386 U.S. 547 (1967).

71 *E.g.*, Brief of Cross-Ideological Groups Dedicated to Ensuring Official Accountability, Restoring the Public's Trust in Law Enforcement, and Promoting the Rule of Law as Amici Curiae Supporting Petitioner, Corbitt v. Vickers, No. 17-15566 (Dec. 20, 2019) (No. 19-679), www.supremecourt.gov/DocketPDF/19/19-679/126410/20191220142234327_Corbitt%20v.%20Vickers%20crossideological%20brief.pdf.

72 AVERY, POLICE MISCONDUCT, *supra* note 60 at 318, sec. 3:4.

73 Kisela v. Hughes, 584 U.S. 100, 111 (2018) (SOTOMAYOR, J., dissenting).

74 Harlowe v. Fitzgerald, 457 U.S. 800 (1982).

75 Anderson v. Creighton, 483 U.S. 635 (1987).

76 Anderson, 483 U.S. at 640; Hope v. Pelzer, 536 U.S. 730, 741 (2002). Kisela, 584 U.S. at 120 ("[T]hat is not the law, for our cases have never required a factually identical case to satisfy the 'clearly established' standard." Hope v. Pelzer, 536 U.S. 730, 739 (2002)) (SOTOMAYOR, J., dissenting).

77 AVERY, POLICE MISCONDUCT, *supra* note 60 at 339, sec. 3:6.

78 *See, e.g.*, Padilla v. Yoo, 678 F. 3d 748 (9th Cir. 2012) (multiple means of torturing suspect had never been adjudicated as "torture").

79 Ashcroft v. al-Kidd, 563 U.S. 731, 746 (2011) (KENNEDY, J., concurring) ("[Q]ualified immunity is lost when plaintiffs point either to 'cases of controlling authority in their jurisdiction at the time of the incident' or to 'a consensus of cases of persuasive authority such that a reasonable officer could not have believed that his actions were lawful,'" quoting Wilson v. Layne, 526 U.S. 603, 617 (1999)). *See also* City and County of S.F. v. Sheehan, 575 U.S. 600 (2015); Taylor v. Barkes, 575 U.S. 822 (2015) (denying circuit precedent); Carroll v. Carman, 574 U.S. 13 (2015).

80 *See, e.g.*, Gardenhire v. Schubert, 205 F.3d 303, 311 (6th Cir. 2000) ("The ultimate burden is on the plaintiff to show that the defendant is not entitled to qualified immunity"); AVERY, POLICE MISCONDUCT, *supra* note 60 at 455, sec. 3:20.

81 AVERY, POLICE MISCONDUCT, *supra* note 60 at 462, sec. 3:21.

82 *Id.* at 483.

83 John C. Jeffries, Jr., *The Liability Rule for Constitutional Torts*, 99 VA. L. REV. 207, 269 (2013).

84 Monell v. Dep't of Soc. Servs., 436 U.S. 658, 690 (1978).

85 *Id.* at 697.

86 Richard H. Fallon, Jr., *Asking the Right Questions About Officer Immunity*, 80 FORDHAM L. REV. 479, 496 (2011).

87 *See generally* Teresa E. Ravenell & Armando Brigandi, *The Blurred Blue Line: Municipal Liability, Police Indemnification, and Financial Accountability in Section 1983 Litigation*, 62 VILL. L. REV. 839 (2017), https://digitalcommons.law.villanova.edu/vlr/vol62/iss5/1 (reviewing indemnification decisions in Philadelphia and finding that they are seldom dictated by § 1983's elements or indemnification statutes, but instead are guided by policy considerations, which overwhelmingly direct decision-makers towards indemnification).

88 Joanna Schwartz, *Police Indemnification*, 89 N.Y.U. L. REV. 885, 885, 893 (2014) (critically examining the issue central to judicial and scholarly debate about civil rights damages actions: whether law enforcement officials are financially responsible for settlements and judgments in police misconduct cases).

89 *Id.* at 888. ("Punitive damages against municipalities are prohibited in part because, the Court has reasoned, 'neither reason nor justice suggests that such retribution should be visited upon the shoulders of blameless or unknowing

taxpayers,'" *citing* City of Newport v. Fact Concerts, Inc., 453 U.S. 247, 267 (1981).)

90 *Id.*

91 Cheryl Corley, *Police Settlements: How the Cost of Misconduct Impacts Cities and Taxpayers*, NPR (Sept. 19, 2020), www.npr.org/2020/09/19/914170214/police-settlements-how-the-cost-of-misconduct-impacts-cities-and-taxpayers. (Corley notes that cities can face hundreds of lawsuits every year charging, among other things, that police used excessive or deadly force or made a false arrest. Many times, the details of settlements are hidden behind confidentiality agreements.)

92 OFF. OF N.Y.C. COMPTROLLER, CLAIMS REPORT: FISCAL YEAR 2018, 13 (Apr. 2019), https://comptroller.nyc.gov/wp-content/uploads/documents/Claims-Report-FY-2018.pdf.

93 Jonah Newman, *Chicago Spent More than $113 Million on Police Misconduct Lawsuits in 2018*, CHI. REP. (Mar. 7, 2019), www.chicagoreporter.com/chicago-spent-more-than-113-million-on-police-misconduct-lawsuits-in-2018/.

94 For an account of the contemporary market for liability insurance in the policing context and the effects of insurance on police behavior, *see* John Rappaport, *How Private Insurers Regulate Public Police*, 130 HARV. L. REV. 1539 (Apr. 2017).

95 Schwartz, *supra* note 88 at 943.

96 *Id.* at 944.

97 Richard Emery, *Why Civil Rights Lawsuits Do Not Deter Police Misconduct: The Conundrum of Indemnification and a Proposed Solution*, 28 FORDHAM URB. L.J. 587, 597 (2000).

98 *See* Samuel Walker, *Institutionalizing Police Accountability Reforms: The Problem of Making Police Reforms Endure*, 32 ST. LOUIS U. PUB. L. REV. 57, 71 (2012). ("It seems that virtually everyone with an interest in policing – citizens, civic leaders, reform activists, and scholars – believes that police unions are extremely powerful, have a major influence on police practices, and are a principal obstacle to change.")

99 *See* Rachel A. Harmon, *The Problem of Policing*, 110 MICH. L. REV. 761, 763 (arguing that "the problem of regulating police power through law has been shoehorned into the narrow confines of constitutional criminal procedure").

100 Dylan Matthews, *How Police Unions Became So Powerful – and How They Can Be Tamed*, VOX (June 24, 2020), www.vox.com/policy-and-politics/21290981/police-union-contracts-minneapolis-reform.

101 *See* Noam Scheiber, Farah Stockman & J. David Goodman, *How Police Unions Became Such Powerful Opponents to Reform Efforts*, N.Y. TIMES (June 20, 2020), www.nytimes.com/2020/06/06/us/police-unions-minneapolis-kroll.html; Reade Levinson, *Across the U.S., Police Contracts Shield Officers from*

Scrutiny and Discipline, REUTERS (Jan. 13, 2017), www.reuters.com/investi gates/special-report/usa-police-unions.

102 DeRay McKesson, Samuel Sinyangwe, Johnetta Elzie & Brittany Packnett, *Police Union Contracts and Police Bill of Rights Analysis*, CAMPAIGN ZERO (June 29, 2016), https://campaignzero.org/wp-content/uploads/2022/11/Campaign ZeroPoliceUnionContractReport-1.pdf.

103 *See* Thomson-DeVeaux et al., *supra* note 21.

104 *See* Benjamin Sachs, *Police Unions: It's Time to Change the Law and End the Abuse*, ONLABOR (June 4, 2020), https://onlabor.org/police-unions-its-time-to-change-the-law/ (citing studies).

105 William Finnegan, *How Police Unions Fight Reform*, NEW YORKER (July 27, 2020), www.newyorker.com/magazine/2020/08/03/how-police-unions-fight-reform.

106 *See* Matthews, *supra* note 100.

107 *Id.*

108 *Id.* (quoting Aaron Bekemeyer: "It's a broader white ethnic politics that uses the language of tradition, neighborhood integrity, hard work, etc., to defend segregated institutions that they benefit from, from schools to certain union jobs in the trade to religious institutions").

109 *See* James C. McKinley, JR., *Officers Rally and Dinkins Is Their Target*, N.Y. TIMES (Sept. 17, 1992), www.nytimes.com/1992/09/17/nyregion/officers-rally-and-dinkins-is-their-target.html. ("The officers alternated chants of 'No justice! No police!' with slogans like 'The Mayor's on Crack.'")

110 Finnegan *supra* note 105.

111 Deneen L. Brown, *"Detroit" and the Police Brutality that Left Three Black Teens Dead at the Algiers Motel*, WASH. POST (Aug. 4, 2017), www.washingtonpost.com/news/retropolis/wp/2017/08/04/detroit-and-the-police-brutality-that-left-three-black-teens-dead-at-the-algiers-motel/.

112 *See* Kim Barker, Michael H. Keller & Steve Eder, *How Cities Lost Control of Police Discipline*, N.Y. TIMES (Dec. 22, 2020), www.nytimes.com/2020/12/22/us/police-misconduct-discipline.html. *See also* Steve Greenhouse, *How Police Unions Enable and Conceal Abuses of Power*, NEW YORKER (June 18, 2020) www.newyorker.com/news/news-desk/how-police-union-power-helped-increase-abuses.

113 RON DELORD, JOHN BURPO & MICHAEL SHANNON, POLICE ASSOCIATION POWER, POLITICS, AND CONFRONTATION: A GUIDE FOR THE SUCCESSFUL POLICE LABOR LEADER (1997), *quoted in* Michael H. Keller & Kim Barker, *Police Unions Won Power Using His Playbook. Now He's Negotiating the Backlash*, N.Y. TIMES (March 10, 2021), www.nytimes.com/2021/03/10/us/police-unions.html?referringSource=articleShare.

114 *Id.*

115 *Id.*

116 Eric Umansky, *How the N.Y.P.D. Quietly Shuts Down Discipline Cases Against Officers*, N.Y. TIMES (June 27, 2024), www.nytimes.com/2024/06/27/nyregion/how-the-nypd-quietly-shuts-down-discipline-cases-against-officers.html.

117 H.R. 1280, 117th Cong. (2021).

118 *Id.* at § 103.

119 *Id.* at § 102.

120 *Id.* at § 101.

121 MARIAME KABA, WE DO THIS TIL WE FREE US: ABOLITIONIST ORGANIZING AND TRANSFORMING JUSTICE (2021).

122 *See, e.g.*, Economic Opportunity Act of 1964, Pub. L. No. 88-452, 78 Stat. 508; Law Enforcement Administration Act of 1965, Pub. L. No. 89-197, 79 Stat. 828; Prisoner Rehabilitation Act of 1965, Pub. L. No. 89-176, 79 Stat. 674 (codified at 18 U.S.C. § 4082); Correctional Rehabilitation Study Act of 1965, Pub. L. No. 89-178, 79 Stat. 676; Law Enforcement Assistance Act of 1965, Pub. L. No. 89-197, 79 Stat. 828; Omnibus Crime Control and Safe Streets Act of 1968, Pub. L. No. 90-351, 82 Stat. 197.

123 Omnibus Crime Control and Safe Streets Act of 1968, Pub. L. No. 90-351, 82 Stat. 197.

124 *See* JOSHUA MILLER, REIMAGINING CRIMINAL JUSTICE: LEVERAGING FEDERAL GRANTS TO FOSTER COMMUNITY-BASED CRIMINAL JUSTICE PROGRAMS, Rutgers Center on Law, Inequality and Metropolitan Equity (Oct. 22, 2024), https://static1.squarespace.com/static/5b996f553917ee5e584ba742/t/671803f23d3c954d6ba8484e/1729627123060/Reimagining+Criminal+Justice.pdf.

125 Exec. Order No. 14288, 90 Fed. Reg. 18907 (Apr. 28, 2025) ("Strengthening and Unleashing America's Law Enforcement to Pursue Criminals and Protect Innocent Citizens").

126 Jacey Fortin, Devlin Barrett, Ernesto Londono & Shaila Dewan, *Justice Dept. to End Oversight of Local Police Accused of Abuses*, N.Y. TIMES (May 21, 2025), www.nytimes.com/2025/05/21/us/trump-police-consent-decrees.html?smid=nytcore-ios-share&referringSource=articleShare.

127 Mike Scarcella & Sara Merken, *Trump Executive Order Seeks Law Firms to Defend Police Officers for Free*, REUTERS (Apr. 29, 2025), www.reuters.com/legal/government/trump-executive-order-seeks-law-firms-defend-police-officers-free-2025-04-29/.

128 Steven Rich, Tim Arengo & Nicholas Bogel-Burroughs, *Since George Floyd's Murder, Police Killings Keep Rising, Not Falling*, N.Y. TIMES (May 24, 2025), www.nytimes.com/2025/05/24/us/police-killings-george-floyd.html?smid=nytcore-ios-share&referringSource=articleShare.

129 U.S. DEP'T OF JUST., CIV. RTS. DIV., INVESTIGATION OF THE LOUISIANA STATE POLICE (Jan. 16, 2025), www.justice.gov/crt/media/1384626/dl.

Chapter 6

1 J. David Mcswane, *Dismissed by DEI: Trump's Federal Purge Made Black Women with Stable Jobs an "Easy Target"*, PROPUBLICA (June 4, 2025), www.propublica.org/article/trump-dei-black-women-minorities-careers-jobs-dismissed.

2 Jeffrey McKinney, *April Jobs Report: Black Women Lost 106,000 Extra Jobs, Most Among All Workers*, BLACK ENTERPRISE (May 8, 2025), www.blackenterprise.com/black-women-loss-extra-106000-jobs-april-unemployment/.

3 Grace Manthey et al., *Colleges Look Less Diverse as Admissions Officers Seek Ways to Adapt Post Affirmative Action*, CBS NEWS (June 2, 2025), www.cbsnews.com/news/colleges-less-diversity-admissions-post-affirmative-action/.

4 Aarti Iyer, *Understanding Advantaged Groups' Opposition to Diversity, Equity, and Inclusion (DEI) Policies: The Role of Perceived Threat*, SOC. & PERSONALITY COMPASS (Apr. 13, 2022), https://compass.onlinelibrary.wiley.com/doi/full/10.1111/spc3.12666.

5 Daniel Bergner, *"White Fragility" Is Everywhere. But Does Antiracism Training Work?*, N.Y. TIMES (July 15, 2020), www.nytimes.com/2020/07/15/magazine/white-fragility-robin-diangelo.html.

6 *Corporate America Promised to Hire a Lot More People of Color. It Actually Did*, BLOOMBERG (Sept. 25, 2023), www.bloomberg.com/graphics/2023-black-lives-matter-equal-opportunity-corporate-diversity/.

7 *See* Janice Assam Gassare, *How DEI Helps Everyone – Even White People*, FORBES (Aug. 30, 2023), www.forbes.com/sites/janicegassam/2023/08/30/is-dei-anti-white/.

8 Iyer, *supra* note 4.

9 Ashley Jardina & Spencer Piston, *Trickle-Down Racism: Trump's Effect on Whites' Racist Dehumanizing Attitudes*, 5 CURRENT RSCH. ECOLOGICAL & SOC. PSYCH. 100158 (2023), https://doi.org/10.1016/j.cresp.2023.100158; Ashley Jardina & Spencer Piston, *The Effects of Dehumanizing Attitudes About Black People on Whites' Voting Decisions*, 52 BRIT. J. POL. SCI. 1076 (2022), http://dx.doi.org/10.1017/S0007123421000089.

10 Rachel Minkin, *Views of DEI have become slightly more negative among U.S. workers*, PEW RSCH. CTR. (Nov. 19, 2024), www.pewresearch.org/short-reads/2024/11/19/views-of-dei-have-become-slightly-more-negative-among-us-workers/.

11 Parents Involved in Cmty. Sch. v. Seattle Sch. Dist. No. 1, 551 U.S. 701, 748 (2009).

12 Nadra Kareem Nittle, *The Short-Lived Promise of "40 Acres and a Mule"*, HISTORY (Nov. 9, 2022), www.history.com/news/40-acres-mule-promise.

13 JILL LEPORE, THESE TRUTHS: A HISTORY OF THE UNITED STATES, 317 (2018).

14 Tera W. Hunter, *When Slaveowners Got Reparations*, N.Y. TIMES (Apr. 16, 2019), www.nytimes.com/2019/04/16/opinion/when-slaveowners-got-reparations.html.

15 Regents of Univ. of Cal. v. Bakke, 438 U.S. 265, 398 (1978) (Marshall, J., dissenting).

16 Jackie Mansky, *The History Behind the Supreme Court's Affirmative Action Decision*, Smithsonian Mag. (June 22, 2016), www.smithsonianmag.com/history/learn-origins-term-affirmative-action-180959531/.

17 Exec. Order No. 8802, 6 Fed. Reg. 3109 (June 25, 1941).

18 Off. Fed. Cont. Compliance Programs, *History of Executive Order 11246*, U.S. Dep't of Lab., https://web.archive.org/web/20241231063227/www.dol.gov/agencies/ofccp/about/executive-order-11246-history.

19 *Milestone Documents: Executive Order 9981: Desegregation of the Armed Forces (1948)*, Nat'l Archives, www.archives.gov/milestone-documents/executive-order-9981.

20 Off. Fed. Cont. Compliance Programs, *supra* note 18.

21 Exec. Order No. 10925, 26 Fed. Reg. 1977 (Mar. 6, 1961).

22 *Id.* at Sec. 301.

23 Melvin I. Urofsky, The Affirmative Action Puzzle: A Living History from Reconstruction to Today 35 (2020).

24 Exec. Order No. 10925, *supra* note 21 at Sec. 201.

25 Judson MacLaury, *President Kennedy's E.O. 10925: Seedbed of Affirmative Action*, 2 Fed. Hist. 42, 49–50 (2010).

26 Exec. Order No. 10925, *supra* note 21 at Sec. 301:

> (1) The contractor will not discriminate against any employee or applicant for employment because of race, creed, color, or national origin. The contractor will take affirmative action to ensure that applicants are employed, and that employees are treated during employment, without regard to their race, creed, color, or national origin. Such action shall include, but not be limited to, the following: employment, upgrading, demotion or transfer; recruitment or recruitment advertising; layoff or termination; rates of pay or other forms of compensation; and selection for training, including apprenticeship. The contractor agrees to post in conspicuous places, available to employees and applicants for employment, notices to be provided by the contracting officer setting forth the provisions of this nondiscrimination clause.

27 Terry H. Anderson, *The Strange Career of Affirmative Action*, 22 S. Cent. Rev. 110, 115 (2005).

28 President Lyndon B. Johnson, Commencement Address at Howard University: To Fulfill These Rights (June 4, 1965), *made available online by* Gerhard Peters & John T. Woolley, Am. Presidency Proj., www.presidency.ucsb.edu/node/241312.

29 Urofsky, *supra* note 23 at 59–60.

30 *Id.* at 87.

31 Anderson, *supra* note 27 at 116.

32 *Id. See also,* Mehrsa Baradaran, *A Bad Check for Black America,* Bos. Rev. (Nov. 9, 2017), www.bostonreview.net/articles/how-nixon-swindled-black-businesses/.

33 Urofsky, *supra* note 23 at 91.

34 *Id.* at 127–28, 258 (citing studies). Roland G. Fryer, Jr. & Glenn C. Loury, *Affirmative Action and Its Mythology,* 19 J. Econ. Perspectives 147 (Summer 2005); Harry Holzer & David Neumark, *Assessing Affirmative Action* (Nat'l Bureau of Econ. Rsch., Working Paper No. 7323, Aug. 1999), www.nber.org/system/files/working_papers/w7323/w7323.pdf.

35 Urofsky, *id.* at 35.

36 *Id.* at 39–42.

37 *See* Hunter, *supra* note 14; John Tateishi, Redress: The Inside Story of the Successful Campaign for Japanese American Reparations (2020).

38 Kimberlé W. Crenshaw, *Race, Reform, and Retrenchment: Transformation and Legitimation in Antidiscrimination Law,* 101 Harv. L. Rev. 1331, 1347 (1988).

39 Randall Kennedy, For Discrimination: Race, Affirmative Action and the Law 243 (2013).

40 Urofsky, *supra* note 23 at 74.

41 Frank Dobbin, Inventing Equal Opportunity 11 (2009).

42 *Id.* at 6.

43 Regents of Univ. of Cal. v. Bakke, 438 U.S. 265, 306 (1978) (plurality opinion).

44 United Steelworkers v. Weber, 443 U.S. 193 (1979).

45 424 U.S. 405 (1975).

46 Albemarle Paper Co. v. Moody, 422 U.S. 405 (1975).

47 Wygant v. Jackson Bd. of Educ., 476 U.S. 267 (1986).

48 488 U.S. 469 (1989).

49 Adarand Constructors v. Peña, 515 U.S. 200 (1995).

50 Michael Avery & Mark Brodin, *The Federalist Society Just Won Its 40-Year War on Affirmative Action,* TruthOut (July 8, 2023), https://truthout.org/articles/the-federalist-society-just-won-its-40-year-war-on-affirmative-action/.

51 Kweilin Ellingrud et al., *Diversity, Equity and Inclusion Lighthouses,* McKinsey & Co. (Jan. 13, 2023), www.mckinsey.com/featured-insights/diversity-and-inclusion/diversity-equity-and-inclusion-lighthouses-2023.

52 *Id.*

53 *Executive Education Portfolio: Program Finder,* Stanford Bus. Sch. Exec. Educ., https://grow.stanford.edu/browse/. (There is no longer a "DEI Certificate" – the closest comparable program appears to be "Leverage Diversity and Inclusion for Organizational Excellence.")

54 *Id.*

55 *E.g.*, Coal. for TJ v. Fairfax Cty. Sch. Bd., 68 F.4th 864 (4th Cir. 2023); Students for Fair Admissions v. United States Naval Acad., 758 F. Supp. 3d 423 (D. Md. 2024); Chislett v. N.Y.C. Dep't of Educ., 723 F. Supp. 3d 285 (S.D.N.Y. 2024); Diemert v. City of Seattle, No. 2:22-cv-1640, 2025 U.S. Dist. LEXIS 23601 (W.D. Wash. Feb. 10, 2025).

56 *Equity, Diversity, Inclusion, and Belonging Leadership Graduate Certificate*, HARV. EXTENSION SCH.: HARV. DIV. CONTINUING EDUC., https://extension .harvard.edu/academics/programs/equity-diversity-inclusion-and-belonging-leadership-graduate-certificate/#outcomes.

57 *E.g.*, ONEYA FENNELL OKUWOBI, WHO PAYS FOR DIVERSITY: WHY PROGRAMS FAIL AT RACIAL EQUALITY AND WHAT TO DO ABOUT IT (2025); Cheryl R. Kaiser et al., *Presumed Fair: Ironic Effects of Organizational Diversity Structures*, 104 J. PERSONALITY & SOC. PSYCH. 504 (2013), https://psycnet.apa.org/doi/10.1037/a0030838.

58 *See, e.g.*, Tanya K. Hernandez, *Can CRT Save DEI?: Workplace Diversity, Equity & Inclusion in the Shadow of Anti-Affirmative Action*, 71 UCLA L. REV. DISC. 282 (2024) (arguing for incorporation of Critical Race Theory methods).

59 KENNEDY, *supra* note 39 at 99–100.

60 Jennifer W. Tsai et al., *Evaluating the Impact and Rationale of Race-Specific Estimations of Kidney Function: Estimations from U.S. NHANES, 2015–2018*, 42 ECLINICALMEDICINE 101197 (Dec. 2021), https://doi.org/10.1016/j.eclinm.2021.101197.

61 Crystal Gwizdala, *Abandoning a Race-Based Tool for Kidney Diagnosis*, YALE SCH. MED. (Oct. 10, 2022), https://medicine.yale.edu/news-article/abandoning-a-race-biased-tool-for-kidney-diagnosis/.

62 NEWARK PUBLIC SAFETY COLLABORATIVE, https://newarkcollaborative.org/.

63 *See* Michael Friedrich, *A Police Department's Difficult Assignment: Atonement*, BLOOMBERG (Oct. 23, 2019), www.bloomberg.com/news/articles/2019-10-23/what-police-community-reconciliation-can-look-like.

64 Laura Meckler & Josh Dawsey, *Republicans, Spurred by an Unlikely Figure, See Political Promise in Critical Race Theory*, SAN DIEGO UNION-TRIB. (June 20, 2021), www.sandiegouniontribune.com/news/politics/story/2021-06-20/republicans-spurred-by-an-unlikely-figure-see-political-promise-in-critical-race-theory [https://perma.cc/CXH2-S92K].

65 Cheyanne Mumphrey & Jocelyn Gecker, *Colleges Cut Ties with The PhD Project, a Nonprofit Targeted by the Trump Administration over DEI*, PBS (Mar. 21, 2025), www.pbs.org/newshour/education/colleges-cut-ties-with-the-phd-project-a-nonprofit-targeted-by-trump-administration-over-dei.

66 Karen Yourish, *These Words Are Disappearing in the New Trump Administration*, N.Y. TIMES (Mar. 7, 2025), www.nytimes.com/interactive/2025/03/07/us/trump-federal-agencies-websites-words-dei.html?smid = nytcore-ios-share&referring Source = articleShare.

67 *See* Saida Grundy, *Trump Is Terrified of Black Culture. But Not for the Reasons You Think*, THE GUARDIAN (June 22, 2025), www.theguardian.com/us-news/ng-interactive/2025/jun/22/trump-black-arts-culture-crackdown?CMP=oth_b-aplnews_d-1.

68 Texas v. Johnson, 491 U.S. 397, 408-09 (1989), *citing* Terminiello v. Chicago, 337 U.S. 1, 4 (1949). *See also* Cox v. Louisiana, 379 U.S. 536, 551 (1965); Tinker v. Des Moines Independent Community School Dist. 393 U.S. 503, 508–09 (1969); Coates v. Cincinnati, 402 U.S. 611, 615 (1971); Hustler Magazine, Inc. v. Falwell, 485 U.S. 46, 55–56 (1988).

69 Snyder v. Phelps, 562 U.S. 443, 451–52 (2011).

70 303 Creative LLC v. Elenis, 600 U.S. 570, 595 (2023).

71 Reed v. Town of Gilbert, 576 U.S. 155, 163–64 (2015); Sorrell v. IMS Health, Inc., 564 U.S. 552, 263–565 (2011); R.A.V. v. St. Paul, 505 U.S. 377, 382 (1992); Ward v. Rock Against Racism, 491 U.S. 781, 791 (1989); Thornhill v. Alabama, 310 U.S. 88, 95–96 (1940).

72 Simon & Schuster, Inc. v. Members of N.Y. State Crime Victims Bd., 502 U.S. 105 (1991).

73 Keyishian v. Bd. of Regents, 385 U.S. 589, 603 (1967).

74 Chicago Women in Trades v. Trump, No. 25-2005 (N.D. Ill. 2025); American Federation of Teachers v. U.S. Department of Education, No. 25-628 (D. Mar. 2025); National Education Association v. US Department of Education, No. 25-91 (D.N.H. 2025); NAACP v. U.S. Dept. of Ed., No. 25-1120 (D.D.C. 2025); Southern Education Foundation v. United States Department of Education, No. 25-1079 (D.D.C. 2025); San Francisco A.I.D.S. Foundation v. Trump, 4:25-cv-01824 (N.D. Cal. 2025); Perkins Coie LLP v. U.S. Dept. of Justice, 1:25-cv-00716 (D.D.C. 2025); Wilmer Cutler Pickering Hale and Dorr LLP v. Executive Office of the President, 1:25-cv-00917 (D.D.C. 2025); Jenner & Block LLP v. U.S. Dept. of Justice, 1:25-cv-00916 (D.D.C. 2025).

75 Adam Bonica, *The Supreme Court Is at War with Its Own Judiciary*, SUBSTACK, July 25, 2025, at https://data4democracy.substack.com/p/the-supreme-court-is-at-war-with.

76 National Association for Law Placement, *The Demographics of Jobs from 1991–2021, Part 2*, July/August 2023, www.nalp.org/0723research.

77 Crenshaw, *supra* note 38 at 1349.

78 Procunier v. Martinez, 416 U.S. 396, 427 (1974) (MARSHALL, J., concurring), *rev'd on other grounds by* Thornburgh v. Abbott, 490 U.S. 401 (1989).

Chapter 7

1 Hills v. Gatreaux, 425 U.S. 284 (1976).

2 See David D. Troutt et al., *The Vibranium Study of African-American Wellbeing*, www.clime.rutgers.edu.

3 *Facts: Income Inequality in the United States*, INEQUALITY.ORG (2021), https://inequality.org/facts/income-inequality/.

4 Rakesh Kocchar & Anthony Cilluffo, *How Wealth Inequality Has Changed Since the Great Recession, by Race, Ethnicity and Income*, PEW RSCH. CTR. (Nov. 1, 2017), www.pewresearch.org/short-reads/2017/11/01/how-wealth-inequality-has-changed-in-the-u-s-since-the-great-recession-by-race-ethnicity-and-income/.

5 Basel Musharbash, *Messing with Texas: How Big Homebuilders and Private Equity Made American Cities Unaffordable*, BIG NEWSLETTER (May 30, 2025), www.thebignewsletter.com/p/messing-with-texas-how-big-homebuilders.

6 David D. Troutt & Katharine Nelson, *Who Owns Newark? Transferring Wealth from Newark Homeowners to Corporate Buyers*, CTR. ON LAW, INEQUALITY & METROPOLITAN EQUITY (May 2022), www.clime.rutgers.edu/publications-filtered/who-owns-newark.

7 MATHEW DESMOND, EVICTED: POVERTY AND PROFIT IN THE AMERICAN CITY (2016).

8 Katharine L. Nelson & David D. Troutt, *Homes Beyond Reach: An Assessment & Gap Analysis of Newark's Affordable Rental Stock*, CTR. ON LAW, INEQUALITY & METROPOLITAN EQUITY (Feb. 2021), www.clime.rutgers.edu/publications-filtered/homes-beyond-reach-an-assessment-and-gap-analysis-of-newarks-affordable-rental-stock.

9 Troutt et al., *supra* note 2. See also KEEANGA-YAMAHTTA TAYLOR, RACE FOR PROFIT: HOW BANKS AND THE REAL ESTATE INDUSTRY UNDERMINED BLACK HOMEOWNERSHIP (2019).

10 Lance Freeman & Frank Braconi, *Gentrification and Displacement: New York City in the 1990s*, 70 J. AM. PLAN. ASS'N 39 (Winter 2004), https://doi.org/10.1080/01944360408976337.

11 Troy Closson & Nicole Hong, *Why Black Families Are Leaving New York, and What It Means for the City*, N.Y. TIMES (Jan. 31, 2023), www.nytimes.com/2023/01/31/nyregion/black-residents-nyc.html.

12 Mussab Ali, Katharine Nelson & David D. Troutt, *The "Other" Cities: Migration and Gentrification in Jersey City, Newark and Paterson, New Jersey*, CTR. ON LAW, INEQUALITY & METROPOLITAN EQUITY (Apr. 2025), www.clime.rutgers.edu/publications-filtered/theothercities.

13 Bruce C. Mitchell et al., *Displaced by Design: Fifty Years of Gentrification and Black Cultural Displacement in U.S. Cities*, NAT'L CMTY. REINVESTMENT COAL. (May 2025), https://ncrc.org/displaced-by-design/.

14 Vincent Basile, Adam York & Ray Black, *Who Is the One Being Disrespectful? Understanding and Deconstructing the Criminalization of Elementary School Boys of Color*, 57 URB. EDUC. 1592 (2019), https://doi.org/10.1177/0042085919842627.

15 *Neighborhood Profiles: Fort Greene/Brooklyn Heights*, N.Y.U. Furman Ctr. Real Estate & Urb. Pol'y, https://furmancenter.org/neighborhoods/view/fort-greene-brooklyn-heights.

16 Rolanda J.W. Spencer, *Blaxit: An Exodus in Los Angeles*, Ark Republic (Oct. 1, 2019), www.arkrepublic.com/2019/10/01/blaxit-an-exodus-in-los-angeles/.

17 Lauren Helper, *The Hidden Toll of California's Black Exodus*, CalMatters (July 15, 2020), https://calmatters.org/projects/california-black-population-exodus (quoting University of Maryland Professor Willow Lung-Amam).

18 Yusuf Ransome, Insang Song, Linh Pham & Camille Busette, *Churches are Closing in Predominantly Black Communities – Why Public Health Officials Should Be Concerned*, Brookings Inst. (May 3, 2022), www.brookings.edu/articles/churches-are-closing-in-predominantly-black-communities-why-public-health-officials-should-be-concerned/.

19 Liam Dillon, Ben Poston & Julia Barajas, *Black and Latino Renters Face Eviction, Exclusion Amid Police Crackdowns in California*, L.A. Times (Nov. 19, 2020), www.latimes.com/homeless-housing/story/2020-11-19/california-housing-policies-hurt-black-latino-renters.

20 Chelsea Helena, Nora Salem, Alexandra Reyes & Steven Graves, *NOT JUST STOPS: Mapping Racially Biased Policing in the Antelope Valley*, Neighborhood Legal Services of L.A. Cnty. (Oct. 2021), https://nlsla.org/wp-content/uploads/2021/10/Mapping-Racially-Biased-Policing-in-the-AV_compressed.pdf (in Partnership with California State University, Northridge); Emily Elena Dugdale, *As Palmdale Grapples with a Hanging Death, Locals Recall the Area's Racist History*, NPR (June 30, 2020), www.npr.org/2020/06/30/884654954/as-palmdale-grapples-with-a-hanging-death-locals-recall-the-areas-racist-history; Kelly McLaughlin, *The Town Where Robert Fuller Was Found Dead Has a History of Racism that Has Fueled Speculation over His Death*, Bus. Insider (June 25, 2020), www.businessinsider.com/palmdale-california-history-of-racism-robert-fuller-death-2020-6; Donna Kiesling & Laurie Goering, *South Holland Homeowners Fears' Cross Color Lines*, Chi. Trib. (Dec. 17, 1992), www.chicagotribune.com/1992/12/17/south-holland-homeowners-fears-cross-color-lines/.

21 Tracee Wilkins, *Charles County Surpasses Prince George's as Wealthiest Black-majority County in U.S.*, NBC Washington (July 7, 2022), www.nbcwashington.com/news/local/prince-georges-county/charles-county-surpasses-prince-georges-as-wealthiest-black-county-in-us-post/3095774/. *See also* Andrew Van Dam, *Is Prince George's Still the Richest Majority-Black County in America?*, Wash. Post (June 29, 2022), www.washingtonpost.com/business/2022/06/29/dept-of-data-prince-georges-richest-black-county/.

22 Karyn R. Lacy, Blue-Chip Black: Race, Class, and Status in the New Black Middle Class (2007).

23 William H. Frey, *A "New Great Migration" Is Bringing Black Americans Back to the South*, BROOKINGS INST. (Sept. 12, 2022), www.brookings.edu/articles/a-new-great-migration-is-bringing-black-americans-back-to-the-south/; Emmanuel Felton, John D. Harden & Kevin Schaul, *Still Looking for a "Black Mecca," the New Great Migration*, WASH. POST (Jan. 14, 2022), www.washingtonpost.com/nation/2022/01/14/black-migration-south/.

24 TED, *The Case for a New Great Migration in the US | Charles M. Blow*, YOUTUBE (Nov. 28, 2023), www.youtube.com/watch?v=HJtbtEn0-uk&ab_channel=TED; Brakkton Booker, *Why We're Covering the Next Black Exodus*, POLITICO MAG. (Dec. 7, 2021), www.politico.com/news/magazine/2021/12/07/black-great-migration-series-523619.

25 Ben Sprung-Keyser, Nathaniel Hendren & Sonya Porter, *The Radius of Economic Opportunity: Evidence from Migration and Local Labor Markets* (U.S. Census Bureau, Ctr. Econ. Stud., Working Paper No. 22-27, July 2022), https://opportunityinsights.org/wp-content/uploads/2022/07/migration_paper.pdf.

26 Shelly Henderson, *Charlotte vs. Raleigh: Comparing the Carolina's Top Real Estate Markets*, HENDERSON PROPERTIES (Oct. 2024), www.hendersonproperties.com/2024/10/charlotte-vs-raleigh/.

27 Noah Smith, *Why Charlotte and Raleigh Work for Black Residents*, BLOOMBERG (Mar. 28, 2018), www.bloomberg.com/opinion/articles/2018-03-28/why-charlotte-and-raleigh-work-for-black-residents.

28 Kendrick Marshall, *"All the Things a City Can Have." Here's Why Some Are Calling Charlotte a "Black Mecca"*, CHARLOTTE OBSERVER (Mar. 1, 2023), www.charlotteobserver.com/living/article272162667.html.

29 Felton et al., *supra* note 23.

30 Charles M. Tiebout, *A Pure Theory of Local Expenditures*, 64 J. POL. ECON. 416 (Oct. 1956), https://fbaum.unc.edu/teaching/PLSC541_Fall08/tiebout_1956.pdf.

31 *See* CAMILLE ZUBRINSKY CHARLES, WON'T YOU BE MY NEIGHBOR? RACE, CLASS AND RESIDENCY IN LOS ANGELES (2006); MARY PATTILLO-MCCOY, BLACK PICKET FENCES: PRIVILEGE AND PERIL AMONG THE BLACK MIDDLE CLASS (1999).

Epilogue

1 *See* David D. Troutt, *Urban Renewal's Grandchildren: Remedying the Persistent Effects of Post-War Race Planning*, 52 FORDHAM URB. L.J. 91 (2024).

2 *See* David D. Troutt, *Trapped in Tragedy: Childhood Trauma, Spatial Inequality and Law*, 101 MARQUETTE L. REV. 601 (Spring 2018).

3 *See* David D. Troutt, *Taking the Knee No More: Police Accountability and the Structure of Racism*, 79 WASH. & LEE L. REV. 1765 (2023).

4 *See generally* JANE CLAYTON, LIFTING THE BLUE VEIL OF SILENCE: LEGISLATIVE PROPOSALS TO IMPROVE TRANSPARENCY IN POLICING

AND BUILD COMMUNITY TRUST, NATIONAL POLICE ACCOUNTABILITY PROJECT (Feb. 6, 2024), https://engage.nlg-npap.org/node/156767.

5 SAMUEL R. GROSS, MAURICE J. POSSLEY, KAITLYN JACKSON ROLL & KLARA HUBER STEPHENS, GOVERNMENT MISCONDUCT AND CONVICTING THE INNOCENT: THE ROLE OF PROSECUTORS, POLICE AND OTHER LAW ENFORCEMENT, NATIONAL REGISTRY OF EXONERATIONS (Sept. 1, 2020), www.law.umich.edu/special/exoneration/Documents/Government_Misconduct_and_Convicting_the_Innocent.pdf.

6 KALLIE COX & WILLIAM H. FREIVOGEL, *Police Misconduct Records Secret, Difficult to Access*, AP NEWS (May 12, 2021), https://apnews.com/article/us-news-police-reform-police-government-and-politics-fa6cbd7e017 b85aa715e23465a90abbe; *see also* Innocence Staff, *What You Need to Know About Police Misconduct and Wrongful Convictions*, INNOCENCE PROJECT (Sept. 30, 2020), https://innocenceproject.org/police-misconduct-wrongful-convictions-what-you-should-know/.

7 TOM MCEWEN, NATIONAL DATA COLLECTION ON POLICE USE OF FORCE, DEPARTMENT OF JUSTICE & NATIONAL INSTITUTE OF JUSTICE (April 1996), https://bjs.ojp.gov/content/pub/pdf/ndcopuof.pdf.

8 Stephen Rushin, *Using Data to Reduce Police Violence*, 57 BOS. COLL. L. REV. 117, 118–20 (2016) (detailing the three different federal initiatives – the Death in Custody Reporting Act, the FBI National Use-of-Force database, and the Bureau of Justice Statistics pilot program scanning the internet for reports of police incidents).

9 Staff, *Police Use Force Against Hundreds of Thousands Annually, New Data Reveals*, UPRISERI (Aug. 28, 2024), https://upriseri.com/police-use-force-against-hundreds-of-thousands-annually-new-data-reveals/.

10 Jamiles Lartey, *A Legal Doctrine that Shields Police From Many Lawsuits May Be Losing Support*, MARSHALL PROJECT (May 25, 2024), www.themarshallproject.org/2024/05/25/police-mississippi-courts-judges-qualified-immunity.

11 Gary S. Gildin, *Legislative Efforts to Abolish Qualified Immunity Yield Mixed Results*, STATE COURT REPORT (May 30, 2024), https://statecourtreport.org/our-work/analysis-opinion/legislative-efforts-abolish-qualified-immunity-yield-mixed-results.

12 *Id.*

13 *Community Schools Playbook*, Partnership for the Future of Learning, 4, https://communityschools.futureforlearning.org/assets/downloads/community-schools-playbook.pdf.

14 Josh Bivens, Celine McNicholas, Kyle K. Moore & Margaret Poydock, *Unions Promote Racial Equity*, ECONOMIC POLICY INSTITUTE (July 31, 2023), www.epi.org/publication/unions-promote-racial-equity/.

15 Aurelia Glass, David Madland & Christian E. Weller, *Unions Help Increase Wealth for All and Close Racial Wealth Gaps*, CENTER FOR AMERICAN PROGRESS (Sept. 6, 2021), www.americanprogress.org/article/unions-help-increase-wealth-close-racial-wealth-gaps/.

16 *Id.*

17 Annie Brickley, *New Report Finds Inequities in Early Child Care and Education Access Among Black Children and Families*, FIRST FIVE YEARS FUND (June 18, 2024), www.ffyf.org/resources/2024/06/new-report-finds-inequities-in-early-child-care-and-education-access-among-black-children-and-families/.

18 Jonathan Koltai, Jess Carson, Tyrus Parker & Rebecca Glauber, *Childcare Remains Out of Reach for Millions in 2021, Leading to Disproportionate Job Losses for Black, Hispanic, and Low-Income Families*, CARSON SCHOOL OF PUBLIC POLICY (Dec. 23, 2021), https://carsey.unh.edu/publication/childcare-remains-out-reach-millions-2021-leading-disproportionate-job-losses-black-hispanic-low.

19 Bryce Covert, *New Mexico Just Became the First State to Make Child Care Free for Nearly All Families*, THE 74 (May 26, 2022), https://earlylearningnation.com/2022/05/new-mexico-just-became-the-first-state-to-make-child-care-free-for-nearly-all-families/.

Index

Printed by Integrated Books International,
United States of America